Key management questions

FT Prentice Hall
FINANCIAL TIMES

In an increasingly competitive world, we believe it's quality of thinking that will give you the edge – an idea that opens new doors, a technique that solves a problem, or an insight that simply makes sense of it all. The more you know, the smarter and faster you can go.

That's why we work with the best minds in business and finance to bring cutting-edge thinking and best learning practice to a global market.

Under a range of leading imprints, including *Financial Times Prentice Hall*, we create world-class print publications and electronic products bringing our readers knowledge, skills and understanding which can be applied whether studying or at work.

To find out more about our business publications, or tell us about the books you'd like to find, you can visit us at
www.business-minds.com

For other Pearson Education publications, visit
www.pearsoned-ema.com

Pearson
Education

Key management questions

Smart questions for every business situation

Tom Lambert

Prentice Hall
FINANCIAL TIMES

London ■ New York ■ Toronto ■ Sydney ■ Tokyo ■ Singapore ■ Hong Kong
Cape Town ■ New Delhi ■ Madrid ■ Paris ■ Amsterdam ■ Munich ■ Milan ■ Stockholm

PEARSON EDUCATION LIMITED

Edinburgh Gate
Harlow, Essex CM20 2JE
Tel: +44 (0)1279 623623
Fax: +44 (0)1279 431059
Website: www.pearsoned.co.uk

First published in Great Britain in 2003

ISBN 0 273 66153 1

British Library Cataloguing in Publication Data
A CIP catalogue record for this book can be obtained from the British Library

10 9 8 7 6 5 4 3

Typeset by Northern Phototypesetting Co. Ltd, Bolton
Printed and bound in Great Britain by Biddles Ltd, King's Lynn, Norfolk

The Publishers' policy is to use paper manufactured from sustainable forests.

Contents

Introduction

*you deserve
state of the art*

Any fool can offer you answers. It takes genius to ask the right questions.
Albert Einstein

- Why you need to have this book – but don't need to read it!

- The unique concept of the book is described and the reader is given guidance in its *use*.

- Applied thought leadership requires the asking of the right questions of the right people at the right time. This book provides the essential questions and clear guidance on how to implement the answers to greatest effect.

What you will gain from this introduction

- How this book is best used.

- The difference between reading a book and really using it.

- How to make a concise, comprehensive assessment of your whole business with a few well-chosen questions.

- Why the best person to question is often yourself.

- The key difference between knowledge and wisdom.

- How to build and nourish wisdom in your organization.

- How to successfully meld tactics and strategy.

I recently realized the awful truth. I have now spent as many years as a consultant as I did as a senior executive – or in a "real job" you may think. The realization that the only way that I could have spent so much time in two careers set me thinking about what I have learned over the last thirty odd years in business. One conclusion came very readily. Whatever success I have enjoyed has come when I have had the good sense or good luck to ask the right questions of myself or of others. The right questions, asked of the right people at the right time are the keys to success.

As a consultant I find that if I ask the right questions of my clients they are generally able to solve their own problems or exploit their best opportunities with little or no further help from me. This leads them to believe that they are getting exceptional value so they choose to use me again and again. I waste neither my time nor theirs and we both learn valuable lessons. Questions enable me to deliver what a consultant is best placed to deliver. I am able to help my client to think in a more focused way while he or she thinks more broadly using better information. What is more, clients implement their solutions and initiatives with considerable confidence and enthusiasm since they are "all their own work".

In my role as a mentor to top executives questions play a wider part. In addition to helping the client to find the action that best suits them I am often able to suggest the questions that they should be asking others in their corporations to ensure that they too are able to think things through effectively. The right questions frequently turn people who are new to a subject area into perceived experts. The chairman fulfils his or her role as consultant to their board with confidence. This accelerated growth of knowledge and experience can do wonders in getting subordinates to think things through and get optimal results where they might have courted mediocrity by making inappropriate assumptions based on insufficient thinking. The right questions asked in the right way of the right people at the right time are the key to quality throughout the business and it is quality that costs virtually nothing beyond an enquiring mind. Excellence lies already in people's minds and capabilities awaiting the right questions to draw it out and turn thought into action.

As a non-executive director the role is one that can be described as "asking the right questions at the right time and insisting on complete answers". Had NED's asked the right questions of the right people at the right time and insisted on full answers, the problems currently besetting great firms as diverse as Marconi, Kuomi and Enron might have been avoided or at least mitigated.

As an executive with international responsibilities I found that if I asked the right questions I could accelerate my learning and I made better and quicker decisions. Today, when the business cycle is accelerating with a crazy velocity and the risk of failure is growing greater almost daily, asking the right questions is becoming the factor that differentiates between success and disaster. Too many so-called business gurus appear to have concluded that the faster pace of business life makes thinking obsolete. This is nonsense. Executive or consultant, manager or committed employee, we all need to hone our thinking skills so that we can think and act faster and be ever more effective. The only way to do that is to ask the right questions not only of others, but also of ourselves.

This book is a collection of the questions that I have found lead directly to the best results in all aspects of my work. What they do for me they will do for you.

Key questions to be considered by every senior executive every day

In their groundbreaking work on market dominance, *Competing for the Future*, Chris Prahalad and Gary Hamel suggested some questions that ought constantly be mulled over by businesspeople. I paraphrase, but the key ideas remain.

- How can we best use our present competencies and strengths to better exploit today's most profitable markets and ensure that we are building a firm foundation to enjoy ever-increasing prosperity in the future?
- What new skills and competencies do we have to acquire to better exploit today's most worthwhile markets?
- How can we apply our current strengths and competencies to take a leading role in the best, most profitable markets of the future?
- What new skills, knowledge and competencies do we have to develop or acquire to create the rules by which others have to play in the most profitable markets of the future?

I will now examine each question and outline the advantages that come from even the most cursory, but regular, consideration of each.

Using competencies and strengths

How can we best use our present competencies and strengths to better exploit today's most profitable markets and ensure that

we are best placed to enjoy ever-increasing prosperity in the future?

There is massive and compelling evidence that makes it clear that leveraging the strengths of a business increases profitability far more than even the most assiduous identification and eradication of weaknesses. If you have but one loyal customer you have a clear indication that you are doing something right. Giving people more of what they value is the fastest and most effective way to build profitable business by attracting other worthwhile customers with similar desires, needs and expectations. Asking the question as framed by Prahalad and Hamel ensures that you and those that you influence are concentrating on the important rather than fretting over any perceived shortcomings most of which have no discernible effect on the way or the degree to which you delight your customers. "Do what you already do well only do more of it and do it better" should be the mantra of all businesspeople. Problems can and will be solved, weaknesses will be eliminated, but the negatives are most readily dealt with when the business is generating good profits and clients and customers are expressing their delight at the service that they experience day after day. Then the attitude is one of "let's get this problem out of the way because we can" rather than "let's swap war stories and grievances because it is only being miserable that makes us happy".

Research has shown time and time again that firms can spend millions of dollars or pounds and an almost unlimited number of hours trying to eliminate every little perceived weakness without increasing profitability by a single penny. Companies, such as the Figgie Corporation have gone from prosperity to bankruptcy as they sought out-of-reach perfection, rather than simply identifying and delivering what the most valuable customers wanted. Ask yourself and others the question that will ensure that you are still there, stronger than ever before, when you decide that the time has come to deal with every minor flaw.

My small addition to Prahalad and Hamel's question is aimed at ensuring that no reader falls victim to short-term thinking. Every success that we enjoy today should be part of a strategic and tactical process to build the best possible springboard for our future. Every time that you have a great idea for present action it will almost certainly become a better idea if you also ask yourself or others "how does this contribute to the future that we (I) want?" The answer that "it helps us to survive for long enough to enjoy the future" is fine, but usually it is incomplete. Today's successes, like today's skills, competencies, behaviours, learning and knowledge can, creatively applied, provide a sound platform for future triumphs.

Subsidiary practical questions

- Who, by name are the 20 per cent of customers that provide 80 per cent of our profits?

- What specifically do they tell us that they appreciate about the way that we serve them?
- What do they see as their key needs for the immediate future?
- What is changing?
- How often do we ask them?
- Where can we find similar customers, equally worthwhile, with similar needs?
- What do we have to do to win them?
- What do we have to do to keep them?

What new skills and competencies do we have to acquire to better exploit today's most worthwhile markets?

Arie de Geus has shown that the real business survivors, those companies that prosper for centuries rather than decades, are learning organizations that attract the best people and practise frugality with their resources. Considering this question should lead to other, equally valid, questions.

Subsidiary practical questions

- Is it better to develop such skills through training or development or to buy them in?
- How do we build a real learning community?
- Do we reward the sharing or the hoarding of knowledge and skill in this company?
- How can we reward the sharing of knowledge and skills?
- How do we ensure that what is learned by our people is relevant to our business needs and is used rather than forgotten?
- How do we optimize the growth of our people at every level?
- Can we attract and keep the best people?
- Who do we need to attract to get ahead and keep ahead of competition?
- What is the quickest and most economical way to attack the most profitable markets?

(For a short cut to some of the most important answers to these questions you might like to look at pages 250–267 of *Key Management Solutions* published by Pearson under the Financial Times/Prentice Hall imprint.

We have moved beyond the knowledge economy into one in which the key differentiator is the application and extension of knowledge to deliver wisdom. You do not have to take it on trust. You know from your own experience. Consideration of the right questions by the right people at the right time and application of the answers is the key to wisdom, and with the business cycle spinning ever faster, the survival of the fittest has become the survival of the wisest.

The knowledge organization

Many thinkers have been concerning themselves with the growth and application of knowledge. Along with the great names of business thought, even a humble contributor has his or her place. So I offer some brief thoughts on the work of Nonaka, Tacheuchi, de Geus, Lambert, du Toit, Peters and Drucker and many others.

- The knowledge age is already past. Knowledge is no longer enough.
- The sole lasting competitive edge is wisdom.
- Wisdom comes initially from asking the right questions of data.
- Data is raw information.
- Information is data considered in the context of a meaningful strategic plan that is consistent with the existing and developing strengths, competencies and culture of the organization.
- Knowledge is information applied to the achievement of the strategic plan.
- Wisdom is knowledge reconsidered and tested in a changing environment to instil appropriate flexibility into the strategic plan.

(Perhaps sagacity is the implementation of wisdom such that the organization is increasingly able to shape the future of the sector(s) in which it competes such that others have no choice other than to play by the new rules and, in their efforts to merely catch up, lose money or withdraw – in a couple of words dominance strategy.)

- Knowledge in an organization is of two types: *Explicit* knowledge which is the effective and efficient application of data based knowledge – facts, measurements, observable behaviours, skills, shared, communicated values and norms.
- *Tacit* or *implicit* knowledge consists of the hunches, creativity, ideas, beliefs of the committed people who are employed in the business at every level. As Tom Peters said a short while ago "the challenge we now face is how to manage the imagination of our people". Imagination can only be directed by those who are ready to pose the right questions.

- Wisdom can only come from the balanced, effective application of tacit and explicit knowledge. The firm can only access and exploit tacit knowledge if it takes specific steps to:
  - Demonstrate that people and their thoughts are respected;
  - Build commitment around an inspirational and shared vision;
  - Develop a culture in which ideas and learning are daily realities at every level and communication is genuinely two way.

- The imagination of our people can be stimulated by the successes of others if, and only if, we develop a "leapfrog mentality". Benchmarking, as it is usually practised, leads only to a "me too" attitude which can only succeed if the competition stands still, kindly waiting for us to catch up. They do not, so the question: "how do we do it better and cheaper?" is one that cannot be asked too many times or of too many people.

- Rather than trying to identify best practice, managers should be designing better than best practice. "Managers must not attempt to manage change, it is too late for that. They must strive to get ahead of change" (Peter Drucker at a conference, 11 December 1998). We get ahead of change only by initiating it. To initiate change we need to ask timely, relevant questions.

- The "strategic knowledge unit" is analogous to putting strategic planning into the hands of specialists. It becomes worse than a dry, academic exercise, it becomes somebody's turf, because in an organizational setting "power flows to she or he who knows". What is known must be shared and since people are generally less than inclined to share they must be questioned – and rewarded for giving pertinent answers.

- If reward, sanctions and legitimacy are decreasingly becoming the bases for organizational power then expert power, status power (through experience and assumed knowledge), and referent power (the power that comes from being the chosen role model because of past success – a consistently over-hyped example is Jack Welch), will increasingly tempt those who wish to progress more than they want the firm to prosper, to be a barrier to creating the learning organization.

- Team success depends increasingly on consensus and consensus only works where change is so fast and so different that the past is not a reliable guide to the future and where relevant knowledge is spread among the population in such a way that even the knowledge holders are unaware of the utility of what they know until other pieces of the jigsaw are available. The effective executive directs the assembly of that jigsaw by asking the killer questions.

- In a changing world the tendency of a winning team to freeze is the biggest danger facing successful corporations. Winning teams readily succumb to the temptation to seeing themselves as "having the one-size fits all formula" for success. They remain winning teams only when they are forced to think through the answers to questions relevant to a rapidly changing situation.

- De Geus argues that the learning organization must be more than a repository of acquired knowledge. It must apply what is learned in order to be flexible in strategic and tactical thinking and action. What is known must constantly be questioned to ensure that it remains relevant. More, the learning organization must practise frugality so that it always has adequate financial resources with which to meet an emergency or a strategic sea change.

- Established companies (those that had survived beyond five years from launch), only a decade ago, had a life expectancy averaging 60 years. In today's fast moving markets that average has fallen to twelve years and is still declining (Harvard Business School Global Research, 1999). Survival depends, as never before, on building and fostering an appropriate culture and doing it more quickly than ever before. Again that demands that the right questions are asked.

Questions arising from the research to make it meaningful to your company today

Looking outward to the marketplace

- How does an organization such as this move from where we are to where we have to be at the lowest possible cost in the shortest possible time?
- What is our key competitive edge in the eyes of our most worthwhile customers right now?
  - How can we apply that edge to gain more customers like them?
  - How can we use our advantage to set the rules by which others have to play?
  - If we manage to get ahead of the pack, how will we stay ahead?

Looking inward at ourselves

- How can we best use explicit knowledge in our organization?
- Can we leverage explicit knowledge in order to be able to direct, without stifling, tacit knowledge?

- Have we got a "leapfrog mentality"?
- Do we want to be better than the best?
- Are all our people, not just top management, determined to become and remain the best of the best?

■ What is the key contribution that our people can make today?

- What will it take to get them to make that contribution? (Try not to think in terms of concrete rewards. Research in psychology has shown again and again that what people are pleased to contribute because they share a vision and the values that drive it, is devalued in their eyes by concrete reward systems. Once a contribution has been devalued it is continued only for bigger and bigger rewards. Let people benefit from success, but ask yourself constantly whether concrete rewards are either necessary or desirable.)

■ If we have organized our business in such a way as to have a department of planning professionals, how can we get everybody contributing to the future direction of the company?

■ How do people in our organization achieve, wield and recognize power?

- Is the basis of power the right one in a world in which we may have to learn how to manage the imagination and creativity of all?

■ Do we really understand how and when to use consensus? (See *Key Management Solutions*, pages 73–75 and 117–122 for some facts and ideas.)

- How can we get across to people how to use consensus decision-making for best effect? (If you have real experts in your organization it is usually cheaper and more effective to let them get on with what they are best at. Consensus decision-making is only effective when the team is committed and the situation is so novel that the information that could lead to a high quality decision might lie anywhere in the team. That is why training people use such unlikely scenarios – Lost on the Moon, Lost in the Desert or whatever for consensus decision-making exercises. Only by creating a situation in which it is highly unlikely that there will be an expert in the group are they able to practically ensure that the team decision is better than that of individuals. The trouble is that they then claim that consensus decision-making is the best option. It usually is not.)

■ Are we careful enough with money and other resources so that we ensure that we can always invest in a change of direction or resources when the need arises?

How can we apply our current strengths and competencies to take a leading role in the best, most profitable markets of the future?

Strengths bring in revenues and profits when they are intelligently applied in the real world. In this question Gary Hamel and Chris Prahalad are again virtually forecasting Arie de Geus's much later findings. Companies that survive and prosper are those that apply their strengths flexibly in a volatile business environment. They never re-invent the wheel for the sake of novelty. Their primary strategy is always to use what they have already proved to be of value in the real world of business. They are frugal in their approach to change for change's sake and they are frugal in their use of resources. They are not averse to change. They change when change is dictated by the changing desires of their customers. This approach and the question that drives it enables them to build prosperity and conserve resources until the need to invest is compelling. Then they have a massive advantage over those who have failed to ask the right questions and have been profligate to the point that they cannot even afford to spend what they must to prosper in changing circumstances.

As usual this question, like people named in the Bible, begets others that are equally valid.

Beyond the organization

- What will be the most profitable markets of the future?
- Which will be the easiest for us to exploit?
- How will we know when it is time to change direction?

Within the business

- How can we be sure that we take all our people with us?
- What specific steps should we take to minimize risk?
- How do we maximize the return on our growing resources, financial and otherwise, in the meantime?

What new skills, knowledge and competencies do we have to develop or acquire to create the rules by which others have to play in the most profitable markets of the future?

This question makes at least two key points. Either you choose to be a leader in the markets that you serve or you risk allowing others to make the rules so they are consistently ahead of the game and forcing you to play follow-the-leader. If you choose to dominate your markets, whether your chosen market is a sector, segment or a small niche, you can develop the standards to which others have to aspire. Playing a game of "me too" in the marketplace can often lead to high expense, low market share and in some cases to total withdrawal and financial collapse.

Being either first to market or the "best of the best" can, if you move too quickly, attract the attention of strong competitors before you are ready for the fight. In the long run, market dominance is the only game worth playing, but considering the right questions at the right time is the best way to get the timing right.

Remember that although there may be "two sides to every question" only the least practical person seeks three and there is usually one right answer for you right now. That answer may no longer be right at some time in the future (which is why you need to keep asking the question), but as an example of stretching questions that have only one right answer for you right now you might like to think about the following as they relate to your company. Be prepared to challenge the implied answers to these questions that have been the drivers of policy and strategy in the past.

Conceptualizing

- What business are we really in?
- How do others see us?
- Are we innovators or augmenters?
- What are our thinking patterns?
- What are our resources?
- What are our assumptions?
- Do we reward creative thinking and associated risk-taking?
- How does the future look?
- What are the appropriate risks to take?
- How do we develop our key goal(s)?
- What are our most attractive alternatives?

- Should we consider starting over?
- Do we have the courage to confront what the marketplace is telling us?

Key questions to really challenge the top team's thinking

- Is there a top-team consensus around the important issues of:
  - Are we thriving or surviving?
  - Are we growing or stagnating?
  - Are we leading or following?
- Are we in danger of calling agreement consensus when it is merely "groupthink"?
- Do we share an absolute determination to be the best of the best and the company that shapes the future of our industry?
- Do we have, and believe in, a real vision of our future – or have we put together a few fine-sounding words which are variously interpreted by individuals, divisions, departments or at different organizational levels?
- Do our people share our vision, ignore it, or are they simply unaware that it exists?
- If we have an inspirational vision is it backed by a mission that tells every stakeholder from customer to society at large, the customer desires that we exist to fulfil, what makes us different from the herd, what challenges us to become and remain the "best of the best", how we treat people and the values that drive every decision that we make?

Strategizing

- What is our best strategy?
- What do we *want* to happen?
- What is the organizing principle behind our business?
- Are we too complex for easy focus?
- What segments, sectors or niches are we aiming at?
- What attracts us to these?
- What are our resources?
- What are the trends?
- How good are the omens?
- Are we proposing high risk innovations?
- How does our proposed strategy limit and control the level of risk?

- What special factors influence our business environment?
- What are the consequences of our strategy?
- Whom are we addressing as stakeholders?
- How ready are we?
- What processes do we have for feedback, evaluation and review?
- What are our strategic options?
- Would we be comfortable as low risk trend followers?

Key questions to challenge the thinking of every member of management

- In developing our strategy have we considered a sufficient number of alternatives?
- Are we psychologically (emotionally) at ease with our strategy?
- Is there general agreement that our strategy is appropriate to today's and tomorrow's business environment?
  - Have we built into the strategy sufficient flexibility to meet rapidly changing needs?
  - Does our performance feedback system give us adequate warning of the need to change direction?
  - Are our management and people at every level capable of flexible response to emergent conditions?
- Are we free of any danger that past success makes our people believe that they have a "one size fits all" strategy suitable for all situations? ("We live in a rapidly changing world in which nothing fails like success" – Richard Pascal.)
- Is there a general understanding that the strategic goals *must* be achieved, even if the route to them is fine tuned to changing circumstances?

Tactics

- What are the key activities?
- Where are the bottlenecks?
- What kind of managers do we need?
- How do we maintain control?
- What is our power base?
- How do we communicate the vision?

- How do we "walk the talk"?
- How do we maintain our values?
- How do we stay focused?
- How do we communicate change?
- How do we celebrate success?
- How do we reward desired behaviours?
- What standards of performance are necessary to keep our best customers?
- How do we increase productivity?
- How do we get/give feedback?
- How do we allocate resources?
- How do we avoid blame-fixing?
- What is the right management style?
- How do we build commitment?
- How do we decide on useful measurement?
- How do we recognize the need for objectives?
- How do we clearly differentiate between efficient and effective behaviour?

Key questions to invite every committed individual to think about their contribution

- Are we building a firm base today from which we will make our strategic plan a reality?
- What are the important skills, knowledge and competencies that we need to make the most of today's most profitable markets?
- Have we, or are we building, the skills, knowledge and competencies that we will need to fully exploit the most profitable markets of the near future?
- Are we working now to ensure that we have the knowledge, skills and competencies to design, develop and dominate the most exciting markets of the future?

Summary

The above questions are part of a small toolkit that I send to the boards of companies who are considering developing a market dominance strategy prior to our first meeting. They are designed to enable the board to easily answer the questions:

– Where and what do we want to be?

– Where and what are we now?

– What is likely to be our preferred route for getting from where we are to where we want to be?

– Is our strategy capable of being implemented in the real world?

– Will our tactics provide the best platform for achieving our strategy?

– Can we carry all stakeholders – employees, customers, suppliers, distributors and the society in which we operate – with us?

– Can we turn stakeholders into proactive advocates for our business?

– Are we convinced that we have identified the best, most economical way forward?

We will have much to say about strategy and tactics later, but in the meantime the above is a taster. If you would like to take a look at the best, proven tools and techniques for developing a strategy pages 16–35 of *Key Management Solutions* will give you some ideas.

Life-long learning – just-in-time

The second point encapsulated in the question is that of building and sustaining a genuine learning community. Arie de Geus's Harvard research makes it clear that, without exception, long-lived and prosperous corporations build genuine learning communities rather than paying mere lip service to the concept. They practise what I have described as "life-long learning – just-in-time". The questions that Hamel and Prahalad raise may lead you to consider the following.

Life-long learning strategy

■ Do we encourage our people to value learning?

– Do we encourage them to share what they learn with their colleagues?

- Do we ensure that what is learned is relevant to our needs and is applied before it is forgotten?
- Do we give our people adequate time to integrate new learning?
- Do we measure the return on our learning investment and insist that trainers, internal or external, take responsibility for people using what they have learned?

■ Do the training people that we employ or hire fully understand and use their knowledge of how people learn?

Bruce Joyce of Columbia University, New York conducted a respected study in which he showed that only some 5 per cent to 15 per cent of what is taught is actually learned sufficiently well to apply it in the workplace. Fortunately we each tend to learn and use different parts of any programme, so if we initiate a programme of supported peer coaching we can massively increase what is learned and used. Seward and Gers conducted a twelve-year longitudinal study based on supported peer coaching and showed that they were able to raise learning and application to better than 90 per cent and keep it at that kind of level for the period of the study. Details of the total package are described in my book *Making Change Pay* (Pearson) as well as in *Key Management Solutions* (pages 250–267).

They call it the law

It is flattering for any writer when businesspeople and journalists take enough interest in something to name it after the author. Thus "Lambert's Laws of Business" were born. I try to look modest when this is mentioned and mutter something about wondering where I stole it from many years ago, but the fact is that like most people I enjoy the flattery no matter how ill-deserved it may be. The so-called "laws" can be expressed – indeed are most usefully expressed – as a short series of questions. I believe that "my" laws ought to be in the forefront of any serious businessperson's mind, in question form. When faced with any decision that requires the investment of time or money I believe that we ought to ask those who propose the investment:

■ What significant contribution will it make to the achievement of the tactical or strategic objectives?

■ When will it pay for itself?

■ How clearly and compellingly can it be explained to those who will have to make it work?

Any doubts about the answers to any of these questions means that you are not ready for the implementation of the idea. Lambert's Laws of Business state that:

Nothing should be done in a business unless:

- It makes a significant impact on achieving goals.
- It will pay for itself in a reasonable time.
- It can be explained in simple and inspirational terms to all those who need to make it work.

The laws refer to tactical matters, so there is much to be gained by asking some tactical questions.

It makes a significant impact

- Who are the 20 per cent of customers that deliver 80 per cent of our profitable business?
- What is the lifetime value of these customers?
- What is the lifetime value of the average customer?
- Who specifically are the customers that we need to keep?
- What do they want from us?
- When did we last ask them what they require from us?
- How well do our goals reflect our need to keep these customers?
- How will this activity play a significant role in enabling us to bind our key customers to us?
- How precisely will this attract new, profitable customers?
- If it does not build our business, why are we proposing to do it?

It pays for itself

- How long is the payback period?
- What is the anticipated return on investment?
- When will the cash flow become positive if we invest?
- What other demands on resources do we have?
- Is this the best way to use our resources right now?

It is meaningful and inspirational

- What do our people care about?
- When did we last ask them?
- Who specifically is crucial to making this work?
- Do they understand the importance of their role?
- Could I explain this change effectively to a four-year-old child?
- Does what is proposed really excite me?

Devil's advocate or devil's disciple?

Consultants frequently misuse questions. I will guarantee that when any consultant says: "Let me play devil's advocate", they don't have a single idea in their heads and grope to find fault with the client's reasoning rather than put their own meagre contribution under scrutiny. If a consultant suggests that this is their preferred role I invariably say: "I am paying the bills and I will ask the questions". The Gestapo in the old wartime movies were no fools and when it comes to dealing with over-priced fools I have a streak of the Gestapo in me.

Through the use of questions it is easy to establish whether the consultant is of any use or is simply spinning his or her wheels at your expense. The questions that a consultant asks should be carefully planned to help the client to widen their thinking. They often should contain the germ of a rough idea that the client can adapt to their own circumstances and adopt if it seems to be the right thing to do. Devil's advocate is almost invariably a destructive role that contributes nothing. Constructive questions open new horizons.

---

mini case study

The killer question

More years ago than I care to remember I had a wonderful opportunity to learn from a real master of the art of using questions. I was working with Don Thain at that time Professor of Marketing at the University of Western Ontario. Don was the most effective teacher that I ever knew. He made wonderful use of the case study. Every morning before the classes that we, in theory, conducted together, he would clip and photocopy key items from that day's *Wall Street Journal* and *Financial Times*. They were his case studies. From his encyclopaedic and detailed knowledge of what was happening in business at home and abroad he would frame questions that brought out the essential learning points of each story – topical, relevant and real world. Students would work industriously to provide insightful answers to each question, but they knew that Don had the killer question waiting and that was the important one. Students and top executives of blue-chip corporations alike would deliver their hard won wisdom. Don would nod sagely and then ask, *"What is your evidence for that?"* I suggest that if you simply develop the habit of asking that question or a variant of it each and every time that you receive a smooth, credible answer from a peer or subordinate that you will do more for the quality of thinking and the reduction of bull in your business than all the training specialists and expensive consultants in the world.

As a quick aside, Don had a habit of scribbling meaningless squiggles on the white board while explaining the world of business with compelling enthusiasm. Before wiping the board clean of the unreadable hieroglyphics he would politely ask if we had all copied all that we needed to. It may sound like a silly habit, but I never saw any groups of more devoted and thorough note-takers than in Don's classes.

When you believe that the answer to any question that you ask is too glib or too vague ask the killer question.

- *What is your evidence for that?*

  You will improve the quality of thinking in your organization at a stroke.

Congratulations

You are almost far too busy to read the remainder of this book right now and you have no need to try to find the time. You have completed the reading requirement. From this page on it is a toolkit of questions with references to proven tools and techniques and the occasional relevant case study. The idea is that you keep the book constantly to hand and dip into it when you need some thought-starters, examples and implementation tools. You have no need to wade through hundreds of pages to get to one or two key ideas. Key ideas are strategically repeated throughout the book in different question forms so that you can safely dip in and out as you choose and ask the right questions in all important business situations.

You can easily and rapidly get to what you want and spend the real time doing what you do best, using your brain to deliver the best outcome for you right now. If you use, rather than read, this book you will:

- Focus on the key issues in all important business situations.
- Make quicker and better decisions in all aspects of the business.
- Build the capability of your people to think things through effectively.
- Make consistent best use of the best people.
- Ensure speedier and more effective implementation of key initiatives.
- Exploit otherwise unforeseen business opportunities.
- Build the business in good times and bad.

And it will be "all your own work" – so congratulations are doubly appropriate!

To encourage you in your position of "boss" you might like to consider the following questions:

- How do I connect my people with my purpose?
- How could I build commitment even more effectively?
- How can I encourage "ownership" through and within my team?
- How can I focus efforts on working smarter in the interest of the individual, the team and the business?
- How can we build competence without wasting time or money?

- How do I recognize the achievements of my people and encourage them to build strength on strength?
- How do I show my respect for the individual?

If you do all of these things effectively you are what one research team calls "a best boss". As a best boss you will want to become better yet and then better still. You will find in these pages the thought starters, case studies, research findings, key questions and even some of the answers that will enable you to build strength on strength.

Success will be yours and what is more thinking through and asking the right questions of the right people at the right time does not only keep you in control, it is fun.

Questioning skills

The value of asking questions cannot be overemphasized. You can effectively manage a person's thinking by asking the right questions. Psychiatrists, psychologists and the most effective salespeople think deeply about the questions that will direct thinking along the lines that are appropriate.

If you want a person to think about how they think or how they feel about something ask them open questions. These are simply questions that cannot be answered briefly or with a "yes" or "no".

- What keeps you awake at night?
- What's your evidence?
- If it were your responsibility what would you do?
- How do you feel about it?
- What do you think should be our next steps?

– and the most widely used open question of all:

- Why?

Although it is usually easier to begin by asking open questions and then focus down on to what is important by asking closed questions, psychologists know that to ask open questions of somebody who feels threatened only adds to the pressure and frequently causes them to clam up or mutter things like "I don't know" or "I'm not really sure". To get shy people or people under pressure to talk freely, ask closed questions first and then open up the discussion when they show signs of feeling comfortable. In the case of very stressed people make sure that the closed questions that you ask initially are "safe" ones even though you probably know the answer. Help them to feel that it is safe to talk to you.

- Do you enjoy your job?
- Are your friends helpful to you?
- Are you comfortable talking about this?

Other closed questions that direct the thinking of others as well as enabling you to draw out more detailed information might include:

- Who are our best customers?
- What were the production figures last month?
- When will it be ready?
- Who is responsible?
- Where did the problem first show itself?
- Which would you choose?
- How does that affect you?
- What excites you personally about our vision statement?

Questions that invite the answer "yes" or "no" are simply extreme forms of closed questions. "Yes" or "no" questions are a powerful tool for restraining garrulity and for forcing another person to stick to the point which is why they are so popular with lawyers. They are dangerous, however, because the answer is seldom complete and can be, as some lawyers wish them to be, very misleading.

One further form of question that managers find useful in terms of ensuring mutual understanding is called the progress test question. When asking such questions, be careful always to take responsibility for what Webster's Dictionary calls "the transfer of meaning".

- Have I made that clear enough?
- Does this raise any questions in your mind?
- Does what I have said make complete sense to you?

If you want honest answers never put the responsibility on the other person by asking questions such as "are you with me so far?" They are likely to answer "yes" no matter how confused they feel. (For a more complete psychological overview of questions the interested reader may wish to refer to *The Power of Influence*.)

To make your life a little easier

Anybody like me who makes a living from asking the right questions knows that the answers can give rise to equally important supplementary questions. In this book I have inserted many logical supplementary questions. I have indented these a little further on the page to make it easier for you to follow the development.

You will have the advantage of listening to and carefully considering the answers to the questions that you pose. This will lead to further supplementaries and give you the full picture wherever you choose to investigate. The supplementaries that I suggest enable you to dig a little deeper and, as you dig, you will become ever more certain of what, given your individual needs and intentions, you want to know.

Summary

The key skill of questioning is to ask the right question of the right people at the right time. That is why the chapters of this book should be referred to and used when the time is right rather than read and put back on the shelf.

1

The big picture

questions of vision and mission

Build bridges – below the waterline. Tom Peters

It is not enough to succeed. Others must fail. Gore Vidal

- Strategic questions that take you from where you are to where you want to be.
- Tactical questions that ensure that you survive long enough to get there.

What you will gain from this chapter

- How to develop a superior strategy.
- How to succeed today while planning far enough ahead to dominate tomorrow.
- How to use questions and other tools and techniques to make the competition play to your rules.

Some numbers that you may need to check out as background to your thinking

- ✓ What is the average customer lifetime?
- ✓ What is the lifetime value of the average customer? (Average revenue divided by average customer lifetime.)
- ✓ What is the average customer lifetime profit?

☑ What is the lifetime value of the top 20 per cent of customers?

☑ What percentage of customers are below average in delivering revenues and profit?

☑ What customers, by name, are more trouble to serve than they are worth?

The big picture

Every great leader of every great business that has ever spoken or written on the subject of success has declared that the one essential attribute is to have a clear view of the big picture. From McKitterick and Watson to the two Jacks, Welch and Smith the story is the same – know precisely where you are going and passionately pursue your dream.

The first step in developing a meaningful strategy for success is to create your ideal future in such detail that all of your five senses can experience it right now. The passion is important so until you have the answers to these questions you have no foundation for your strategy and, without a foundation, you will never have a strategy worth pursuing or the energy to make it a reality. Unless you have what it takes to make your dream a reality, you have nothing and if you are incapable of developing a dream worth the effort you might just as well drift and let the world give you as much or as little as chance dictates. So either take the following questions seriously, or forget the whole business, because in a very real sense you will have no business. (For the tools of strategy building see *Key Management Solutions* pages 14–36.)

In writing this section I am, as always addressing an individual reader. This should in no way be taken to mean that strategy building is anything other than a team activity. Teams, however, need leadership and it is my firm resolve that my reader should be at the very least, a "thought leader".

Step one – the ideal future – where I want us to be

■ What is my ideal future?

■ Assuming all things to be possible and knowing that I will come back to a realistic assessment and plan later, where do I intend to be in the future?

■ How large will the company be in 5–10–15 years' time?

■ What customers will be beating a path to our door?

■ Who will they be, how big will they be, what will be their position in their own sectors?

- Why will they beat a path to us rather than to our competitors?
- What will we provide them with that the others cannot?
- Who will we employ?
- What will be their qualifications, attitudes, capabilities and behaviours?
- What will they say about us as an employer?
- What will our customers say about us?
- How will suppliers and distributors, if we have them, feel about being associated with us?
- What will they tell others about us?
- What will they tell us about our products and services?
- How will the communities in which we operate respond to our presence?
- Why specifically will they welcome us as a model employer and good neighbour?
- What will get *me* out of bed every morning bursting with the desire to get to work?
- What will make others as passionate about this as I am?

Summary

Unless you are clear about where you are going you have no way to assess how far you have come, how far you still have to go or whether your ambition has been too modest. The Japanese have a saying: "aim for a tree and you may only hit the ground, but aim for the sky and at least you will hit the tree". Building a picture of your ideal future is the basis from which all else, vision, mission, strategy, goals and tactics flow. Do not see this as an abstract exercise in wishful thinking. Make your future a reality that you can see, touch, hear, taste and even smell and you will enable others to share your dream and work for its realization.

Step two – the start of the journey – where are we now?

Concerns

- What are the important concerns that have to be resolved before we can succeed?
- How specifically will each halt or stall our progress to my ideal future?

- What is my evidence that they are really important barriers to progress?
- How exactly are important customers affected?
  - What complaints do we get from important customers?
  - How many complaints did we have last month?
  - What have we already done?
  - What is the evidence that we have already done all that is required?
- In team discussions how can I ensure that my colleagues and I concentrate on the important concerns and set aside hidden agendas, old grievances, favourite gripes and the rest?
  - Who are the regular complainers?
  - What do they complain about?
  - Are their complaints justified?
  - How can I handle their justified concerns so that they will not be raised again?
  - How can I pre-empt the old, meaningless war stories without losing their goodwill?
- Who is best qualified to resolve each of the key issues that are really important?
- What is in it for them if they resolve them now?
- Why haven't they been resolved before now?
- Who will share my passionate desire to deal with the key obstacles and only the key obstacles?
  - How can I organize them to work with me to ensure the best outcomes?
- How can I bring together the skills, knowledge and passion needed to remove the barriers?
- *What steps can I take today to start to resolve the key concerns?*

Summary

Research shows that resolving concerns rarely adds significantly to profits. Resolving those few key concerns that will actually bar your progress toward achieving your ideal future is essential. The above questions are designed to enable you to probe deeply enough to be sure that the concerns that you choose to address are those that are a significant barrier to getting where you want to be.

Opportunities

- What are the most exciting opportunities that the market offers today?
- Which are we currently ready to pursue?
  - What are the key strengths, capabilities, competencies, knowledge and attitudes that are required?
  - Which do we have in abundance?
  - Which can we rapidly build?
- Which opportunities would give us the best return on resources used?
- Which would give us the quickest return?
- Which should we pursue right now?
- What are likely to be the most exciting opportunities of the future?
- Which future opportunities should we be preparing ourselves for now?
- Which can wait until later?
- Which are not valuable enough for us to bother with in the foreseeable future?
- What current skills, capabilities and knowledge could we apply to get a head start in developing and exploiting these opportunities?
- How can we build additional skills, capabilities and knowledge needed to pursue them ahead of our rivals?
- Can we list those opportunities that we should start to exploit immediately?
- Can we list those that we should be planning to exploit as soon as we have built the capability?
- Which should we put to one side to avoid being distracted from our main task of achieving our ideal future?
- *What will I do today to take this forward?*

Summary

In a volatile business environment opportunities will arise frequently. Not all opportunities are worth pursuing, however, and asking the right questions enables you to make the best use of your always limited resources.

Strengths

■ What are our key strengths? (List them all. Write them down. Disregard your competition that may or may not share similar strengths. Discipline yourself and your colleagues to only look inwards. This is no-navel gazing, it is an approach that ensures that you identify all that you have going for you even if you need to use considerable creativity when it comes to making it work for you. At this stage your purpose is to clearly establish ALL that you have going for you. Nothing is too trivial to be included unless its inclusion trivializes the whole activity – see the Case Study on page 11 for an example.)

■ Why do our present customers choose to do business with us?

■ What specifically do they say about us?

■ To whom do they say it?

■ If they say good things about us, how can we get them to talk more widely about our products and services? (A repeated warning from the psychologist in me. Never pay for anything that people are prepared to do freely to demonstrate their regard for you. Payment devalues the generous action and turns it into something that becomes conditional on payment. In Howard Shenson's words, "to pay me is to insult me. If you choose to insult me, you'd better insult me thoroughly, regularly and more and more expensively".)

■ What skills, knowledge, competencies, attitudes, values or behaviours cause customers to want to come to us first and stay with us?

■ What current strengths could we apply to take more profit out of today's markets?

   – What potential are we missing?

   – How much is the total market worth?

   – What is our market share?

   – How much more could we realistically take?

   – From whom can we take it?

   – What would it cost us to do it?

   – How much more money could we be making?

   – How will we use that additional profit to pursue our ideal future?

■ What strengths do we need to build or acquire to be most effective in the key markets of the future?

   – What will be the key markets of the future?

- – Which of our current strengths are also relevant to those markets?
- – What should we be doing right now to develop and promote those strengths?
- How will we most effectively and economically build or acquire those essential strengths that we lack?
  - – Should we consider working with strategic allies who have strengths complementary to ours?
  - – Do we know any potential allies whose strengths complement ours?
  - – Who are they and how should they be approached?
  - – If we do not know of any potential allies how do we go about finding them?
- *What is the most important single thing that I can do today to enable the effective application, building or leveraging of our strengths?*
- How precisely will that action move us forward toward our Ideal Future?

Summary

> Strengths are the key to tactical and strategic success. It is by building, leveraging and promoting your strengths that you create and keep customers. The above questions enable you to fully appreciate your strengths and apply them most effectively to achieve your present and future prosperity. The effective acquisition and application of strengths is so important that it is worth your while to consider whether you have the answers to some key questions.

Do not stop listing strengths until you are absolutely confident that you are able to answer the following additional questions fully and accurately.

- Where is your company better than average in terms of operational excellence, service to customers and keeping costs down?
- Where does your company have superior knowledge of customers and their emergent needs and desires?
- Why will your customers mandate you to increase that knowledge and feed you information?
- What makes it easy to attract and keep above average staff?
- What do they enjoy about their work?
- What makes them feel personally committed to the company?

- How do they show that they take a real pride in communicating with, understanding and serving every customer?
- How successful are you at building customer loyalty?
  - Can you keep at least 90 per cent of profitable customers for at least ten years. (Research by Bains and Company indicates that profitability is optimal where companies are able to achieve the above figures.)
- What precisely gives you that ability?
- What specifically and concretely are you particularly good at doing, in the eyes of your customers, which enables you to make your highest profits and create the highest level of customer delight at the lowest possible cost?
- Where do you already have the greatest ability to communicate on a one-to-one basis with your delighted customers?
  - Who does the communicating?
  - How reliable is their feedback? (If you rely solely upon your sales and marketing people to communicate with your most profitable customers you are in danger of receiving biased feedback on what customers want and how well you provide it. It is a senior management responsibility and a considerable strength to remain in frequent contact with every vital customer.)
- Which are the strengths and competencies that you have now that will enable you to win more profitable business in those parts of today's markets which you currently serve?
- Which are the strengths and competencies that you need to build quickly in order to more fully exploit the most profitable markets today?
- Which are the strengths and competencies that you have which will enable you to prosper in the most exciting and profitable markets of the foreseeable future?
- What strengths and competencies must you build to create some of the most profitable, exciting and sustainable markets of the future?
- What strengths and competencies must you build to set the standards for your industry in the most exciting markets of the future?

Control the instinctive belief that the priority is to correct your weaknesses. The priority is always to give the profit-producing customer more of what they already like about doing business with you. Any real strength that you have is playing a part in delighting at least one customer somewhere. What delights one can be leveraged to delight many so make sure that your list is comprehensive and that you are confident that you know where and how every strength can be better applied to give you a sound highly profitable, springboard today and massive prosperity tomorrow.

The twin secrets of the successful strategic thinker are to never become so committed to easy profits today that you lose sight of the bigger picture tomorrow and to never ignore low hanging fruit today that will give you the investment capability to turn dreams into reality. The activity of analyzing, building and applying strengths is a subtle balancing act in which you need to be careful neither to overvalue nor undervalue those attributes through which your ideal future will be delivered. Your ability to achieve your ideal will be a direct function of how effective you are at questioning how well you are applying your strengths today and building those that you will need tomorrow speedily and at the lowest possible cost. The essential questions are not to be asked once a year and then forgotten until the next planning meeting. They are a part of day-to-day management.

Threats

- What external threats could jeopardize our progress?
- Which could be avoided if we take the appropriate steps now?
- What should we start today to remove these threats from the picture?
- What threats could materialize regardless of any steps that we take in advance?
- What would be the warning signs?
- How can we be sure that we see the warning signs in sufficient time?
- What is our detailed contingency plan to ensure that we will not be knocked off course by any threats?

Threats to a business fall into two distinct types. There are those that can be avoided by taking the right steps today and there are those that, if you fail to ask the right questions, could take you by surprise. The first demand swift and effective tactical decisions and action today. The second require effective strategic contingency plans that can be implemented at the first sign of trouble. In a business world where the business cycle has been shown to be accelerating, being prepared to take effective and timely action is the essential success factor. This depends on asking the right questions and on building the answers into all planning, both strategic and tactical.

Summary

Threats fall into two categories, those that can be avoided and those that cannot be circumvented by any action taken in advance. Ask enough questions to ensure that everyone is clear about the difference and that today's actions and tomorrow's contingency plans are robust.

COST analysis

The above is a COST Analysis. It performs all of the capabilities of a SWOT Analysis with the additional advantage that it is designed to be action oriented and therefore integrated from the start into an effective planning process. It also avoids the emotional problems that research has shown are frequently associated with the better known, but less useful SWOT Analysis. Just in case you revere the sequence of the four letters S-W-O-T you may be interested to know that the concept first saw the light of day at the Stanford Research Institute as SOFT Analysis (Strengths, Opportunities, Failures, Threats). The change to SWOT was for commercial, rather than practical or conceptual reasons and was not made by the inventors of the concept.

The reader will be fully familiar with SWOT Analysis, but on an analogy with the writer of concert programme notes who has to assume that someone is listening to Beehoven's Fifth for the first time let me explain what goes wrong. The first activity is to establish STRENGTHS. This means that most planners try to identify this most important factor before they are "warmed-up' mentally. As a result they miss a number of strengths that the business has and which, with a little thought could have been exploited to deliver superior service and win business. A weak list of strengths makes it easy to dwell on inessentials when considering WEAKNESSES. As a result the planners identify a wide range of confidence sapping weaknesses. If, on the planner's paper at least, the organization has a limited number of strengths and a considerable catalogue of weaknesses, OPPORTUNITIES appear to be few and hardly worth bothering with. Finally an organization that has been defined as strong only in terms of weaknesses is perceived to be subjected to many and varied THREATS. In short the emotional effects of conducting the SWOT Analysis can be to drain rather than to build enthusiasm and motivation. At best the work that has been put into the development of the lists of Strengths, Weaknesses, Opportunities and Threats is ignored during the rest of the planning development and where work is done and then set aside the whole process is devalued.

How trivial can who(?) get?

I would have expected the board of a major international corporation to be more dedicated to quality outcomes, but it was soon clear that they had no intention of doing any work. They were treating the strategy planning workshop as an outing and a child's outing at that. They resolutely refused to do any serious thinking for the first hour and a senior group tried to outdo each other in facetiousness giving flippant and meaningless answers to any question put to them. On being asked to list the key strengths that drove their business one sub-group had only come up with "the tightness of our girls' skirts" before subsiding into giggles.

It was clear that I had to do something drastic. I stopped the activity and asked the chairman to stand by the window. I invited the CEO to join him and so on until I had a group of grinning board members in rough order of seniority queuing at the window behind the top man. The window was on the top floor of a skyscraper hotel. I then behaved in a less than professional, but highly effective manner. Addressing the chairman, I asked him to open the window. (Unfortunately he couldn't. It was sealed to optimize the air conditioning and obviate suicide attempts. But I didn't let that stop me. I was angry.) Then speaking to the whole group I suggested in the strongest possible terms with some use of language inappropriate to the consultant–client relationship that since they were clearly of no use to their stockholders, employees, customers or anyone else they should jump regardless of the state of the window.

As I finished my tirade the door opened and an hotel employee entered with refreshments and a message from one of my publishers to tell me that a major international business magazine had referred to me that day as "the world's *friendliest* guru".

The irony was not lost on any of us and we all dissolved into fits of laughter. After the laughter subsided we got on with the job and my clients, determined to show their mettle did a superb job that has been instrumental in their massive global success.

Had I only asked the right questions at the right time the humour of the situation might have been lost, but in the greater scheme of things we would have saved time and reached the final splendid outcome possibly with less expense and less acrimony. When faced with a group determined not to work effectively or at all, use your questioning skills to get them back on track quickly and with good humour. (Please refer to the last few paragraphs of the introduction for a few ideas on how to use questions to manage behaviour.)

Step three – the vision thing

The vision is not a short sequence of fancy words with little meaning, nor is it a long sequence of even fancier words with even less meaning. It is, in Tom Peters' carefully chosen expression, the tool that will "get everybody to the barricades when the chips are down". You have defined, refined and committed your team to your Ideal Future. Your task now is to encapsulate that future in a short, pithy, meaningful, inspirational phrase that will excite and motivate everybody from employee to customer to come to the barricades when the chips are down. This is by no means an easy task and many strategic planning sessions have seen top businesspeople sweating well beyond midnight on a simple task that they started early that day. A couple of questions might help.

- What is it about our Ideal Future that genuinely excites and inspires us?

- How can we express that, preferably in words of not more than two syllables so that others will share our excitement?

- What do our people like to do that is implicit or explicit in our Ideal Future?

  - Do they like to "kick ass"? (A Japanese earth-moving competitor has the vision statement "Surround Caterpillar". This may not sound important, but it does two key things. It exploits the employees' desire to be aggressively competitive and it channels that aggression against the competitor that must be beaten if Komatsu is to enjoy market dominance.)

  - Do they want to protect the environment?

  - Do they want to serve their neighbours and their neighbourhood?

  - Do they want to be respected as the best of the best? (A banking client has "Ultimate in Service – Anywhere".)

- What will make all our stakeholders determined to support our progress and proud to be part of what we truly are?

- How will we test what we develop to ensure that it is truly inspirational?

  - How will we know that it will "get people to the barricades when the chips are down"?

- How will we communicate it to all those who have a part to play in making our vision reality?

Communicating the vision and mission in such a way that they promote action is a tough task. It is a task that demands as much consideration as the writing of either or both. Be careful to avoid anything that has failed in the past. If the video of the chairman fell on deaf ears, do something different this time.

Ensure that the words used in both the vision and the mission statement are carefully checked to ensure that ambiguities are excluded. Go a step further and assure yourself that, where necessary, definitions are agreed. When you communicate, try to ensure that everyone receives the same information at the same time and give people a chance to publicly demonstrate their commitment. See "Our mission" below.

Summary

> The vision serves the same purpose as did the banner on ancient battlefields. It provides a rallying point for all when things look bad. If it does not do this, it is nothing but empty words. Be sure to ask enough questions to develop an inspirational vision.

Step four – the mission

While some firms are increasingly seeking to replace the mission statement with something more "modern", others are simply trying to ensure that the mission statement is more than a series of fine sounding words. In fact, both are trying to achieve the same outcome. Both are attempting to create a living, breathing, *useful* tool to which their people will refer and which is capable of communicating what the organization is really about. We have two pathways to a single goal and each is equally valid.

Let me start with the "mission that is not a mission statement". Some years ago Andersen Consulting (now Accenture) began to advise their clients to do something other than write and publish a grandiose mission statement. They suggested instead that the client company should list all the key values that drove their business and that all major decisions should be taken on the basis of how well the values would be satisfied. In my company, we use the same system. Any major decision is subjected to how well a decision to act would satisfy our key values. If, for example, I were to suggest to my colleagues on the board that I should set up an office on a beach in the Maldives I would be required to indicate to them in considerable detail how such a move would:

■ Make the best possible use of the best people.

■ Offer superior client service at the most economic cost.

■ Be global in scope and application.

■ Add to life-long learning – just-in-time for all our people.

■ Be frugal with our resources.

■ Avoid building "monuments to bankruptcy".

■ Move consultancy a step nearer to being a genuine and respected profession.

It seems that I may have to rethink the Maldives strategy, but hopefully, the reasons why are clear. In the early days Andersen advised their clients to have proposal forms printed with the key values so that any idea could be readily planned around them. In this way the foundation of the mission became a tool that was always accessible to the people who were working to achieve it.

We are something of a belt and braces (suspenders) organization. We have a list of key values and a mission statement. The values inform those of us lucky enough to be part of the organization how we will behave while the Mission Statement tells all our stakeholders (clients, suppliers, employees, strategic allies and the people of the countries in which we operate), all that they need to know about us to enable them to make an informed decision whether they choose to work with us.

Our mission

To enable our clients to develop and implement superior strategic and tactical solutions through effective networking. What makes us different is that we combine practical experience with state-of-the-art research to develop superior tools and techniques designed to add value at every stage of the implementation process and to do what we do at the lowest possible cost. We ensure growing client autonomy by building their ability to use our unique tools and techniques to attract, win and retain customers.

We are committed to making the best use of the best people and to life-long learning applied just in time. Where our clients are concerned we stick firmly to the principles that: **Nothing should be done in a business unless it:**

- *Adds significantly to the ability of the business to attain its objectives.*

- *Will pay for itself in a reasonable time.*

- *Can be explained in simple terms to those who have to make it work.*

Our stakeholders, suppliers, employees, consultants, clients and members of the communities in which we work are treated as unique, creative individuals that have inalienable rights to be treated as valued on their own terms.

Decision-making at every level is driven by our core values of making the best use of the best people in understanding, adapting and delivering state-of-the-art information to our clients to massively increase value.

I hope that although far from ideal (I have yet to see an ideal mission statement), you will agree that our mission statement tells those who are interested the essential things they need to know about our business. What do they need to know?

- What do these people do?
- What needs and desires of ours do they exist to satisfy?
- What makes them different?

- Why should we approach them first?
- Why are we likely, having come to them, to want to stay with them?
- What challenges them to become and remain the best of the best at what they do?
- What drives their people to constantly develop and hone their capabilities?
- How do they treat their employees, clients, suppliers, strategic allies and the societies in which they operate?
- What are the key values that drive decision-making in their business?
- If I had a problem and an unsupervised employee of this organization was helping me, what values, beliefs and attitudes would drive their decision-making, advice and actions?

Summary

Only if your mission statement gives credible and reasonably comprehensive answers to the above questions, does it serve its key purpose of being a useful, and frequently used tool.
If it is not a frequently used tool it is merely an expensive piece of decoration.

In summary the purpose of any mission statement is to:

- Tell your customers, clients, patients (anyone who uses your products or services), those needs and desires of theirs that you exist to satisfy.
- Indicate what makes you *different* and why the most worthwhile customers, the best employees and the most exciting strategic allies should beat a path to your door.
- Indicate what challenges you and all your people to become and remain the best in the business.
- Tell all stakeholders how you intend to treat them.
- Clarify the key, essential values to the degree that any person working on their own initiative is able consistently to make decisions coherent with, and supportive of the mission.

If you are either in the throes of redesigning or of "re-visiting" your mission (the mission is not for all time, it is a flexible goal that should be subject to constant improvement), I strongly suggest that you put yourself, in turn, in the position of each and every category of stakeholder and ask the above questions on their behalf. If the mission statement that you end up with provides the answers that you wish it to and if those answers are credible from your new standpoint as a stakeholder you have a tool. Of course having a tool and using it effectively are two different things, so there is more work to be done.

- How will we communicate the mission to all who have a role to play in achieving it?
- How can we build their commitment?
- How can we gauge their commitment?
- How can we keep the mission before their eyes and in their minds and hearts without them becoming habituated to it?
- How can we ensure that they refer to the mission when faced with a difficult decision under pressure?

American corporations in particular, have, in the past, created a formal acceptance of a new mission statement by holding some kind of social gathering where the mission, writ large, is paraded before an applauding, enthusiastic multitude of stakeholders prior to be signed by every employee with due ceremony. If this seems over the top to you, consider, if you will, the oft repeated and confirmed experiment summarized below.

Before looking at the research it might help if I add a word on this matter of habituation and the mission. Our brains are wired to disregard those things that are not of crucial interest to us at the time. If they did not we would be overwhelmed with irrelevant information as was the unfortunate Sherevski, a Russian "memory man" whose brain lacked this vital feature. "S" as he is called in the annals of psychology, could not manage a simple task such as buying a pack of cigarettes. The merest hint of a desire to smoke and his mind was filled with complete memories of every brand on the market and every cigarette that he had smoked in his life. He simply could not, under such a barrage of irrelevant information, step into a shop and ask for a pack of his favourite brand. In fact he was incapable of having a favourite brand. So our brains are doing us a considerable service when they filter out the non-essentials. This "habituation" process is the reason why anything that becomes routine becomes unnoticed after a while. So, for example, if you have a picture on the wall for a longish period, after a while you no longer notice its presence. Ironically, you are only likely to "notice" it again if it is removed. A similar thing happens when you put your mission statement on the wall in what used to be the style of Japanese corporations. Soon nobody notices that it is there. Give it to your people on paper and the same thing tends to happen. It "disappears" from consciousness. You need to use your creativity to find a way in which your people will "rediscover" the mission frequently so that they don't habituate to it.

One of my clients used phrases from the mission on a random basis as screen savers with some short-term success. Your challenge is to find a better way, and believe me it will be no walkover. You are effectively taking on millions of years of evolutionary development. But research into psychology may help. A variable or frequent stimulus is more noticeable than a stable one.

You may wish to ask yourself:

- How can we make the mission both a practical tool and something that is "new" every time that it is seen?

Research – Robert Cialdini and many others worldwide

Take your mind back, if you will, to your student days. Were you a swot who worked consistently and hard? Or were you, as I was, one who skipped lectures, sweated on deadlines to deliver work, but took a pride in your ability to wing it? If you were the latter type, how did you feel as the dreaded final examinations approached and you found that after three or four years of "work" your mind was a blank and you were doomed to failure. It gave little comfort that many of your friends, barroom buddies and the like, were in the same alarming situation. You and they were potentially in deep "doodoo" and you would jump at any way out – or would you?

Bob Cialdini an American professor of psychology and global expert on the behaviour of used-car salesmen (I'm not joking, he really is the leading expert on what used-car sales people, the ultimate "compliance professionals" get up to in order to win a sale), would approach his students with the solution to their examination problem. He would offer them some additional tuition, based firmly on the key topic areas almost certain to appear in the forthcoming examinations. To half his students he would explain that he would have to put his neck on the line with the Senate to ask for the additional resources, so he needed their absolute verbal assurance that they would attend every one of any additional tutorials that he was able to schedule. The students gave, hand on metaphorical heart, the assurance that come hell or high water they would be there. To the second half, Cialdini put a slightly different condition. He asked them to sign a paper to confirm that they would attend every session.

He would then hold his extra tutorials at the most anti-social hour, in the most inaccessible part of the university in the most uncomfortable room that he could find in the early hours – preferably a room that was consistently freezing even on a summer dawn. The tutorials were certainly of great value to all attendees, but after the first, those who had given their word verbally to be there began to miss sessions. After a few meetings a mere 10 per cent to 20 per cent of the "word only" students remained and these drifted away until only one or two diehards were in evidence. Those who had publicly signed to be there, however, continued to attend in full force, shocked that some of their peers could so readily break their word.

Asking people the simple question: "will you commit to this?" is easy and leads to easy answers. If you really want people to commit your question needs to be more along the lines of "will you publicly commit in a provable manner?" The difference is subtle, but in behavioural terms it is far from being trivial.

Is signing the mission statement "over the top" after all?

Strategic alternatives

- What alternative strategies would enable us to achieve our mission?
  - What is the fastest, most economical way to create our ideal future?
  - What is our evidence that any alternative will work in the real world?
  - What has been tried in the past?
  - What worked?
  - What failed?
  - What has changed since they were tried?
- What are the levels of risk associated with each alternative?
  - Are we seeking low risk?
- Which alternative is likely to lead us to a position of market dominance?
  - Do we really desire market dominance?
- Which alternative is most consistent with our desired company image?
- Which strategy is most likely to appeal to our current most worthwhile customers?
- Which will be most feasible, attractive and novel and appeal most strongly to us?
- Which will excite and motivate our people?
- Which will we pursue?

Summary

There is always more than one path that leads to where you want to be. Choose the one that is the shortest route that offers novelty, because the market and those who will make it work respond to novelty; feasibility, because unless a strategy is feasible it is nothing but hand-waving argument and dreaming; attractive, because you and all who are involved in making it work will do better if you enjoy the process; and economical, because achieving the same goals with greater economy leads naturally to greater profit. You need to ensure that everyone who plays a part in achieving your strategy asks not, "how can we do this?" but always, "how can we do this at the lowest possible cost?"

Strategy

- Does the strategy that we have chosen offer a rational, even if unconventional route to sustainable success in the real world?
- How will we communicate the strategy to those who have to make it work?
- What objectives does it imply?
- Does it make the optimal use of our strengths, competencies, capabilities and resources?
- Will it make a significant contribution to the sustainable prosperity of the organization in the short term as well as in the longer term?
- Will it pay for itself in a reasonable time?
- Can it be explained in simple terms to all those who will make it work?
    - In short, does it meet all the requirements of Lambert's Laws?

Summary

Tactics are usefully defined as, "making sure that we do the right things today". A strategy must ensure that you are still doing the right things ten years down the track. That means that you have to regard it as tentative and flexible yet robust enough to deliver success in a volatile environment.

Comparative/competitive analysis

- Do we really know what our best customers in each segment want?
- Specifically, how good are we at satisfying their needs?
- Taking each major competitor individually by name, how good is each in comparison to us?
- Where do our competitive advantages lie?
- Who are our weakest competitors?
- Who are their most worthwhile customers?
- What is our strategy for attracting those customers?
- How do we gear up our marketing and sales operation to ensure that we attract the best customer's business?
- Which competitors do we attack next, and next and . . . ?
- How do we dump those of our customers that are more trouble than they are worth and concentrate our resources on worthwhile business?

- How do we protect our reputation for service?
- How do we ensure that we retain our best customers?

■ How do we improve all that we do *at lowest possible cost* to ensure that we become and remain the best of the best?

(For the tools and techniques of Comparative analysis in a handy single page format please refer to *Key Management Solutions*, pages 172–174.)

Summary

Adrian Furnham has shown that some business ideas work best if you reverse them. Perhaps to the businessperson the most useful saying would be, "if you can't join 'em, beat 'em". Comparative analysis is a unique tool that tells you whom you can beat, when you can beat them and how to go about it. Do not underestimate the questions that give you competitive advantage.

PEST+ (political, economic, social, technological and legislative) analysis

Entry into new markets overseas demands careful prior assessment. But this assessment should not be used only as a prelude to foreign adventures. Political, economic and social changes have major effects at home and the strategy is designed to be flexible, but relevant, over a considerable period of time.

Political analysis

■ What are the levels of political stability in all markets that we serve?

■ What effect are changes of government likely to have on our business prospects?

■ What are the effects of any instability on our threat and opportunity analysis?

Economic analysis

■ What are the global economic trends?

■ How may these affect our business?

■ Have we taken full account of them in our thinking?

Social analysis

- What are the social conditions in all the markets that we serve?
- What opportunities or threats do they suggest?
- Have we integrated these into our strategic thinking?

Technological analysis

- What are the likely technological developments?
- How can we best exploit these at lowest cost?

Legislation

- What legislation is probable in each of the key markets where we operate?
- How could such legislation affect us?

The downside

Most organizations, if they complete a PEST analysis at all, look to avoid trouble. That makes sense. But it is not the end of the story. Nor is it necessarily the most important reason for getting complete answers to all questions.

- Does it suggest any threats or weaknesses of which we have taken insufficient note?
- Do we need to adjust our strategic contingency and avoidance plans?

The upside

In all situations it should be nothing less than a well-practised habit to look for areas of competitive advantage. The effective businessperson will look at all situations with one question firmly in mind.

- *Does anything that I have learned suggest an additional area of competitive advantage that we need to plan to exploit?*

And since advantage without action is meaningless:

- Do we need to draw matters to the attention of divisions/departments to ensure that tactical plans will best reflect the advantageous and disadvantageous factors in each market?

Summary

Too many planners look at markets either in too simple or too complicated a manner. PEST+ analysis delivers the questions that ensure that you consider all that is important without becoming excessively academic.

Strategic objectives

- Given the mass of information that we now have what are our strategic objectives?
- What are our priorities?
- Do the objectives state clearly exactly what we must do?
- Are we clear on how we will measure the success of each?
- Is every objective meaningful in that it makes a significant contribution to the success of the strategic plan?
- Is each achievable in the probable market and economic conditions?
- Is each attainable with the resources and people that we have or can acquire?
- Have we included any necessary development of people or resources?
- Have we used expert inputs from departments and divisions to ensure that we will have, for example, a training and development plan, a production and productivity plan and so on that fully supports the strategy?
- Are all objectives clearly time-framed?
- On the basis of our strategic objectives can every department and/or division identify their contribution?
- Have we taken full account of our contingency and avoidance plans?
- Have we decided how often the top team will review the strategic objectives?

Summary

Strategic objectives are a jigsaw puzzle that break down into tactical objectives and actions. They should be comprehensive to ensure that if they are achieved then the total strategy is achieved. They are then split into tactical objectives designed so that if each is achieved the strategic objectives are achieved. They are the cornerstone of long-term prosperity.

Tactical implementation plans and tactical objectives

- Have all business units reported on their contribution to achieving the strategy in terms of clear and precise tactical objectives?
- If all objectives are achieved will the strategy be achieved?
- Are all tactical plans clearly specific, measurable, achievable, realistic and time-framed?
- All responsibilities clearly allocated including personal and departmental accountability, support plans from other departments/business units, communication plans, authority levels for essential expenditure and feedback, evaluation and review?
- Have all duplications of responsibility and effort been avoided?
- At the lowest level is everybody clearly aware of who is to do what, with no omissions?

Summary

Strategic planning is a business activity. It is not an academic exercise to be played out in ivory towers by specialists who tend toward the predictions only possible in the world of theory. It should be conducted by the top team with inputs from specialists as required. Those HR specialists who suspect, or have good reason to believe, that the standing of their specialism is in decline may wish to consider whether they will prepare themselves for the vital role of "process leaders" as might any other manager with, or capable of attaining, the appropriate skills. Strong process leadership is often essential if the result is to be meaningful. When I was with General Motors I learned the trade of consultant. Whether you choose to use internal or external process skills is a judgement based on the availability of training or talent. Process skills are essential.

External or internal consultants can afford to lack neither a detailed knowledge of the strategy nor exactly what questions were asked, and answered, as it was prepared. The well-known capacity of some consultants to do high-quality work in one part of the operation while they ignorantly do harm elsewhere would greatly diminish if all activities were to be judged by asking the question: "What does this contribute to achieving the strategy?"

2

The best use of the best people

questions of people and purpose

Civilization and profits go hand in hand. Calvin Coolidge

- Questions that enhance your people skills and that enable you to attract and retain the best.
- Questions that will protect you from Corporate Alzheimer's and the Auschwitz syndrome.
- Questions that will enable you to "right-size" any organization.
- Questions to motivate and questions to reduce risk.

What you will gain from this chapter

- How to attract and keep the best people.
- How to make the best use of the best people.
- How to have people assess their own performance and keep striving to be "the best of the best".

Essential numbers

- ☑ What is our annual labour turnover as a percentage of our total workforce?
- ☑ What is the turnover for our industry?
- ☑ What is the number one cause for people leaving us?

The best use of the best people

If a business chooses to dominate its markets it must also choose to make the best use of the best people. This means that you must plan to attract, retain and make the best possible use of the best people available. Thirty years ago Frederick Herzberg said that we need to differentiate between how we treat people and how we use them and, surprisingly it is how we use their skills and initiative that motivates them.

This section is therefore devoted to the following key factors:

- How do you recognize the best people?
- How do you attract them into your business?
- How do you select them?
- How do you use their capabilities?
- How do you retain them?

The best use of the best people begins with you

It may sound like an impertinent question to ask so early in an acquaintance, but are you in the right job? Please note I am not asking whether you are the right person for the job. What is important is does the job that you are doing make the best use of your skills, knowledge and capabilities. You are probably one of the "best people" in the right position. So I ask again is the job right for you?

- Do you go to bed happy at the thought of the next day's challenges and sheer hard work?
- Or are you anxious in the evening as you consider the prospect of work next day?

- Do you "talk shop" with colleagues because it is exciting stuff?
- Or do you talk obsessively with your partner about the trials and tribulations of working life?
- Worse perhaps, are you unnaturally reticent, responding aggressively to innocent enquiries from your nearest and dearest?

- Can you pace your activities sensibly?
- Or do you work late frequently and skip lunch because you have been given or have assumed too much work?

- Are you readily approachable by your team and peers?
- Or do you treat people with ill-temper or with off-hand indifference?

- Are you clear where your job is taking you and do you want to go there?
- Or are you drifting and hoping that something will turn up?

- Do you actually enjoy your job?
- Or is working what you have to do in order to afford rare moments of relaxation?

- Does work empower you?
- Or does it imprison you?

- Do you admire your colleagues and bosses?
- Or do you think that they are incompetent and ought to step aside for a better man or woman – you?

- Do you feel pleasantly superior when friends talk about their jobs?
- Or do you feel pangs of envy and discontent?

- Do you delegate with confidence?
- Or are you sick of people pushing their work onto you?

- Do you enjoy perks, responsibility, challenge and opportunities to travel?
- Or do you feel generally hard done by?

- Are you paid what you earn?
- Or are you underpaid and overworked?

- Do you feel relaxed and self-confident?
- Or do you feel stressed and worn out?

- Do you enjoy hobbies and interests outside of work?
- Or have you given them up in order to work longer hours?

- Are you ambitious?
- Or are you resigned?

If you feel dissatisfied with work be very clear what it is that you really want. Nothing is more frustrating than to jump from the proverbial frying pan only to find how hot the fire can be. Answer the following questions with care, but remember that you have needs beyond work. You have social needs, domestic and family needs. You may well have needs to pursue a hobby or sport and areas of learning beyond work. Most of us, whether we willingly admit to it or not, have spiritual needs. Some people have found the following planning template is useful. We use it in our *International Executive Stress Management* workshops to great effect.

Life plan

The next ten years

My life goals

I have a vision of becoming in the next ten years:

Personal objectives

Family:

Home:

Wealth:

Relationships within and beyond the family:

Learning, both formal and informal:

Spiritual:

Essential life values that will drive all that I do:

Business objectives

Type of work and/or industry sector:

Position:

Country or countries where I intend to work:

Time out – sabbaticals, child care, time with loved ones:

Learning – how will I keep my mind active and avoid descending into a rut:

Net worth – how much do I need in cash and property to fulfil my dreams. Will I work to live or live to work?:

Exit strategy – how will I turn my assets into a forum that will support my long-term goals:

Use of my retirement – how will I remain young as I grow old:

Property:

Investment(s) – think beyond the merely financial. How will you invest your talents, abilities and ambitions?:

Essential business values:

Personal strategies

As a wife and mother or husband and father or as none of these

Relationships:

Ideal family size:

Role in children's development and education:

Home life

Type of home:

Where:

Home atmosphere:

Lifestyle and health

Hobbies and interests:

Sports and outdoor pursuits:

Health and care of the self:

Wealth:

Income:

Net worth:

Using wealth for the care and comfort of others:

Spiritual growth

Areas of study:

Key values that drive my spiritual journey:

Business strategies

Specializations:

Clients or customers:

People (specific or the kind of) that I want to work with:

Geographic areas that I want to work in:

Business marketing strategies – how I will play my part and use my talents to grow any business that I am part of:

Self-marketing strategies – the specific steps that I will take to ensure that I will fulfil my ambitions:

Personal and professional strengths that I can leverage to succeed right now:

Personal and professional strengths that I will need in the future:

Languages that I will master:

Professional development/conferences/seminars and training that I will attend:

Mentors and advisors:

Who am I?

My philosophy of life:

My psychological profile – how I see myself and how others see me:

Strengths I can develop and use to enrich my life and that of those I love:

Weaknesses I should be aware of:

Resources outside myself:

Things that I love to do

Consider the things that you love to do and separate them into those that

Need planning:

Can be done spontaneously:

Cost nothing:

Cost more than I can always easily afford:

Need to be done with others:

Can be done alone:

When was the last time you did the really important ones?

Then plan to build more joy into your life. Start with the easy ones first perhaps, spontaneous, low cost activities that you can enjoy alone. What Jack Welch calls, in business terms "low hanging fruit". Gradually seek opportunities for all the others and get their richness back into your life.

Summary

Robert Burns called on the Gods to give us the gift of seeing ourselves as others see us. My work in psychology suggests that the way that others see us is a function of the way that we see ourselves. The best bosses and the most successful people know where they are going and how things will be when they get there. Research shows that the drifter is subject to major stress and is a prime candidate for a heart attack. Ask yourself the key questions that will uncover to you who you really are and you will do a much better job of understanding and managing others.

Making the best use of the best people

A few jobs are best done in splendid isolation, some demand superior teamwork, but I believe utterly and completely that whatever else a business might need it must attract, recruit and retain the very best people and then make the very best use of their capabilities. When you know yourself and know how to be true to yourself the following very practical questions will help you to make the key decisions.

Do we need to recruit?

- We appear to have a vacancy, but are the team coping without any loss of motivation, productivity or morale?

- A team member is leaving, but could we streamline systems or redistribute tasks among the team and still get the work done to standard and on time?

- Some people appear to be overloaded, but are there others with too little to do?

- Do we have a bureaucratic approach to responsibility that denies people the opportunity to make the contribution that they could and would make if they were allowed? (This may seem to be a somewhat odd question, but in many firms that I have advised over the years people with some or even considerable free time have declared time and time again that they would willingly help their colleagues, but management insists that they stick to their knitting even when they have neither wool nor pattern. So massive potential productivity is lost and the overwhelmed become increasingly dispirited as they see their colleagues with little to fill their time. As those who need the help suffer from the form of stress that we call "burn out", those who might help to solve their problems suffer from an equally dangerous type of stress that we call "rust out".)

- There is a backlog of work, but is the most economic solution to bring in temporary staff to clear it?

- We have created a new responsibility, but could a member of the team fill it?

- Specialist expert knowledge is needed, but would a consultant or external advisor be the best and cheapest solution?

- We appear to need someone, but is the value of their contribution going to outweigh the total costs of recruitment and employment?

- I want to enhance the scope and size of my team, but am I planning to meet important company needs or am I thinking of empire building?

Why do we need to recruit? – job purpose

If a firm is to recruit, equip, train and pay an employee that is a major investment. If the selection process is inappropriate or if the good employee is not retained and used effectively the cost is massive. Before considering the investment ask:

- Why is the company prepared to spend this money?

- What is the specific outcome that we expect from an employee in this position?
  - Given that outcome, what is likely to be our return on the total investment over time?
  - Does the return justify the investment?
  - Do we need to re-think and raise our expectations of the employee's contribution?

What key activities or major accomplishments are essential?

- What exactly will the jobholder have to do to achieve the job purpose?

Please note carefully the wording here. The question is "what will they DO" – not "be able to do". Anything that an employee can do, but doesn't actually do delivers no benefit to the firm.

Bob Mager, the leading thinker in the field of job performance had a very effective way of assessing whether an employee could perform the job or not. He suggested that the supervisor should load a pistol, cock it and hold it to the employee's head with the words, "Now do it or else!" If the jobholder still failed to perform the task to the necessary standard he or she needed training. If they could do it under such extreme circumstances they lacked motivation to perform.

If, for example, you were considering the replacement of an existing employee who may be performing below standard and replacement is a major expense you might first ask yourself:

- What is my equivalent of Mager's loaded pistol?
- How do I convince any employee of my willingness to pull the trigger?
- Do I have the authority to use my equivalent of a pistol?
- Does the employee really understand what is expected of them?
- Have they ever been told why the company is willing to invest in them?
- Is there anything that I or others are doing that distracts this employee from doing what is necessary? (Task interference.)
- Do we provide the employee with a working environment in which the task can be performed effectively? (Working environment.)
- Is timely, accurate and relevant feedback provided on job performance? (Feedback.)
- When they receive training how will I ensure that they use what they have learned on the job with appropriate levels of peer and supervisor coaching?

Summary

I have written "task interference", "working environment" and "feedback" in brackets because Mager's research over many years and in many companies and cultures suggests that poor performance results from these rather than lack of training or ability with a factor of around nine to one.

---

mini case study

The big "G's"

In General Motors for many years every employee has, in theory at least, enjoyed the benefits of a Bill of Rights.

Every employee has the right:

- To know what is expected of them.

- To work in an environment free of unnecessary distractions and task interference.

- To receive timely and effective training.

- To be supported in using what they have learned by their supervision and colleagues.

- To know how well they are doing.

- To receive appropriate monetary, career and psychological awards for their performance.

In General Electric under Jack Welch all employees enjoyed the same rights with this addition:

- *To be challenged at every appraisal interview to demonstrate how they intended to achieve more in the next period using less resource.*

Jack Welch aimed this addition specifically and personally at every member of his top team at a comprehensive and regular performance debriefing session. Nobody in the organization, Welch included, was ever allowed to demand of others what they were not able to do themselves. By asking the right questions you can establish whether people lack motivation or capability or whether, God forbid, you are the prime source of others' failure to perform.

Do not be seduced into asking employees simplistically, "do I interfere with your ability to do your job?" Few will have the guts to tell you that you make a mess of ensuring that they know what is expected of them, constantly change priorities and fail to give feedback on performance accurately or in good time to enable them to do something about it.

How well must the jobholder perform? – job standards

- How well does the jobholder need to do each of the key major accomplishments to ensure the delivery of the job purpose?
- How much are we likely to have to spend on training a newcomer to achieve the job standards?
- Is there a cheaper or better way than recruiting from the street?
- How quickly do we need to have this jobholder "up to speed"?
- From where are we likely to be able to attract the kind of person who is able to deliver the essential standards of performance most quickly?
- What will it cost us to attract such a person?
- Does recruitment offer us the best return on investment?

(See *Key Management Solutions* pp 57–62 for full details of how to continue to use the answers to these questions beyond recruitment for self-administered, motivating job performance appraisal system that instils self-discipline, pride in performance and the motivation to become and remain the "best of the best".)

What variations on the recruitment process have been successful?

mini case study

Michael Gerber

Michael is a best-selling author, but his day job is to lead one of the most successful consultancies supporting small businesses in the United States. When he seeks to recruit consultants he accepts that since his methods and systems are unique he will need to train every recruit thoroughly. He therefore needs to attract those who are committed to what he does and who are eager to learn and to apply what they have learned.

His recruitment strategy is simple and very effective. He runs an advertisement that states his consultancy's vision with the additional "strap line" which reads, "If this excites you join us for a chat and a cup of coffee at (name of location) on (date)."

Having greeted his applicants and offered them coffee and pastries Michael delivers a short talk in which he explains what the firm does and, most important, the values that drive their services. At the end of his presentation he invites his guests to make a simple decision. If they are excited by what they have heard they are invited to take further refreshment and stay on to meet their prospective colleagues. If what they have heard fails to ignite their enthusiasm they are invited to enjoy the refreshments before leaving with Gerber's sincere thanks for taking the trouble of coming. Those who decide to stay are advised that they face an interview. The interview will be carried out neither by Human Resource professionals nor by senior management. Their potential colleagues will interview prospective members of the team and the applicants will be asked only two questions:

- What excited you about what you have heard today?
- What is the contribution that you intend to make?

The applicants are advised, however, that they should take every opportunity to quiz the interviewers so that they fully understand what will be expected of them, what it is like to work in the company and how people are assessed and rewarded.

Please think about it for a moment. What do you really need to know about people beyond that they share your dream and are clear about what they can and will do to make it a reality?

Leaders who see merit in Gerber's approach need to ask themselves the following essential questions:

- Are we able to attract the best in our business to work for us?
- Do good people apply to us when we are not advertising vacancies?
- If we cannot attract the very best and if people don't beat a path to our door, should we consider a different approach?
- How might we improve on Gerber's ideas and make them relevant to our operation?
- Is the Gerber approach something that we could adapt and adopt?
- Can I think of an even better approach?
- Are our vision and mission sufficiently inspirational to appeal to the very best in our industry if they were to have no other information than the written word?
- Do our values, vision and mission consistently get all our people to the barricades when the chips are down?
- Do all our best people confirm that they are proud and happy to work with us when talking to friends and families?
- Are we known in all the local bars and clubs to be the best employer and the best company in the area?
- Do our best people stay with us in spite of constant attempts by competitors to lure them away?
- Do we know whether competitors are trying to poach our best people?

- Are our best people constantly challenged to perform and proud to accept the challenge?
- Do all our stakeholders, shareholders (stockholders – USA), employees, suppliers, distributors, customers and the community that we serve, act as advocates for our business?
- Am I personally proud of what we achieve here?
- Am I effective in communicating that pride to others? (Webster's used to define communication as the transfer of meaning. The transfer of feeling is equally important.)

Summary

The job purpose is a clear but concise statement of why the firm is prepared to pay the costs of employment of any individual. Major accomplishments show what must be done to achieve the job purpose. Standards show how well they must be performed. Job purpose, major accomplishments and job performance standards must be the same for all holders of the same job, regardless of experience. The effective manager needs to understand all three, as does the employee. After the job purpose is achieved, the motivated employee will deliver more, much more. Any failure to understand means that the employee will deliver something different – much different and usually much worse.

In addition to knowing what is expected of him or her, the employee must be provided with the tools to do the job, an environment as free as possible of task interference and timely feedback on performance.

Should we advertise? – if so, where?

Ask your HR or other appropriate managers:

- Do we need to advertise or are you aware of suitable candidates?
- If we have a policy of advertising all positions internally first have we done that – with what results?
- Have we interviewed all internal applicants?
- What is the quality of internal applicants?
- If no-one satisfactory has applied why not? (Some years ago I was headhunted by a very angry company chairman to head their executive development operation after he had been told, to his utter disgust, that there was nobody in the organization ready to step into the Managing Director's shoes. He was right to be angry. Succession planning is a key responsibility at every level. It is also a prerequisite of getting yourself promoted.)

- What do we need to do to build a pool of internal talent?
- How do we keep talented and capable people committed while they await opportunities for advancement?
- Where should we advertise?
- Why is that the best publication?
- What others have we tried?
- What is our ideal candidate likely to read?
- What is the evidence that advertising in that publication delivers the best results?
- What should our advertisement say?
- How will we catch our ideal candidates' attention with the header?
- What "offer" will attract the best candidates?
- What evidence do we have that we can deliver what we promise?
- What action do we want the best people to take on seeing our advertisement?
- If you haven't already thought through the answers to these questions what do we need to do to ensure that you will be in a position to answer them readily next time?

Should we use recruitment specialists?

- Are there companies that specialize in our business?
- Do we have clear evidence that they deliver superior candidates rather than over-charging to save our HR department a little work and a deal of thought?
- What evidence do they supply to back up their claims of expertise in our business?
- If I were thinking of looking for a change of employment would I trust them to find my ideal job?
- Would you?
- Would we do better to offer our employees a cash incentive to find good applicants from among their friends?

Summary

Advertising and the use of recruitment specialists should be actions of last resort. Too often existing employees are demotivated because they are denied opportunities and terms and conditions that are offered to newcomers.

Succession planning, training and development and the building of experience should be planned to ensure a qualified and committed pool of labour at every organizational level.

Should we poach from a competitor?

This is in many ways an ethical decision and some readers may have rather strong feelings one way or another. Personally I believe that part of the strategy is to find ways to weaken competition. Where skilled and knowledgeable workers are in short supply, attracting and retaining the best is an essential contribution to maintaining a competitive edge. I see no more wrong in taking key staff from competitors than I do with winning and keeping their best customers. Of course, you have every right to believe that my attitude is unethical. Once ethical considerations are out of the way, however, there are practical considerations that need to be thought through.

- Do I know enough about my competitors, their customers and staff to attract the best people?

- Would I have any concerns that those that can easily be attracted away from their present firms would be loyal to us?

- Are we doing enough to build and sustain the loyalty of our present employees? (This should include building customer loyalty. Research by Bain and Company shows that loyal customers means loyal employees means loyal customers – the "Loyalty Cycle".)

- Can we attract people from the competition without raising the stakes so high that we create dissatisfaction among our current best people?

- Do I know enough about our competitor's employees to be able to contact their very best people?

- Am I prepared to accept that whereas poaching people and customers is ethical, expecting new hires to provide confidential information about their previous employer's products and plans is not?

- Am I confident that I will not, through the interview process, provide my competitors with sensitive information about this company?

Summary

Poaching from a competitor is a fine balance of risks and benefits. Make sure that you ask the right questions to minimize the first and maximize the second.

What is the job worth? – pay and conditions

- What is this job really worth to the company in terms of quantifiable outputs?
- If we offer an exciting package to a new hire, how will that effect our present best people?
- Do our remuneration policies fully reward our best, most loyal employees?
- How does the relationship between pay, qualifications, responsibilities and capabilities stack up?
- What would our most effective competitors pay for this position?
- If we can't compete on pay, what can we offer our ideal candidate that is better than money? (More people than you might expect value personal and professional development beyond mere financial gain as long as the money is enough to enable them to do a little better than just get by.)
- What makes us different as an employer?
- Is there something so exceptional about this need that we must offer an exceptional package to attract the right person?
- Are we limited by pay scales?
- Is there any really good business reason why we should be?
- What is your evidence for that?

(This last question is added as a reminder of the real "killer question". It should be asked any time that the answers that you get sound too glib or any other time that you feel like using it. No other question that I have ever come across or found myself having to respond to has been so influential in making me really think things through rather than simply being "fast on my feet" under pressure. Being fast on my feet is an attribute that I, like most good business people, tend to overvalue.)

Summary

Attracting the best people is one thing, retaining the best people is quite another. Salaries and perks may not motivate directly, but they are the symbols of the value of their contribution. The right questions often save a manager from the difficulties that arise from demotivating staff.

Can we save time screening applications?

- Who should do the initial screening of applicants?
- What evidence do we have that they won't screen out the best candidates?
- Does the job purpose really demand the qualifications or is that merely the re-application of old requirements because it has always been thus?
- If psychometric tests are to be used what is the evidence that they are *reliable* (if given to the same person on different occasions would produce the same result), *credible* (applicants will take them seriously and complete them honestly) and most important, *valid* (they actually measure what they claim to measure).

Psychometric tests

All tests are, or should be, supported by research papers and those that are offered commercially should have summary research papers attached that are comprehensive and readily understood by the layperson. In my day in industry it was not uncommon to find that:

- The research specifically stated that the test used could not be relied upon for recruitment purposes.
- The test was valid and reliable, but those using it lacked the training to interpret the test effectively.
- The test had been rushed into the market without proper testing. (The "Ohio – Fleischman" leadership test, a relatively simple test of leadership style, although useful to professional psychologists from its inception, took almost twenty years to perfect for wider use.)

For those readers qualified in psychology who are asking the question, the answer is "yes, I do know that there are other important forms of reliability". For example, in the laboratory it is often necessary to check that if the test were presented in a different form the results would be consistent. I suspect, however, that these recondite areas are unlikely to be meaningful to the average manager. So please bear with me while I move on – except that you may wish to ask yourself:

- In what business situations might alternative form reliability be important to the manager? – Partially sighted or blind candidates won't do as Braille is a normal written language adapted to be read by touch.

---

mini case study

Did we get it right?

Smith Kline French (now GlaxoSmithKline) used to take the business of recruitment more seriously than most. For management and executive positions they would use a regular questionnaire to follow-up on those whom they had rejected for a position and check their progress in their new firms against that of the hires. This gave them a reliable indication of the effect of their hiring practices and indicated where key questions needed to be asked.

You have only to consider the lifetime cost of one major error and you will see that the cost of sending out annual questionnaires for a few years is easily justified. This method is not fast, but it is thorough and those that ally methods such as this to constantly asking the right questions are able to make value-building improvements incrementally. At the very least, what we test we usually try to ensure that we do right first time and every time.

What questions should I ask? – final preparation for recruitment interviewing

Unless you have detailed knowledge and probably experience of the job *as it is now* and *as it is developing* it is wise to talk to current jobholders where possible to ensure that you can develop the key questions.

- What would you look for in a colleague?
- What are the minimum qualifications someone would need?
    - Why precisely would they need them?
    - Are qualifications more important than personality or vice versa?
    - Why do you think that?
    - Can you give me an example? (Another way to ask, "what's your evidence?")
- What skills and experience are essential?
    - How are they used day-to-day in the job?

- What kind of personality should a fellow team member have?
- Which is more important, teamwork or individual skill?
  - Why?
- What is more important, nerve or brain?
  - Why?
- What training should a candidate have already had to hit the ground running?
  - Why?
- If you were interviewing me for this job what would you ask me?
  - What answers would get me the job?
  - Why?

General guidelines for interviewing

- Stick to meaningful questions related to the job function and career prospects.
- Avoid irrelevant or impertinent questions.
- Experts on writing cv's and resumés usually advise "keep it brief", so probe those areas of the candidate's cv that are important to the job function.
- Ask questions that may reveal a person's ethics, but try to avoid the well-worn, artificial questions to which any given answer is wrong. "Have you stopped beating your wife?" – tells you nothing in the real world.
- Take notes after explaining to the candidate why it is important that you have an accurate record of your discussion.
- Ask all candidates the same questions as far as possible so that you are comparing apples with apples.
- Use open, but safe questions to have the candidate talk about what they think and feel.
- Encourage openness with nods and signs of real interest.
- Thank the candidate occasionally for providing the information.
- Probe with more closed questions.
- Put an end to waffling with straight "yes/no" questions if necessary.
- Probe answers with "describe how?" questions.
- Make sure that all the candidate's questions are answered to their satisfaction.

Consider carefully the degree to which the candidate's questions reflect the skills, knowledge or attitudes that you are seeking. (The effective questioner takes every opportunity to analyze and learn from the questions posed by others.)

What should I ask every candidate?

Select from the following those questions that are truly relevant to the situation and the job and those that are essential to any employee who has a role to perform in helping to achieve your company's mission. Where appropriate, follow all answers with a request for specific examples from the candidate's own experience.

To avoid wasting time

- How did you hear about the job opportunity?
- What do you already understand about the job?
- What do you know about the company?

To assess the level of interest

- Why are you interested in our company?
- Have you seen our mission and vision?
- Do they excite you?
- What specifically excites you about this company and its future?
- What contribution would you expect to make?

To qualify whether the person can make a contribution explain the job purpose, major accomplishments and standards of performance and give the candidate these as a job definition, then ask:

- Is there anything that would stop you from performing the essential duties of the job?
- How quickly do you believe that you would perform to the required standards?
- Why do you believe that you could consistently achieve the job standards by the time that you suggest?
- If hired, when could you start?
- Have you any obligations or trips planned that will take you away at any time during the next twelve months?
- Are there any problems working either at weekends or early or late in the day if necessary?

- How do you feel about travel?
- Would you have any problems travelling out of town at short notice?
- Are there any limits on where you would be willing to re-locate if your career demanded it?

To understand the candidate's job experience

- In a couple of words what would you say is/was the purpose of your current/last job?
- What was the key output that you were expected to achieve?
- Can you describe a typical day?
- What did you do yesterday?
- Of what accomplishments are you most proud?
- How did you manage that?

To understand the person

- Can you just tell me about yourself?
- How would your friends describe your personality?
- What, if anything, causes you serious concern?
- What gives you the greatest satisfaction in life?
- Why have you chosen to work in this field?
- What was your most exciting and useful earlier job?
- Have you ever been fired?
- Why?
- What did you learn from the experience?
- Will you please tell me about your last/current job?
- What are/were the key outcomes?
- What did you love about it?
- What did you hate about it?
- What kept you awake at nights? (I love this question. As a consultant the outpouring or denial that I get in return usually takes me right to the heart of the matter so that I can focus on what the client really feels is important rather than what was deemed to be an "acceptable" problem.)
- What achievement makes you most proud?
- Is/was the pressure great?

- How did you manage when the going got tough?
- What is your favourite way of relaxing?
- Please can you give me specific examples?

To understand how the person learns

- What were the key things that you learned on your first job?
- Where do you learn most easily? With your colleagues, in the training room, on the job sorting out problems, from books or where?
- Can you give some examples of problems that you have solved?
- How did you go about it?

To understand the person's judgement and decision-making abilities

- From your knowledge of our business, what would you think is our most important product or service?
- What seem to you to be our strong points?
- How well do you think that we exploit our strengths?
- What would you do that is different?
- What are our weak points?
- What would you suggest that we do to improve?
- What is the biggest crisis that you have faced at work?
- What did you do?
- What has been your greatest professional challenge?
- What risks have you taken in your career?
- What was the biggest ethical conflict that you have faced at work?
- How did you resolve it?

Attitudes to supervision and leadership

- Tell me about the best boss you ever had?
- How did the worst boss that you have known behave?
- If you were to complete your own performance review what might you say about you?
- What motivates you?
- What gets you to the barricades when the chips are really down?

- When are you happiest?
- What upsets you?
- What is your preferred reward?

Level of commitment

- How long do you plan to be in this position if it is offered?
- What are the next steps in your career plan?
- What is your ultimate goal?
- What do you see as the benefits of a loyal workforce?
- How should loyalty be rewarded?
- In an ideal world where anything is possible what would you be doing today?
- Do you have life goals?
- Do you write them down?
- How often do you check your progress against your goals?
- How do you measure personal success?
- What do you dream about?
- What do you have in mind when you think "some day I'll . . ."?

If creativity and original thinking are important

- What is the most creative thing that you have ever done?
- If you were to write a book what would it be about?
- What did you dream of when you were a kid?
- Do you enjoy fantasy?

To bring things to a conclusion

- What would you like to ask me that we haven't covered?
- Why, after all that I have asked, do you still want this job?
- Why are you the right person for this job?
- What do you think that you bring to us that we need and don't yet have?

As the law expands there will be an increasing number of things that you cannot ask. Questions that relate to age, sexual orientation and ethnicity are increasingly, and rightly, taboo. The rule, however, remains simple: only ask questions that lead to uncovering information that is totally relevant and pertinent. There is no room in the recruitment of quality people for those who simply enjoy putting others through some form of third degree or seek information because "I just want to know". Do your preparation and stick to the point and you cannot go far wrong.

How do I check references?

There are legal concerns about references and many are not prepared to criticize former employees in writing. Even the most glowing written reference is therefore unlikely to be really helpful. It may tell you nothing but the plain unvarnished truth or it may, and this is more likely, be over-generous. Most professionals, if they take up references at all, tend to prefer to talk to someone in authority and to stick to factual questions rather than seek opinion. Opinions may emerge if they are strongly held.

- How long did the candidate work for the company?
- What were their main duties?
- What was the salary level?
- Why did they leave?
- Did you try to keep the candidate?
- Why (or why not) as the case may be?
- Did this person have to work under severe time pressures?
- Did this person ever cause problems?
- Would fellow employees speak well of this person?
- Did this person enjoy promotions while with you?
- Is there someone else that I might call who has detailed knowledge of this person?

If references are important to you, you need to understand that the information that you get is only of value to the degree that it is consistent and confirmed by others. Pursuing references can be a time-consuming business of limited value in which it is not the direct answers that are important so much as the asides, tone of voice and other subtle cues.

How do I get the most out my hiring practices?

Ensure that every new team member feels that he or she is a valued member of the team from the first moment on the job.

- Who will show them the ropes and answer their early questions?
- Who will introduce them to the people that they need to know and show them around the place?
- Who will take them to lunch and make the social introductions?

- If we have an induction process does it inspire enthusiasm or boredom?
- Does our approach to initial training consistently enable new people to "hit the ground running"?
- What were my concerns when I was last a new hire?
- What do we do that would have resolved such concerns?
- How have times and attitudes changed since I was last a new hire?
- What does this mean to us right now?

How should I approach job performance appraisal?

Some real-life appraisal comments

Continued employment of this man is depriving a village somewhere of its idiot.
Should his IQ ever rise to 50 he should sell!

The grand old man

Years ago I was lucky enough to attend a conference where the doyen of Total Quality, W Edwards Deming was the keynote speaker. He had chosen as his theme performance appraisal and was arguing that appraisals as carried out in most organizations, at best, encouraged mediocre performance. He suggested that a "box ticking mentality" did more to encourage satisficing behaviour than it did to promote excellence. His arguments, delivered in an excruciatingly slow monotone, were strong, but the effect on his audience, mainly HR directors and managers, was stronger. They were getting mad.

Finally, a gentleman close to me, his face purple, his eyes bulging with rage, could take this assault no more. He leapt to his feet and screamed, "If I can't carry out appraisals what can I do instead?"

The great man stood in silence for what seemed a very long time. When he spoke it was even more slowly than was his normal lugubrious style. "Forgive me sir, if I check that I understand your question." "You are asking me to tell you how else, if you do not carry out appraisals, you may find ways to humiliate people?"

In that moment I became a fan for life of Deming and a tireless promoter of Bob Mager's approach to building job performance to an ever-growing spiral of self-motivated, self-driven achievement by people that value themselves and the business. Mager's approach is outlined on page 35 above and described in detail in *Key Management Solutions*. The essence is as follows:

- The company through its management makes a clear decision about precisely what they are paying for when they carry the costs of employing me. They detail the specific outcome that they expect of me and of all others who fill the same job.

- My manager and I discuss exactly what I must do to achieve the outcome expected of me. These key activities are rarely more than half-a-dozen to eight, but they are essential to achieving the job purpose.

- My manager and I establish the minimum standards of performance that are essential to consistently achieve the outcomes that I am being paid for. We agree that in appropriate situations 100 per cent is a reasonable standard.

- We record all the above, purpose, key activities and job performance standards on one single sheet of paper.

- All who have the same job must achieve the same job purpose to the same standards. Old hand, new hire or clockwork mouse, no allowances are made. If I cannot reach the standards I am clearly not doing what I am paid to do and I know I must improve.

- All necessary training (see "loaded pistol" above) is provided and I work in an environment that is, as far as possible free from task interference. I have the necessary resources to do the job and the time in which to do it.

- I will be given timely and effective feedback on my performance and, more important, I will frequently test my own performance against the standards and will seek help and advice if I believe that I am falling short of the standards required.

- I will be encouraged to do more and deliver other outcomes on my own initiative, but not at the expense of my core responsibilities.

- All of my achievements will be recognized and celebrated.

- Above all, doing the right things to the right standard is my responsibility and I am expected to consistently review my own performance and progress.

The result is that I am equipped and motivated to perform. I take a pride in "my job" rather than "the job" and my manager has the freedom to provide true leadership where and when it is most needed. Since I am daily in a position to compare what I am doing with what is required, my appraisal interviews can be frequent, professional, brief, motivational and carry no surprises or fears for either of us. This is real empowerment.

Can I motivate other people?

The manager is well advised to dismiss arguments of the "angels dancing on the head of a pin"-type about whether you can motivate others or whether they can only motivate themselves. Any manager at any organizational level has the responsibility to deliver a working environment in which people are motivated.

- Do my people know what is expected of them and why it is important?
- Do they receive feedback on performance that is timely and focused on actions rather than personality?
- Do they work in an environment as free as possible of changing deadlines, changing priorities and interference with their ability to get on with the job?
- If such an environment is not a practical possibility have I taken steps to ensure that those who work here are motivated by challenge?
- Do they have the resources to do the job? (But see little case study below.)
- Do they experience a challenge that is inspirational, but not overwhelming?
- Are they encouraged to set themselves challenging, but achievable goals?
- Do I know the individual members of my team well enough to understand what their best contribution is likely to be?
- Do I understand what excites them in and out of work?
- Do I constantly seek to offer them new challenges that are exciting, but within their capabilities?
- Do I give people opportunities to use their key strengths in line with the needs of the business?
- Do I encourage learning and the sharing of what is learned?
- Do I act as a coach and trusted advisor to all my people?
- Do I immediately recognize achievement and reward it?
- Do I promote the achievements of my team to other executives as team achievements rather than assuming them for my own?
- Do I ensure that my people get the salaries, status and promotions that they deserve?
- Do I risk giving a little too much too soon rather than too little too late whether it is responsibility or reward?

- Do I delegate effectively and, having delegated, do I really leave them free to get on with the job confident that they will seek help if they should need it?

- Do I involve my people in decisions where they have the knowledge and commitment to make sound judgements?

- Do I involve people in consensus decisions when the situation is one that is so new that there is no way of knowing where valuable expertise lies?

- Do I make fast decisions when necessary and communicate them effectively?

- Do my team trust my decisions and feel confident that I involve them when that is appropriate?

- If I go out to bat for my team do I make sure that I win? (See Idiosyncrasy Balance, page 89 of *Key Management Solutions* if you are not sure why this is important.)

- Do I encourage creativity while avoiding "change for change's sake"?

- Do I share information when I can and do my people accept that when I keep things to myself there is an essential business reason for so doing?

- Do I beat the grapevine or the scuttlebutt to the punch and make sure that my people take pride in being the first to know?

- Do I encourage people to come to me with solutions rather than problems while ensuring that in the case where they need my help they have no qualms about laying the problem on my desk?

- Do I refrain from seeking to change "attitudes" other than by having people change their behaviours to those that work so adding to their understanding and allowing them to change their own attitudes?

- Do I make sure that my team are and remain winners?

- Do I ensure that they never fall into the rut of believing that they have the "winning formula" for all occasions? Do I encourage them to look for what is different in new situations and deal with them creatively? (See pages 78–80 of *Key Management Solutions*.)

- Do I keep my best people without standing in the way of their career progress?

- If one of my brightest team members one day became my boss could I take an honest pride in his or her achievement?

Summary

"Can I motivate other people?" looks like a good question, but it is the wrong question. Two things are essential. You need to be sure that you understand what actually motivates your people and to use that knowledge to create an environment in which they will be motivated, regardless of where that motivation may come from, and in so doing, you need to ensure that as much as possible of what demotivates is swept away.

mini case study

The know-it-all

When I was bright-eyed, bushy-tailed and thought that I knew it all I was an area marketing manager with an automotive dealer on my patch with a parts and accessories department that was a disgrace to the good name of General Motors.

Bins had an amazing variety of different parts thrust into them. Major items were strewn on the floor where it was almost impossible for anyone other than the extremely agile to avoid falling over them. There may have been a place for everything, but nothing seemed to be in its appointed place. The department was far too small for the business that it was doing. In short it was a disgrace and I, the great Pooh Bah of a GM District Manager no less, had no intention of putting up with it. In spite of the difficulties under which they were forced to work the team was cheerful, helpful, efficient and led the whole of the Region in terms of profitable sales. I decided that they deserved better. I argued, cajoled, threatened and finally had my way.

A brand new, wonderfully equipped Parts Department was built. No less a person than the chairman of GM conducted the opening celebration. It would be an exaggeration to suggest that there was dancing in the streets, but there was a celebratory lunch at which all of the major customers, suppliers and other dealers were represented and expressed their admiration for what we had achieved. It was one heck of a feather in my cap, or so I thought. During lunch the chairman and I had the kind of conversation that makes a young ambitious executive feel that his career is taking off. He did, however, make one small remark that I didn't understand. "I'm sure that you have a plan to re-motivate the team." Of course I decided at once that the chairman was an idiot. Could he not see that the team were delighted and excited by the toys that I had given to them to play with? Why they didn't even need to walk to the storage bins any more. The bins were on a track and came to them. Their motivation would obviously climb to undreamed of heights.

To my amazement the next time that I visited the dealer sales of parts and accessories were falling fast, the team was relatively morose and no-one was whistling as they worked. Some key team members were even muttering about looking for different jobs elsewhere. The enthusiasm had been drained from everybody as if someone had turned on a tap. I had to find out why they were so damnably unappreciative of what I had done for them. It wasn't easy to get them to talk to me, but in the end the reason emerged.

They didn't like the new department. They felt that any darned fool could do the job under these ideal circumstances. All the challenge, all the fun had gone out of their lives. They had been reduced to being no better than anyone else. Next time I decided that I knew what would motivate others I had learned the hard way to ask myself "what motivates them now?" It can be a killer question.

How do I delegate effectively?

As an executive I always found delegation easy. All that I did was to hand over the task and then push my poor subordinate out of the way so that I could show him how it ought to be done. Let's see what I have learned. Today I might ask myself:

- Have I clearly explained the importance of the task without over-stressing it?
- Have I explained the desired outcome?
- Have I told them of resources and support available to them?
- Have I given them the freedom and the time to plan how to perform the task?
- Have I encouraged them to explain their plan to me?
- Have I checked that they really understand what is required?
- Have I encouraged discussion of possible alternative approaches if necessary?
- Have I explained how I approach the task without over-selling my way?
- Have I let them use their own approach if we are clearly at one where the outcomes are concerned?
- Am I realistic about my expectations?
- Have I set challenging but realistic targets?
- Have I explained any intermediate deadlines?
- If I think it necessary have I set times for progress reports?
- Have I warned them of those elements of the task sensitive to error or risk?
- Have I stepped back and let them get on with it?
- Am I ready to give help or advice only if they ask for it?
- Do I give them encouragement from time to time?
- After the task is complete am I prepared to give timely and constructive feedback?

Did someone say "dumbsizing"?

Attracting, retaining and using the best people is vital, but sometimes the realities of the business and economic cycle mean that the headcount needs to be reduced. I am not thinking only of the so-called "packages" when I suggest that downsizing carries with it major and irrecoverable costs. Careful assessment of the results of companies that have been ruthless in "cutting heads" has shown that very seldom do they return to the profit levels of others in their sector that found different ways to reduce costs when necessary and survive. Forget the extreme cases, ignore the tales of hatchet men who have been accused of the "eighteen month goodbye" and, in one case at least, of false accounting. Getting downsizing right is a difficult and expensive process. Before embarking on a downsizing exercise it is essential to obtain reliable answers to the following questions.

- Is downsizing the only way to survive in today's economic environment?
- What is your evidence?
- What other ways have been considered?
- What has been rejected?
- Why?
- Are those who are promoting the idea of downsizing aware of the downside?

Let us look at the downside and the reasons why downsizing rarely is the path to prosperity that it is sometimes touted as being. Downsizing carries within it the seeds of two, often fatal, business diseases.

Corporate Alzheimer's

This is the name that has been given to one disease. It strikes when essential, but unrecorded knowledge walks away in the minds of those who, with the best of intentions, assumed that "everybody knows that". Too often, knowledge that has become the foundation of action that has become habitual is regarded as too obvious to be either recorded or communicated and when those who know it leave, it leaves with them to return only when disaster strikes and someone has the nous to find out what went wrong. A simple example is that of an experienced salesperson who knows better than to call on a certain important customer on Monday, because his foul mood after a weekend incarcerated with a wife whom he hates leads him to cancel orders rather than place them. A new salesperson without that knowledge which everybody is assumed to know walks blithely in on Monday and loses a critical order and possibly an important account. The example, in the interests of keeping it simple, may seem trivial, but the cumulative effect of all the key pieces of information that can be lost is not.

That is part of the reason why knowledge management has grown so much over the last two or three years.

Before anyone leaves the firm the minimum is to ask:

- How will we capture and use all the information that only exists in our people's brains?

- How will we recognize what is important?

- How will we record what is important and ensure that it is communicated to all who need to know?

- How will we ensure that those who receive the information are in an emotional state to use it?

I hope that you consider the last question to be a strange one. I added it to introduce a more complex and insidious disease to which the downsized organization is prone. The immediate effects of downsizing among the survivors include a healthy wish to get and keep their heads down, thank their lucky stars that they still have a job and assume any and all additional responsibilities in the hope that the axe, should it be wielded again, will miss them a second time. Sooner or later, however, another syndrome strikes.

The Auschwitz syndrome

People do more work usually for no more pay. They know of one-time colleagues and friends who are still suffering from the pain of unemployment. They begin to feel guilty that, in taking on additional responsibility they have been complicit in the problems experienced by their former workmates. They feel guilty and guilt, as any psychiatrist knows, must be transferred to someone or something else if it is not to fester and cause serious emotional damage. They begin to blame the company for their new feelings of emotional discomfort. They review the unfairness of their employer in that they are expected to do more without recompense. Unthinking managers or supervisors meet any complaints with the mantra: "think yourself lucky that you still have a job". Discontent increases to the level where it must have an outlet. When it seems safe to do so they start to engage in small acts of sabotage against the firm. Anything from goofing off to stealing stationery supplies to failing to carry out an essential activity serves and to them any such action "serves the company right". To mitigate the effects of the Auschwitz syndrome you may want to consider or ask the following questions.

- What can we do to enable survivors to recognize that we genuinely have done all that we can for those who have lost their jobs?

- How can we ensure that survivors are recognized and compensated for taking on additional responsibilities when money is short?

- How can we give survivors new skills that they will be motivated to employ in the service of the firm?

- How can we make it clear to all that we have considered every alternative before engaging in staff reductions?
- What should senior management do to demonstrate that they are really sharing the "pain"?
- What should we do to show that our policy for reducing staff is fair?
- How can we avoid the idiotic approach of "last in first out", thus losing some of our most necessary, expensively recruited people?

mini case study

A client company had every reason to downsize. The economic cycle was in decline. Their sector was hit hard. They had, through sloppy management in the past, developed a top-heavy, grossly overstaffed organization with much duplication of effort and a massively bureaucratic structure. They had never heard of either the Auschwitz syndrome or of corporate Alzheimer's, but they expected trouble and asked for help even if it was no more practical than having consultants in the business on whom they could pin any blame for the inevitable.

We were able to help. In outline what we did was as follows.

We identified three distinct categories of leavers with different needs.

- Some would be happy to take the "package" and retire. They would need some advice ranging from investment through to ways of filling their time to "keep out from under their partner's feet".

- Some would need to find another job as quickly as possible. They would need help with job-hunting strategies.

- The remainder would look upon this as an opportunity to start their own businesses. They would need help with identifying and applying their key strengths, business planning and marketing.

- We designed and applied psychometric tests to enable people to reconsider the groups that they had put themselves in and backed this up with individual counselling where requested. For example, it was important that those who had opted for an entrepreneurial new career had the strength that it takes to succeed. Our role in ensuring that there were no feelings of guilt among survivors necessitated a "no failure" approach.

- We designed and conducted training in essential skills and knowledge relevant to each group.

- We organized and held internal recruitment fairs and gave free business consultancy to the start-ups.

- Finally, we trained survivors and leavers together in essential influencing and sales skills on the grounds that entrepreneurs need to sell their products or services, job hunters need to sell themselves and employees need state of the art influencing skills so that their valuable ideas are not lost.

■ At every opportunity we raised the matter of unrecorded information that "everybody knows" and gathered the data from the folk tales and friendly discussion passing this to management for recording and communication.

This was completed at a cost per person which was considerably lower than might have been spent using an outplacement agency. The feeling among survivors and ex-employees that everybody had received the help that they needed lasted for years and the image of the firm within their community was enhanced rather than diminished after downsizing.

Summary

I make no apology for the comparative length of this chapter. The number of questions simply reflects the vital importance of getting it right where people are concerned. Business is about people. No technological advance can ever change that. I have a simple creed on which my attitude to business is based and it is this: *consistently making the best use of the best people.* People are not resources, most important or otherwise of the firm. They are growing, independent individuals who can, if they choose to do so, deliver to the business superior skills and knowledge, commitment, quality, economy and high productivity. By attracting the best people and enabling them to make the best use of their many qualities you will succeed.

3

Getting people to work together

questions of collaboration and culture

A man should keep his little brain attic stocked with all the furniture that he is likely to use. Arthur Conan Doyle

- The essential questions that build your ability to create, nurture and manage teams.
- The psychology of teamwork expressed as questions.
- What to ask and who to ask if you want to get things done.
- Questions to save you from the perils of "let my people go".
- Questions that make empowerment work.

What you will gain from this chapter

- How to achieve effective teamwork and build productivity.
- How to build winning teams.
- How to keep on winning.
- How to understand conflict and competition.
- How to analyze how the smarter members of your group will be thinking about you as their leader.

Essential numbers

- [✓] What is the productivity per employee/hour? (If you are not in a manufacturing type of operation you may think that productivity is not a simple matter. It may not be, but it is essential to have high productivity whatever business you are in. In my business, for example productivity is best measured in terms of the time consultants spend doing billable work for clients rather than sitting and thinking. We have a slightly more complex formula that includes the level of customer delight and the time that it took to reach the required outcome. Whatever you have to do to make it make sense measurement is essential.)

- [✓] What was the productivity level last year?

- [✓] How does the growth in productivity compare with the national average? (UK 2 per cent per annum, France 3 per cent per annum, USA 4 per cent per annum (all figures rounded up to the nearest whole number) – in the first quarter of 2002 productivity in the USA rose by 8.6 per cent following a business downturn during which it continued to rise, year on year, at an average of around 4 per cent per annum.)

Understand your teams

When Mike Abrahams headed training for Marks and Spencer he used to perform a little activity that filled his delegates with a sense of wonder. Early in the programme he would administer Myers Briggs, a psychological test designed around Jung's theories of human behaviour. At some subsequent point he would arrange the class into small groups and have them consider a case study. As they worked he would be busy writing on each of the flipcharts that he had available. When the total group reconvened he would ask each sub-group in turn to report their findings. As each reported he would be standing by a flipchart that he would reveal at the end of their contribution. The flipchart contained, almost word for word, what they had said in response to the case study. Magic? Not really. Just a very deep understanding of the way individuals, with different psychological profiles, behave in teams allied with some very careful selection of group membership.

Careful selection is where team building should, in theory, begin. Unfortunately, few have the advantages that Mike enjoyed in the conference room. Most of the time in business we inherit teams and pay scant attention to the effect of addition or removal of members. In a busy life we are often grateful if we have enough heads and hands to get the job done. Team effectiveness, however, is an essential contributor to success and it is worthwhile to consider with some care what you have to work with.

- Do I encourage my people to leverage their strengths rather than attempt to resolve their weaknesses?
  - Do I require them to think about their basic abilities and maximize their contribution based on what they do best?
- Could I write down, right now, the key strengths of each of my people and have every individual agree with what I have written about them?
- Could I use Jung's very simplified personality categories of "Thinker", "Intuitor", "Sensor" and "Feeler" accurately to analyze my team. (Details of the various types are given below.)
- Have I considered the motivational effect of making the best use of the best people?
- Do I actively avoid job mismatching?
- Do I try to keep individuals out of situations where their weaknesses may be exposed?
- Do I actively encourage people to work together formally or informally so that the strengths of each are most effectively applied to the task?
- Do I encourage as part of a learning culture, individuals to support each other informally to enhance productivity and excellence?
- Do I create challenge at a level that enables people to stretch themselves without experiencing damaging stress? (Some stress, at manageable levels is not only unavoidable it is highly desirable. It is the only specific against rust-out and depression.)

Jung's four basic personality types each have an essential role to play in any team. When assigning tasks it may be useful to ask the following questions.

Is he or she:

A thinker

- Someone who enjoys tackling problems with logic.
- Is strong on analysis but often weak on implementing solutions.
- Works methodically, but is largely interested in theory and research rather than action.
- Remains sceptical of others' ideas unless they are backed by a compelling logical argument.
- Good with facts, research, systems analysis, accounting and finance.

A sensor

- Good at getting things done.
- Impatient with theory and planning.
- Is happy to do routine work.
- Hard working and well organized.
- Energetic and somewhat single-minded.
- Finishes one job before starting another.
- Highly sensitive to task interference.
- Stressed by constantly changing priorities.
- Good at initiating projects, setting up deals, negotiating, trouble-shooting, but most of all at converting ideas into action.

A feeler

- Likes other people.
- Warm and sympathetic.
- Overlooks clear evidence in favour of "gut feelings".
- Sensitive to other people's moods.
- Good at holding the team together, counselling, arbitrating, public relations.

An intuitor

- Enjoys playing with ideas.
- Good at seeing the big picture.
- Highly creative.
- Strong imagination.
- Gets hunches that often tend to be accurate.
- Good at long-term, strategic planning, creative writing, lateral thinking, creative problem solving.

Needless to say, most of us do not fall conveniently and exclusively into any one category, but the value of thinking in these terms is that we all have strengths that we enjoy applying and identification of what makes people tick can lead to optimizing both the use of their strengths and increasing the motivation of the individual. Leaders who do this well, often Intuitors or Thinkers themselves, motivate the team and strengthen their own leadership position by delivering success.

Teams should ideally have the right balance of types. That is not to suggest an equal number of each style, but a balance that is relevant to the job to be done. In their research, McCann and Margerison discovered that some of us are what they called "hubs". A hub has the ability to assume the role of any team member as the situation dictates. A hub that is sensitive to the emerging needs of the team is flexible and pragmatic. A hub who lacks that judgement or is not given direction by a knowledgeable leader appears to be inconsistent and capricious. (Research into team behaviour is as prolific a field as is research into leadership. Some of the best, most useful work has been that of Meredith Belbin. My *Key Management Solutions* outlines his team roles and how to make the best of them or you may wish to go directly to his excellent and highly practical books. My *Power of Influence* looks in detail at team/personality types and specifically identifies what motivates team members to become a problem and the most effective solution strategies.)

- Does my team have the right balance?
    - Can I bring in people who can correct the balance where necessary?
    - Do I have a hub in my team?
        - Is he or she aware of the needs of the team at all times?
        - Can I provide guidance and direction when necessary?
        - How can I provide guidance to this individual without creating the sense that I am trying to manipulate his or her personality?
        - Am I ensuring that all my people are given responsibilities that make the fullest possible use of their strengths?

Summary

A balanced team is useful. It is not, however, essential for success. A key strength of some individuals is that they can recognize and respond to the need within the team for certain behaviours and take on the appropriate and useful role. It is worth trying to identify such people and encouraging them to make optimal use of this considerable strength.

Shared values create and sustain successful teams

Two things tend to bind teams together. One is shared knowledge. The reason that jargon is often used within work groups of various types is that the sharing of any knowledge, arcane or otherwise, and particularly, a shared language tends to bring people together. What is true of knowledge is doubly true of values. Difficulties arise when people share things in such a way that they seek to identify and exclude outsiders. The vital thing is to ensure that the members of your team work well together in the interests of the greater team that is the business.

- What are the values that my team share?
  - Are they consistent with the values of the total business?
- Are my team happy to bring in newcomers or do they try to keep them out?
  - Do my team struggle on alone when people are ill or absent even when help is freely available?
  - Have my team created norms or rules of behaviour that are not understood by others?
  - Have they developed little rituals that do nothing other than to identify who is "in" and who is "out"?
  - If I spoke to my team about the old concept of the "internal customer" how would they react?
- Are my people totally committed to the company strategy?
  - What is my evidence?
- Do I need to do anything to integrate my team into the greater team?
  - What level of opposition would I raise if I tried?
- Do I need to discuss this with my peers?
- What values do my team share?
  - Do they value conformity and structure?
- Are we in danger of creating a bureaucracy in turbulent times?
  - Do we value helping others?
- Do we spend too much time and money delivering a service that is far more than is needed or appreciated?
- Do we take on the responsibilities that should rightly fall on others?
- Do my people make conflicting promises to other people and departments?
- Do they fail to keep promises because they offer the same resource to too many "customers" – internal and external?
  - Do my team value freedom?
- Are they mature enough to recognize the difference between freedom and licence?
- Are they disciplined in the exercise of freedom?

- Do we value flexibility?

■ Are my people clear that whereas flexibility is a virtue, especially in a volatile business and economic environment, inconsistency is a problem?

- Do we value achievement?

■ Are we in danger of trying not to let things go until they are perfect?

■ Do we hold on to "our" products, ideas and outputs to stop others from "making a mess of them"?

- Do I give the right example?

- Do I delegate or try to do everything myself?

- Do we value power?

■ Do we use our understanding of power to get things done?

■ Do we look for new responsibilities, challenge and further accountability to show what we can do?

■ Do we attempt to develop power for its own sake rather than to achieve the goals of the organization in shortest time at lowest cost?

- Do we value information?

■ Do we collect information and apply it as quickly as possible to enhance our performance?

■ Do we readily share information, not merely within the team, but beyond?

■ Are we part of a larger learning community?

Summary

Team effectiveness is often a function of combining disparate capabilities and behaviours with shared values.

Values

Values are an important part of the cement that holds people together. If the values that you and your team hold are at odds with those of the organization you have a major problem on your hands. Solving that problem may not be easy. No matter how mature your team may be, no matter how subtle and sensitive your approach, any precipitate attempt to change values directly is likely to lead to a degree of fragmentation. It can turn a team into two or more armed camps. Rather than attempt to change important intangibles like values, beliefs or attitudes directly, it is usually easier to persuade people to test alternative and more effective behaviours. When these new behaviours work, the long-term result is changed attitudes and values. The short-term benefit is that the inappropriate values are no longer shaping the way that we interact with others. Let me try to explain why this approach works.

All through our lives we are experiencing and responding to the behaviour of others. No attitude, belief or value that we hold can ever be illogical to us. They result directly from our experience and knowledge of how the world works combined with our sense of how it ought to work.

- We acquire and build **knowledge** of how other people and other things "tick".
- We use that knowledge to create our **attitudes** to others.
- We refine those attitudes through our moral sense of what ought to be to create our **values**.
- The combination of our attitudes and values dictates our repertoire of **behaviours**.

Because attitudes and values are developed through a lifetime of experience, it is only experience, not admonition that is likely to make us change them. Attitudes and values are not fixed, but they change slowly in the face of our experience. (For example, it is a truism of political theory that many of us become more conservative as we get older.) Behaviour, on the other hand can be seen as being little more than a repertoire of tactics that we apply, relatively flexibly, to operate successfully in the real world. We can be persuaded to try different behaviours. When I am training people this is where I focus. Other people's beliefs, attitudes and values are significant to my understanding, but what I seek is a behavioural change. If I can show them alternative behaviours, enable them to practise them in a "safe" environment until they are comfortable with them, then through peer coaching back on the job I can persuade them to practise them in the real world. Where they are reinforced by success, they will change what they need to as a result of their own experience.

- So they change their **behaviours** toward others.
- Their change of behaviour becomes part of the other's **knowledge** of the world and how it works.
- Their **attitudes** change a little to accommodate their new knowledge.
- Their **behaviour** toward your team is gradually amended as their attitudes become assimilated.
- As a result, your team discover that their new **behaviour** reaps dividends which leads to the slow development of new attitudes and refined values.

It is not an easy process. Effective application of real psychology rarely is. We have no snake oil, but better brains than mine have explored causes, tried and tested solutions and ended with practical approaches that work in the real world. Not only should you consider trying them, but you may wish to enlist the help of your training department. If you do the latter be sure that they recognize that you are a customer and it is their responsibility to meet your needs. That means that unless they can convince you that they know a better way, they either do things your way and get the results that you demand or you spend your budget elsewhere.

Summary

My assumptions and knowledge about how the world works form my attitudes. The logic of that connection means that changing my attitudes is a tough task. If, however, you can persuade me to try a different behaviour I may find that others start to behave differently toward me in return. This changes my worldview, which in turn, influences my attitudes. So my new, more successful behaviour is reinforced and my attitudes change permanently.

Corporate culture

Culture sounds like a rather grand thing. In real life all that it means is "the way that we do things around here". Putting it another way culture is a repertoire of behaviours. From time to time you need to think if those behaviours are appropriate to the organization's present needs, because you understand that the one thing that is relatively easy to change, if necessary, is behaviour. Look for indications that your culture is no longer serving the needs of your business.

- Is there a high turnover of staff?
    - Do you tend to lose the good people?
- Do people tend to do only enough to get by?
    - Is productivity low?
    - Is morale a problem?
    - Is there a general air of pessimism?
    - Do important and urgent things have to wait their turn?
- Do customers complain about the difficulty of talking to a real person who understands their needs?
    - Are lines of communication too long to get things done effectively? (Tom Murphy, an ex-chairman of GM once expressed the problems of the corporation by saying: "We have lines of communication so long that nobody clearly understands what is expected of them or what their levels of authority may

be. Only the chairman feels that he is free to take action. Even the chairman needs about fifteen years to fight his case at every level of the chain of communication. No chairman has ever been appointed who is younger than fifty-five or has retired later than his sixtieth birthday. Gentlemen, you have a problem.")

▣ Does the company have a traditional, bureaucratic structure designed for more stable times?

▣ Have the "let my people go" empowerment gurus had a field day?

   – Do people complain that they do not know what is expected of them?

▣ Is the company perceived to be more interested in products than in people?

▣ Can competition move faster and more effectively than you can?

It is quite impossible to define the right culture for any company without knowing a great deal about its people, technology, customers and other stakeholders, but in general, a healthy culture is one that produces a company that:

▣ Is confident and relaxed.

▣ Has consistently high morale.

▣ Is able to attract and retain the best people in its industry.

▣ Has customers and prospective employees beating a path to its doors unbidden.

▣ Is responsive to customer need and wants.

▣ Is generally ahead of its competition.

▣ Knows global best practice and looks for ways to be better than the best rather than a follower of fashion.

▣ Is autonomous, calling on consultants and the like only in exceptional circumstances.

▣ Develops its people for a role in a well-defined future.

▣ Has the image that it wants in the eyes of all stakeholders.

Summary

The determinants of culture are subtle and complex, but the outcomes of culture are very simple. Culture is the way things are done around here. If generally people are doing the right things in the right way at the right time you have the culture that you need.

Winning teams

Nobody can doubt that there is every advantage in being the leader, or a member of a winning team. Every advantage, but one as it happens. If you were to give three teams the same task in a competitive situation something interesting occurs. The winning team feels good and looks forward with confidence to the next challenge, which is hardly surprising. But it is dangerous. If you then offer them a somewhat different challenge they will try to apply the previously successful tactics, taking scant notice of what is different. They do as so many of us do. They try to force fit the problem to their preferred solution. That rarely, if ever, works so winning teams are on the way to becoming losing teams even as they enjoy their triumph. Look at your team and consider the following.

- Have the team won a reputation for success?
- Do they feel that they have the formula for success?
- Do they look carefully at what must be done to identify what is different?
- Having identified differences do they willingly respond by changing their approach?
- Are they creative in developing creative initiatives?
- Do they actually take pride in finding better ways of doing things?

If winning teams tend to freeze around the winning tactics, losing teams melt. They start the process by looking beyond the team for victims of blame. The boss is a very likely target as are other departments, customers or vague circumstances. If displacing blame for failure turns out to be yet another failure, losing teams start to blame each other and any sense of team spirit evaporates as factions engage in backbiting and aggression. In short, a losing team rapidly becomes no team at all.

- Does my team fail or have they experienced failure up to the time when I took over?
- Do they try to pin the blame for failure on others?
- Do they fight among themselves?
- Are there factions within the team vying to out-blame each other?
- What can I do to pull them together?
- How can I give them an easy victory?
- How will I stop them from believing that a single achievement means that they have a "one size fits all" success formula?

Summary

Everybody wants to be part of a winning team. Teams rarely go on winning for ever. This is usually because they come to believe that they have a "one size fits all" formula that works in every situation. In an increasingly volatile business situation this is a major danger that all managers and team leaders need to plan to avoid.

Competition and conflict within and beyond teams

Most sociobiologists and evolutionary psychologists would argue that the desire to compete and, beyond that, to demonstrate and direct aggression has become so much part of human nature that it is an inescapable part of the life of human groups. As I write this I am looking forward to watching the London Marathon. The world's greatest track long-distance runner Gebrelselassie is running in his first marathon. He has made his intentions publicly clear. Nothing less than a world record at the first attempt will satisfy him. He intends not only to run against the field on the day, but also to pit himself against every great runner who has completed the course in the past. He has no interest in how the others may run. He expects to run faster and better. In psychological and business terms we call his attitude one of "working conflict" (no matter how good you are, I/we will do better). Of course it turned out that Khannouchi could and did run better, but the joy of watching three great runners in a perfect display of the best of working conflict was a joy almost as great as that of seeing Paula Radcliffe, alone at the front of the field for the whole of the women's race. That too was working competition. She ran her own race regardless of what others chose to do and led every yard of the way, running faster and faster in the later stages. Not a team performance, simply a great one.

There is a famous and rather trivial psychological experiment that has been repeated for few better reasons than it is fun to contemplate what happens. When behaviourism went out of fashion and cognitive psychology came in, the cognitive psychologists, in an attempt to show their superiority began to call their colleagues who were somewhat less dedicated followers of fashion, "rat psychologists". The intended insult rankled. A couple of psychologists identified a simple experiment aimed at showing that in certain well-defined ways rats could be smarter than people. Rats are indeed very smart animals. They learn quickly and they learn carefully. For example, if a rat finds a new food substance that it has not tried previously it eats a tiny amount. It then waits for several hours eating nothing else, to see if the new food makes it ill. Only when it is convinced that the food is safe does it return and eat its fill. These are intelligent tactics. The reason why rats are used so extensively in laboratories is based on their intelligent behaviour. One now-famous scientist took somewhat offbeat advantage of the rat's famous intelligence. He decided to pay his way through college by breeding rats and selling them to his fellow scientists. He then concluded rightly that scientists would pay a considerable premium for "super-intelligent" rats. So he labelled a considerable percentage of the perfectly ordinary rats that he bred as super-intelligent and reaped significant extra profit. But it didn't stop there. He followed up the career of the random rats that he had labelled super-intelligent and guess what? His highly trained scientific customers all assessed the behaviour of their top-of-the-range rats as being "superior".

So, a couple of mildly mischievous and slightly disaffected psychologists set up a small experiment to pit rat intelligence against that of the cream of human society, the university undergraduate. Rats are famous for their ability to rapidly learn to run mazes and find a reward of food. Could humans learn as quickly or as well? Mazes were built with the human one an exact, but scaled up replica of that used for rats. The reward for rats was the usual food pellet, that for the relatively impecunious students was a small sum of money. The experiment was completed. Humans and rats learned to run their respective mazes. Let me save human blushes and say that the result was an honourable draw. The experiment was completed and the rats happily withdrew to their cages. The humans kept on running the maze. The rewards had been withdrawn, but the humans continued to run the maze. They were asked politely, then firmly to stop and they continued to run the maze. They were banned from the laboratory, but they snuck in and ran. The doors were locked and barred to keep them out, but they broke in and ran the maze. Another example of working conflict, the desire to be better than competition, no matter how smart the other side.

Warring conflict

One of the most popular books of 2001/2002 has been *Nathaniel's Nutmeg*, the story of how the Dutch and English cheated, tortured and slaughtered each other over centuries as they fought to dominate the nutmeg trade. An extensive example of what in business terms we call "warring conflict". This is conflict in which it matters not at all how hard the opposition try, because our intention is to destroy their best efforts and thereafter take the easy track to ongoing success.

- Do you see signs of conflict and competition within your teams? (If you do you need first to assess whether it is working or warring competition. If it is the former think very carefully before you decide that the challenge is, of necessity, a "good thing". If there are winners there are losers and losing teams melt.)
- Should the conflict be confronted?
- Should it be re-directed at others outside the group?

- How far outside? (Japanese business has traditionally assumed that conflict will exist. They have, therefore, in many cases directed that conflict outside the company at competitors through "warlike" mission statements and a practical respect for the writings of Sun Tse. Don't let the doldrums of the Japanese economy fool you. They exist because of a failure to deal with structural and political factors and not because Komatsu have a mission to "surround Caterpillar".)

- Who are the rivals that we should seek to damage first if that is our decision? (People respond with the greatest energy when they share common cause against a common and specific enemy. Dominance strategy usually means that you pick off carefully targeted competitors one by one. You gain little by an anodyne belief that all outside the group are equally to be attacked. Nothing is gained by exhortations and silly catchphrases. Know your enemy and attack their specific weaknesses. It is both most fun and most effective to do things that way.)

- How will we ensure that our success against one competitor will not lead people to believe that they have a formula that will work against all?

- How will we stop our groups from freezing? (To be the best of the best you have to keep on learning to be better and as de Geus's research has shown, you have to be ready to change track when circumstances have changed enough to make a sea change the best strategy.)

Summary

Managers and particularly management trainers tend to philosophize over whether competition is a better motivator than co-operation. If competition leads to better performance it is undoubtedly useful. When writing their mission statement all companies should consider what it is that will challenge their people to become and remain the best of the best. That is working conflict or competition and is directed where perhaps it ought to be – at competition.

Warring conflict is directed inwards and, as is explained above, is very destructive. Warring conflict destroys its victims, but it also destroys its perpetrators as they are distracted into "playing games" rather than improving performance.

The watcher watched

Companies and corporations often suffer in the long term by perpetuating the one-time strengths that have become weaknesses in a volatile market. Where a superior boss has become the role model for all time, problems often arise. You need to study your boss and to be aware that the smartest people in your group are studying you. This is essential if you are to identify and adopt your best bosses' strengths while they are strengths and to adapt your behaviour to changing circumstances.

- What are your bosses' aims and values?
  - Which do you share?
  - Which do you find difficult to adopt?
  - Why?
  - What is your best strategy in respect to that value?
- Should you discuss with your boss any inappropriate behaviours to which it gives rise?
  - Should you simply create a counterbalance within your team to reduce the effect of any inappropriate behaviours without directing explicit or implied criticism of your boss?

  What is your personal definition of "loyalty"?
  - Where does your primary loyalty lie? (To the firm? To your team? To your boss? To yourself and your career? To your family? To your friends? Think it through carefully. Research by Lickert some years ago showed that a career in management invariably makes you the "man or woman in the middle", subject to conflicting loyalties and expectations. Sooner or later you have to be clear on how you choose to handle these conflicts if you want to sleep at night.)
- How does your boss measure your performance?
- How does he or she measure himself or herself?
  - Is he or she consistent?
  - Does any inconsistency affect the performance of you or your team?
- Who does your boss admire?
  - What do you think of his or her heroes?
- What is his or her leadership style?
  - Is he or she an autocrat demanding unquestioning obedience?
  - Does he or she take a democratic approach expecting you and your team to share values and goals and go after them the best way that you know how?

- What effect does the boss's leadership style have on your behaviour?
- Is there consistency or conflict?
- What does that do to your team?

■ What would you prefer to do about it if anything – doing nothing may be the right choice?
  - What can you do?
  - What limits your power to act?
  - If there is a potential conflict between what you wish and what you can do – and there may well not be – but if there is, how will you deal with it?

■ How can you avoid or manage stress?

■ How can you avoid creating stress for others?

■ What are the pressures on your boss?
  - Do those pressures create pressure on you?

■ What rewards do you personally seek?
  - What is likely to be the best way of achieving what you want?
  - How does that sit with your personal attitude to loyalty?

■ How can you and your boss become part of a superior team?

■ Do both of you accept and understand that you depend on each other for progress?
  - What can you do to ensure that you and your boss recognize your need to work consistently together to achieve goals that are important to both of you?

Summary

The behaviour of teams is complex. Winning teams often fail. Losing teams always fail. The team that comes a good second often has the best chance of being the winner next time, but you cannot hold a team in second place and once they become winners they experience the same potential pitfalls as any other winner. You must ensure that your team recognizes differences where they exist to keep them out of a rut of self-satisfaction. Equally, however, you must ensure that they see differences where none exist.

Conflict is probably inevitable: the manager's job is often to direct aggression to where it can do the most good and it usually does most good when it is directed at competitors outside the organization.

All teams are part of a greater team and you need to understand the expectations that your boss and your team have of you. They may well conflict and to manage a team effectively you often have to manage conflicts that are too near to your heart for comfort.

You and your boss are an essential team that need to work effectively together.

4

"Leadership is what leaders DO!"

questions of business leadership

In defeat unbeatable; in victory unbearable. Winston Churchill (about Field Marshall Montgomery)

- The indispensable questions that enable you to turn Churchill's aphorism into a success formula.
- Questions that ensure that you can be flexible and consistent simultaneously.
- Questions that will give you control in all situations.
- Questions that will give you time to think.

What you will gain from this chapter

- How to establish yourself as a leader.
- The secrets of some of the big names in international business leadership.
- Are you a charismatic leader?
- Does it matter?
- A game plan of success for every type of leader.

Some facts you may need to consider

- ✓ When did you last proactively consider your leadership style?
- ✓ What was the result?

☑ How recent was the test that was used if you used a test? ("Tannenbaum and Schmidt" goes back to the 1950s, Fleischmann to the 1970s and Hersey and Blanchard to the late 1970s. This is not to say that these well-established tests no longer have value – they still can teach us a great deal. It will be interesting, however, to compare them with a test based on the latest leadership research. That is part of what this chapter will enable you to do.)

☑ What has happened to the productivity of your team since you took over?

- Has it increased?
- Decreased?
- Remained static?

☑ How appropriate is your style in today's business?

Introduction to leadership

Few doubt the importance of leadership. Few question the contribution that a strong leader makes to the success of any enterprise. So important is the subject perceived to be that there have been more than 10,000 major studies of leadership carried out since the end of World War II with innumerable minor studies. As I write I am reminded of the story of the student of divinity who, during an examination was faced with a question demanding that the candidate should list the "minor prophets of Judah". The student wrote on his paper: "who am I to decide who is major and who minor? Here is a list of kings". The story is apocryphal no doubt, but it does help me to make a small point about leadership.

One of the greatest leaders that this country has known insisted that leadership is what leaders do and what leaders do is to bring success to their teams whether the "team" is a small work-group or a nation in peril. Leadership is, and must always be, focused on success. A recent book has been written to show how quickly leaders can move in the public mind from heroes to villains. Success is the key and ongoing success is an essential attribute of leadership. Idiosyncrasy balance ensures that leadership failures chip away at credibility and power. Readers of my *Key Management Solutions* will be familiar with the concept of idiosyncrasy balance, the psychological process through which a leader either builds a credibility balance that enables him or her to survive the occasional failure, or dissipates early goodwill and makes it inevitable that informal leaders will challenge his or her position with the group.

The leading Harvard psychologist, Howard Gardner, has recently published his theory that successful leaders are those who are best able to develop and promote a personal myth. For example Margaret Thatcher, an inconsistent, wily and street-wise politician, more adept than most at making the twists and turns that a political career demands, promoted and sustained the myth that the "lady is not for turning". Gardner's ideas are interesting and have re-awakened the argument as to whether leaders are born or made. It should provide any leader with considerable food for thought that Winston Churchill, the consummate mythmaker, fell victim to his own, carefully nurtured, mythology in the immediate post-war election where he was rejected as a "warmonger", yet he consistently avowed that there is no reliable theory of leadership and leadership is simply "what leaders do". Those of my generation are, or should be, grateful that in war at least he did it so well.

Readers may wish to submit themselves privately and at their leisure to the following test which is based partly on current academic theories of leadership, but more on a lifetime spent watching leaders, successful and otherwise, in action and sometimes guiding their thoughts and professional development.

The charismatic leader

A success and style instrument designed by Tom Lambert

Instructions

1. Consider the situations described below. From the actions indicated choose that which most closely approximates to what you would do in real life if faced with the circumstances described. Do not attempt to hedge your bets by suggesting that you would do "some of this and some of that". Leadership is increasingly demonstrated by an ability to think and act quickly in fast-changing environments. Decisiveness counts.

2. Have a trusted and reliable colleague complete the test *on your behalf, as if they were role-playing as you and trying to think as they believe that you think and act as you appear to them to act.*

3. Compare results and discuss particularly any differences of perception concentrating on what it is that you do, or have done in the past, that led your colleague to see you in a different light from that which you chose for yourself.

4. Choose whether to amend any of your own answers in the light of your colleague's view.

5. Choose whether to amend your behaviour in the light of any new information.

6. Read the Commentary and discuss with those of your peers who have also completed the instrument.

7. Consider what you have learned about charismatic and pragmatic leadership and decide what use you will make of your new knowledge in future decision-making.

Situation one

You are offered a promotion that will require you to work in a field in which you have no interest and with people for whom you have little respect. If you accept the promotion it will, of necessity, take you away from the as yet unfinished task of building the best team in your sector devoted to a mission to which you are committed. On the other hand the corporation has a culture of never asking twice and the promotion, should you take it, will not only provide you with greater personal security, but with fast track promotion prospects. In fact it is very likely to take you right to the top in a few years. You have no obvious successor with the ability or commitment to complete your mission where you are at present and the new task will take all your time if you are to succeed.

Choices

1. Take the job. The corporation best understands its needs and if you have been selected you can make your greatest contribution by meeting those needs elsewhere if that is what the company expects.

2. Ignore your very strong understanding that the new job will require your full attention and negotiate a "watching brief" over your old operation with some sort of dotted line reporting structure that will enable you to guide your successor and protect the future of the department to which you are devoted.

3. Refuse the job and complete your present task to such a high standard that your capabilities and committed would be recognized by all and the firm would be crazy to block your future progress.

Situation two

You have developed your team to the point where you are able to push decision-making down to the lowest organizational level capable of making an informed choice. You have communicated your vision, values and objectives to all so that you can be sure of each individual's absolute commitment to shared goals. You have passed a major decision to your people acting as a team. For organizational reasons you have taken their decision to your CEO for her to "sign off" on it. To your surprise the CEO appears to be at best lukewarm. "I think you ought to look at this again. It is your decision and I will back you if you choose to stick with it, but if you are wrong, and I think that you are, your neck will definitely be on the block." You are convinced that the decision is right.

Choices

1. Discuss the situation "from the ground up" with your CEO. Listen to her objections and, if necessary, throw out the original course of action and override your team's decision.

2. Marshall your arguments and, backing your team's decision to the hilt, attempt to win over the CEO, but be willing to accept that, should you fail, the decision will have to be changed, perhaps for something more "politically" acceptable.

3. Invite the CEO to explain her reservations, but make it clear that the decision stands unless she indicates something that your people cannot have known that effects the decision. You make it abundantly clear that you have absolute faith in the capability and motives of your team and that you only pass down decisions to those best qualified to make them.

Situation three

You are the CEO. An opportunity has arisen that will give your firm a considerable short-term advantage over competition. Exploiting it will, however, mean diverting resources from a strategic plan that is on track to deliver your key strategic goals within the planning horizon of three years. The effect of such a diversion will be to delay the achievement of the strategy by at least a year. It will, however, produce a substantial extra profit this year and the shareholders, who at last year's AGM vociferously demanded a quick return on their investment, will be happy.

Choices

1. Your responsibility as a chief executive is to the shareholders. Exploit the short-term opportunity. Keep the shareholders off the Board's back in the short term and try to conserve enough of the extra profit to bring in additional resources to accelerate progress toward the strategic goals next year and thereafter.

2. Keep your focus on the strategy. Avoid anything that diverts attention from the mission.

3. Put the dilemma before the Board. Try to get consensus and go with whatever decision the Board makes.

Situation four

You are marketing director. Your advertising agency has developed a plan that will take you head to head against a bigger competitor. If it is successful the plan will deliver a massive increase in sales and revenues, but given the much greater resources of the competitor it is a high-risk tactic.

Choices

1. Go for it! Business is about risk.

2. Carefully assess your own competitive strengths and weaknesses and develop a series of comprehensive marketing and sales campaigns to pick off weaker competitors one by one, pitting your known strengths

against their identified weaknesses, strengthening the company with worthwhile extra revenues and profits until it is ready to take on the giants.

Part two

Consider how true the following statements are of you.

Please score them as follows:

Absolutely true of me all the time:	4
True of me most of the time	3
Rarely true of me	2
Never true of me	1

1. I think best under pressure.

2. I love volatility and uncertainty.

3. Complexity makes decision-making more interesting.

4. I believe that inspiration is as important as perspiration.

5. I expect my people to pluck triumph out of disaster every time.

6. My people would follow me to hell and back.

7. I take winning very personally.

8. My vision drives others as much as it does me.

9. People buy in readily to my vision.

10. My people believe in themselves because they believe in me.

11. I always exude confidence no matter what the problem.

12. I cut to the chase and ignore trivia.

13. I disregard a person's weaknesses if they have the strengths I want.

14. I make sure that I understand how the enemy thinks.

15. I know what my people can deliver then I ask for a little more.

16. The more my people learn the better I can use them.

17. What my people learn I expect them to apply straightaway.

18. I expect my people to value learning.

19. If my people want to learn Anglo-Saxon poetry I encourage them.

20. When they know Anglo-Saxon I'll find a use for it in the business.

21. I'm prepared to walk a mile in any man's moccasins.

22. If I invent the "talk" I'll "walk it" until everyone believes. _____

23. Faith can move mountains, faith in me can build them. _____

24. My mission in life is to help others to achieve beyond their expectations. _____

25. I have taken the trouble to learn what is best in pretty well any situation. _____

26. I'd back me to the hilt. _____

27. I am building a great future for all my people. _____

28. Nothing will stop me from getting where I want to be. _____

29. I'll go the extra mile to support and protect my people. _____

30. I've had enough of this there is work to be done. _____

Peer assessment

Feel free to copy this to trusted colleagues.

Instructions

You have been nominated by _____

as a particularly trusted colleague. Please help him or her to develop their leadership skills by addressing the situations and statements given as if you were the colleague who has nominated you. On the basis of your knowledge of your colleague and of their normal behaviour please put yourself entirely in their shoes. Ignore as far as you can your own responses to the situations and statements and limit your answers to those that you believe your colleague would give if being totally frank.

Having completed the task and keeping the results confidential between you please return the completed forms to your colleague for their careful consideration. Your colleague will want to discuss your assessment with you so please bear in mind the reasons for the decisions that you make. After you have answered any questions that your colleague may wish to ask of you, you may wish to initiate further discussion around questions such as:

- *What is the most appropriate leadership style for the organization at present?*

- *How does your colleague's leadership style currently affect his or her subordinates?*

- *What is likely to be the most appropriate leadership style for the organization in the future?*

- *What do you both need to do now to make any transition to a new leadership style, now or in the future, as easy as possible?*

- *If you agree that a change of style is or will be appropriate how can that need be best communicated to your teams?*

Instructions your colleague was given

- Consider the situations described below. From the actions indicated choose that which most closely approximates to what you would do in real life if faced with the circumstances described. Do not attempt to hedge your bets by suggesting that you would do "some of this and some of that". Leadership is increasingly demonstrated by an ability to think and act quickly in fast changing environments. Decisiveness counts.

- Have a trusted and reliable colleague complete the test *on your behalf, as if they were role-playing as you and trying to think as they believe that you think and act as you appear to them to act.*

- Compare results and discuss particularly any differences of perception concentrating on what it is that you do, or have done in the past, that led your colleague to see you in a different light from that which you chose for yourself.

- Choose whether to amend any of your own answers in the light of your colleague's view.

- Choose whether to amend your behaviour in the light of any new information.

- Read the Commentary and discuss with those of your peers who have also completed the instrument.

- Consider what you have learned about charismatic and pragmatic leadership and decide what use you will make of your new knowledge in future decision-making.

Situation one

You are offered a promotion that will require you to work in a field in which you have no interest and with people for whom you have little respect. If you accept the promotion it will, of necessity, take you away from the as yet unfinished task of building the best team in your sector devoted to a mission to which you are committed. On the other hand the corporation has a culture of never asking twice and the promotion, should you take it, will not only provide you with greater personal security, but with fast track promotion prospects. In fact it is very likely to take you right to the top in a few years. You have no obvious successor with the ability or commitment to complete your mission where you are at present and the new task will take all your time if you are to succeed.

Choices

1. Take the job. The corporation best understands its needs and if you have been selected you can make your greatest contribution by meeting those needs elsewhere if that is what the company expects.

2. Ignore your very strong understanding that the new job will require your full attention and negotiate a "watching brief" over your old operation with some sort of dotted line reporting structure that will enable you to guide your successor and protect the future of the department to which you are devoted.

3. Refuse the job and complete your present task to such a high standard that your capabilities and committed would be recognized by all and the firm would be crazy to block your future progress.

Situation two

You have developed your team to the point where you are able to push decision-making down to the lowest organizational level capable of making an informed choice. You have communicated your vision, values and objectives to all so that you can be sure of each individual's absolute commitment to shared goals. You have passed a major decision to your people acting as a team. For organizational reasons you have taken their decision to your CEO for her to "sign off" on it. To your surprise the CEO appears to be at best lukewarm. "I think you ought to look at this again. It is your decision and I will back you if you choose to stick with it, but if you are wrong, and I think that you are, your neck will definitely be on the block." You are convinced that the decision is right.

Choices

1. Discuss the situation "from the ground up" with your CEO. Listen to her objections and, if necessary, throw out the original course of action and override your team's decision.

2. Marshall your arguments and, backing your team's decision to the hilt, attempt to win over the CEO, but be willing to accept that, should you fail, the decision will have to be changed, perhaps for something more "politically" acceptable.

3. Invite the CEO to explain her reservations, but make it clear that the decision stands unless she indicates something that your people cannot have known that effects the decision. You make it abundantly clear that you have absolute faith in the capability and motives of your team and that you only pass down decisions to those best qualified to make them.

Situation three

You are the CEO. An opportunity has arisen that will give your firm a considerable short-term advantage over competition. Exploiting it will, however, mean diverting resources from a strategic plan that is on track to deliver your key strategic goals within the planning horizon of three years. The effect of such a diversion will be to delay the achievement of the strategy by at least a year. It will, however, produce a substantial extra profit this year and the shareholders, who at last year's AGM vociferously demanded a quick return on their investment, will be happy.

Choices

1. Your responsibility as a chief executive is to the shareholders. Exploit the short-term opportunity. Keep the shareholders off the board's back in the short term and try to conserve enough of the extra profit to bring in additional resources to accelerate progress toward the strategic goals next year and thereafter.

2. Keep your focus on the strategy. Avoid anything that diverts attention from the mission.

3. Put the dilemma before the board. Try to get consensus and go with whatever decision the board makes.

Situation four

You are the marketing director. Your advertising agency has developed a plan that will take you head to head against a bigger competitor. If it is successful the plan will deliver a massive increase in sales and revenues, but given the much greater resources of the competitor it is a high-risk tactic.

Choices

1. Go for it! Business is about risk.

2. Carefully assess your own competitive strengths and weaknesses and develop a series of comprehensive marketing and sales campaigns to pick off weaker competitors one by one, pitting your known strengths against their identified weaknesses, strengthening the company with worthwhile extra revenues and profits until it is ready to take on the giants.

Part two

Consider how true the following statements are of you. Please score them as follows:

Absolutely true of me all the time:	4
True of me most of the time	3
Rarely true of me	2
Never true of me	1

1. I think best under pressure.

2. I love volatility and uncertainty.

3. Complexity makes decision-making more interesting.

4. I believe that inspiration is as important as perspiration.

5. I expect my people to pluck triumph out of disaster every time. _____

6. My people would follow me to hell and back. _____

7. I take winning very personally. _____

8. My vision drives others as much as it does me. _____

9. People buy in readily to my vision. _____

10. My people believe in themselves because they believe in me. _____

11. I always exude confidence no matter what the problem. _____

12. I cut to the chase and ignore trivia. _____

13. I disregard a person's weaknesses if they have the strengths I want. _____

14. I make sure that I understand how the enemy thinks. _____

15. I know what my people can deliver then I ask for a little more. _____

16. The more my people learn the better I can use them. _____

17. What my people learn I expect them to apply straight away. _____

18. I expect my people to value learning. _____

19. If my people want to learn Anglo-Saxon poetry I encourage them. _____

20. When they know Anglo-Saxon I'll find a use for it in the business. _____

21. I'm prepared to walk a mile in any man's moccasins. _____

22. If I invent the "talk" I'll "walk it" until everyone believes. _____

23. Faith can move mountains, faith in me can build them. _____

24. My mission in life is to help others to achieve beyond their expectations. _____

25. I have taken the trouble to learn what is best in pretty well any situation. _____

26. I'd back me to the hilt. _____

27. I am building a great future for all my people. _____

28. Nothing will stop me from getting where I want to be. _____

29. I'll go the extra mile to support and protect my people. _____

30. I've had enough of this there is work to be done. _____

Commentary

The short self-administered test that precedes this is designed to help senior executives to consider their tendency toward charismatic leadership. Research suggests that although charisma is not an essential factor in leadership it is important and if, in Tom Peters' words: "You need to get everybody to the barricades when the chips are down" or worse, "build bridges under the waterline", there are situations where it is perhaps vital.

It is often demonstrated that for any one successful charismatic leader beloved by the media there is at least one quiet, pragmatic, even self-effacing leader who is no less successful. The important factor then is, as is always the case in business, to play to your strengths and not to try to appear to be something that is uncomfortable for you as an individual.

This instrument will not only help you to establish confidently whether you are a charismatic leader, it will also provide you with proven information and research findings that will enable you to develop a suitable game plan for effective leadership whatever your personality.

Characteristics of the charismatic leader

A leader is charismatic if he or she has all or most of the following abilities:

- To think quickly in a volatile situation.
- To think effectively in a fast changing environment.
- To take effective action in complex situations.
- To inspire followers to overachieve in the face of overwhelming odds.
- To take real enjoyment and satisfaction from pursuing important goals.
- To instil in all their people a belief that they can win, regardless of the forces lined up against them.
- To walk the talk of success even when outcomes are by no means certain.
- To ignore the trivial and irrelevant and focus on outcomes and goals.
- To identify what is important in complex situations.
- To deploy people and resources to leverage strengths rather than mitigate weaknesses.
- To acquire and use essential competitive intelligence.
- To create a business-driven environment of "life-long learning – just-in-time".
- To relate knowledge and skills acquisition clearly to the vision, mission, goals and values of the business.

- To anticipate the knowledge, skills, competencies and strengths that will be required to achieve the strategy.

- To be able to walk a mile in another's shoes whether that other is the customer, employee, supplier, colleague, distributor or competitor.

- To understand all key players in the business environment from their own point of view.

- To be able to create inspirational myths about themselves and convince others to accept those myths as true. (Gardner, Harvard 2000)

If your colleagues and subordinates believe that all of these are true of you, you are certainly a remarkably charismatic leader. If they, or you, do not believe them to be true of you please read on and you will obtain a mass of reliable information that will hone and enhance even the most impressive leadership skills.

The pragmatic leader

A leader is pragmatic if he or she:

- Is adept at accurately assessing rapidly changing situations.

- Assesses the maturity, motivation and commitment of the team accurately.

- Confines decision-making to those best able to make the specific decision.

- Works to transform the organization when necessary through evolution rather than revolution.

- Attracts followers through actions and results rather than personality and beliefs.

- Develops skills of leadership as assiduously as others might pursue operational skills.

- Gives direction and understands how to mould behaviours.

- Works sensitively and effectively with group dynamics.

- Focuses on the long-term goals without losing sight of today's needs.

- Recognizes that leadership is a skill, not a gift.

I am sure that you have realized by now that being a charismatic leader is by no means excluded by being pragmatic. The difference is that although the key skills are by no means mutually exclusive, the charismatic leader who lacks the pragmatic skills can be very effective in leading his or her team into disaster as can the pragmatic leader who lacks judgement. This instrument is designed to help real leaders to develop further their skills and knowledge whether they are charismatic, pragmatic or a healthy mixture of the two styles.

The instrument

It is mere snake oil to suggest that in a complex area of human behaviour simple or simplistic answers are either possible or desirable. The aims of instruments such as this are to:

- Provide information and ideas that the individual can think about, challenge, adapt and adopt or reject.

- Deliver in a simple form an opportunity to see ourselves as at least one other sees us.

- Offer a simple tool that will help to develop a consistent and appropriate leadership style throughout the organization.

- Protect individuals from assuming that they display traits that they do not and being misled into attempting to use strengths that they lack in the eyes of others.

- Offer viable alternative behavioural strategies to those who might find attempts to inflict a "one size fits all model" uncomfortable and unworkable.

- Provide a basis for further personal development through training, coaching, mentoring or through acquiring and practising neglected life skills.

When working through these "answers" please read them all, not only those that reflect your choices.

Comments on your answers and some thoughts that you may want to consider

Situation one

You are offered a promotion that will require you to work in a field in which you have no interest and with people for whom you have little respect. If you accept the promotion it will, of necessity, take you away from the as yet unfinished task of building the best team in your sector devoted to a mission to which you are committed. On the other hand the corporation has a culture of never asking twice and the promotion, should you take it, will not only provide you with greater personal security, but with fast track promotion prospects. In fact it is very likely to take you right to the top in a few years. You have no obvious successor with the ability or commitment to complete your mission where you are at present and the new task will take all your time if you are to succeed.

Choice 1

Take the job. The corporation best understands its needs and if you have been selected you can make your greatest contribution by meeting those needs elsewhere if that is what the company expects.

Commentary

There is much to be said for the general idea that the company needs to deploy its people according to their key strengths. The company pays for all resources including people so that they may be used effectively to make a contribution to achieving the business goals and mission. And here lies a potential problem. Charismatic leaders only function effectively when they love what they are doing – and it shows. A charismatic leader who accepts second best to satisfy personal ambition frequently has been shown to fail. Because neither the job to be done nor the people that he or she must work with excite the leader he or she tends to become increasingly isolated. People experience little or none of the early success that they expect and informal leaders tend to emerge, isolating the leader increasingly from what is happening in the team. A well-established law of managerial psychology is that of *idiosyncrasy balance*.

Idiosyncrasy balance says that:

The team perceives the leader as being worth following, if and only if, that leader brings the team the success that it craves. A new leader has around one hundred days in which to deliver success. Any failure or perceived lack of progress beyond one hundred days reduces the effectiveness of the leader and leads to the emergence of informal leadership. In effect the team "fires the boss".

Questions for discussion

1. In what other sphere of leadership is the first one hundred days considered vital?
2. What examples can you think of where a leader has been effectively fired by the team?
3. Is informal leadership always a problem?

Choice 2

Ignore your very strong understanding that the new job will require your full attention and negotiate a "watching brief" over your old operation with some sort of dotted line reporting structure that will enable you to guide your successor and protect the future of the department to which you are devoted.

Commentary

Research has shown that one of the major causes of conflict within an organization is where the past leader of a team is perceived as "meddling" in things that should no longer concern them. Such interference undermines the new leadership and often causes "warring" factions to develop where some support the old leadership while others support the new. This is exacerbated by the fact that winning teams often mistakenly believe that different situations in a rapidly changing world are in their reality "no different from" situations for which they had the success formula in the past. Interference by a leader from that past reinforces this view and teams become the prisoners of their own success. As Richard Pascale succinctly puts it: "Nothing fails like success".

Charismatic leaders who are consistently successful throw themselves wholly into everything that they do and intentionally avoid trying to cling to the past.

Questions for discussion
1. In your experience does interference from an old leader most frequently stem from insecurity in the new job or love of the old?
2. How often do apparent "personality clashes" in senior management teams boil down to one executive refusing to let go of an old operation in which they experienced considerable past success?
3. Does anything need to be done to avoid this happening in your company?
4. What can be done if action is desirable or necessary?
5. Is there a danger that the successful teams in your organization may "freeze" into a rut of success and assume that all situations are "really just like the old"?
6. How can people be convinced that in a rapidly changing world situations do not repeat themselves exactly and new problems need creative thinking and new remedies?
7. Should a leader encourage his or her people to "think the unthinkable"?
8. If so – why?

Choice 3
Refuse the job and complete your present task to such a high standard that your capabilities and committed would be recognized by all and the firm would be crazy to block your future progress.

This is what charismatic leaders often do. General Lee who led the South in the American Civil War preceded the leadership of his beloved South by turning down an offer of promotion by Lincoln in the Federal Army in 1861. In the southern United States Lee is still seen as a great hero, but had he accepted the job offered by Lincoln the South might not have gone to war, or the war might have been over quickly and deaths of thousands of people and the near total destruction of the economy of the South might have been avoided. The charismatic leader needs to combine clear understanding of the bigger picture to control a personal need for achievement in areas where he or she cares deeply.

McClelland suggested that one of three overwhelming motives drive those of us who seek to lead.

Achievement

Achievement drives us to insist on high standards, sometimes higher than is necessary and since no one can achieve quite as well as we can, being motivated by achievement is often the enemy of effective delegation. Psychological research suggests that achievement motivation is the key to pre-managerial entrepreneurial success, but that carried into management it puts a severe limitation on the development of successful teams. This research is frequently cited as the reason why successful entrepreneurs fail to build or retain control of, major corporations.

The effective charismatic leader always knows when and what to let go and how to make the best possible use of others. The less effective charismatic leader believes his or her myth of superiority and cannot let go. General Lee may be a hero to the southern states even today, but is it possible that his belief in his own considerable ability led finally to disaster?

Affiliation

Nice people sometimes seek leadership responsibility in order to do thoughtful and generous things for others. This can lead to situations where a leader is distracted from the goal because he or she is overly concerned with the effect that some necessary action may have on others and fails to take essential and timely action. The leader driven by affiliation is, at the extreme, paralyzed by the fact that they are so eager to please everybody that they do nothing for fear of upsetting somebody. Such leaders never bring their teams long-term success and invariably are side stepped by the emergence of informal leaders who have their eye firmly on the ball. (Whether it is the right ball is always open to question.)

No successful charismatic or pragmatic leader is mainly motivated by affiliation. Most are effective in how they *use* other people. Not in some manipulative way, but in order to use the greatest strengths of the best people to get things done effectively and at minimum cost. (See *Power* below.) This often demands that more kicks are administered than kisses and those under them often perceive charismatic leaders as hard taskmasters that they would nonetheless follow "to hell and back". A nurturing style of leadership seldom is effective in the cut and thrust world of business.

Power

Research suggests and experience confirms that those who are driven by a desire to understand and make the best possible use of power within the organization for the attainment of organizational goals are most successful as leaders in business. Charismatic leaders and the most successful pragmatic leaders have this in common: they take the trouble to understand power as it pertains to the organization and they use that knowledge to achieve organizational goals in the fastest time at least cost. Then they consider the key sources of power in the organization and assess their ability to strengthen those that they feel are most appropriate and useful in helping to achieve business goals.

Questions for discussion

1. What type of power is most appropriate to your organizational and business needs?

   Reward power: The ability of an executive to reward desired behaviour or results.

   Sanction power: The use or threat of punishments to control behaviour.

   Referent power: Leaders acting as role models for desired behaviours leading to looked-for results. Leaders who are imitated because they are admired. The ultimate charismatic leader.

   Status power: The formal and informal emphasis on age, role, experience and expertise in decision-making.

   Expert power: The exercise of power that comes from being "he or she that knows how".

   Legitimate power: The development of rules, norms, policies and procedures aimed at ensuring that all fully understand that power is a function of organizational position and responsibility.

2. Do any informal or formal rules or traditions exist in your company that get in the way of achieving goals?

3. Where do such "rules" come from?

4. How will you sweep them aside so publicly that everybody realizes that the way the game is played has really changed? As an example you might like to consider Bob Townsend's suggestion that the quickest way to demonstrate that things are going to be "different around here" is to publicly fire some apparently fireproof barrier to progress. (Hopefully something a little less dramatic will suffice in your case after all, Bob Townsend also suggested that personnel managers should be "taken out and shot".)

5. Consider "referent power" again if you would please. Are you aware of any cases where a greatly admired leader has become a role model for all future generations to the degree that pale facsimiles of the original are now practising a leadership style that is out of tune with the present business needs?

Situation two

You have developed your team to the point where you are able to push decision-making down to the lowest organizational level capable of making an informed choice. You have communicated your vision, values and objectives to all so that you can be sure of each individual's absolute commitment to shared goals. You have passed a major decision to your people acting as a team. For organizational reasons you have taken their decision to your CEO for her to "sign off" on it. To your surprise the CEO appears to be at best lukewarm. "I think you ought to look at this again. It is your decision and I will back you if you choose to stick with it, but if you are wrong, and I think that you are, your neck will definitely be on the block." You are convinced that the decision is right.

Choice 1
Discuss the situation "from the ground up" with your CEO. Listen to her objections and, if necessary, throw out the original course of action and override your team's decision.

Commentary
It may come as a surprise, but this is probably the best decision for the charismatic leader. If you are truly charismatic you will have built a substantial fund of confidence in your people that what you do is done for a good reason and usually works. They will accept that you are selective about when you accept their decisions without being arbitrary. In short you will be seen as being "firm but fair" and your decision to override will be accepted without undue concern. If, however, you have not built such a reputation among your people they will believe that you are playing games with them and that their apparent involvement is a charade. In the early stages of developing your team's ability to make unsupervised decisions you need to limit the areas under consideration to low risk situations where you can live with anything that they decide. Only pass major decisions to teams that have proved their worth by making good decisions in the past that have led to successful outcomes, but be sure to emphasize any and all distinctions between the new situation and the old. The charismatic leader stretches people by demanding new ways and better ways of doing things. This is why Jack Welch is famous for congratulating his vice presidents on their achievements prior to demanding to know how they propose to achieve more with less resources in future.

Third-rate training operations and third-rate managers adore consensus decision-making because it satisfies a vague sense of liberal thinking and appears to disperse responsibility and accountability. Leaders should bear in mind that in the real world of work consensus decision-making works best only where the team is mature and where the situation is so novel that it is not known where expertise lies and all available knowledge needs to be brought to the table.

Too often the "let my people go" empowerment fanatics talk about the "tremendous up-swell of creativity" among employees without so much as a thread of tested evidence. Unplanned, ill-thought-through attempts at empowerment lead, in the real world to anarchy and paralysis in roughly equal measure. Where expertise exists the quickest, most economic and best course is to use it. In so doing you get outcomes that deliver success to the team. They learn as a result of the process and become ready for unsupervised decision-making when the circumstances are right.

The feel-good leader who says in effect that "the objectives will look after themselves if we just set people free" has seldom if ever succeeded outside of "business bodice rippers".

Questions for discussion
1. Are there any activities in your company that result more from unsubstantiated doctrine than from fact?

2. How are the results of any such "experiments" to be measured?
3. Does any individual, group or department play a major role in introducing fads and fallacies?
4. Can the company afford to experiment in today's business environment?
5. Can the company afford not to experiment?
6. If you don't experiment how will you avoid getting stuck in the "rut of past success"?
7. Where and how can you obtain solid information that reduces the risk of new ideas?

Choice 2

Marshall your arguments and, backing your team's decision to the hilt, attempt to win over the CEO, but be willing to accept that, should you fail, the decision will have to be changed, perhaps for something more "politically" acceptable.

Commentary

Debate with a well-informed colleague is an excellent way to clear the mind and reach the best decision. Be very careful, however, if you choose this alternative not to let your team know that you battled and lost. As far as they are concerned your responsibility to them is only to battle when you can win. Losing, no matter how bravely, does nothing for your ability to lead your team effectively. Better to simply announce that you have "rejected their decision for the following reasons" (cf. Choice 1), and require them to learn from the experience. Your CEO's expectation of you, however, is that you will battle to get the decision that she reaches with you implemented without hassle. Again you are expected to fight and win, but with this subtle difference: the team would rather that you do not fight at all if you cannot win. They don't like bosses who "make waves" unnecessarily. Your CEO, however, or the shareholder if you are CEO, will always expect you to win when directing your team. That is their definition of leadership.

The decision to avoid any unnecessary conflict can be justified in some situations. If your organizational culture is one in which *legitimate power* is what counts there is little point in challenging that power base unless serious business reasons make it inevitable. To accept the world as it is may be the best strategy for all, employees, shareholders and other stakeholders. The successful charismatic and pragmatic leader seeks the reasons for change rather than pursuing change for its own sake.

Questions for discussion

1. Is the leader always "the person in the middle" subject to usually conflicting expectations from all sides as the research says that he or she must be?
2. How do you manage this conflict in your organization?
3. What can you do, if anything, to reduce this conflict in your organization?

Choice 3
Invite the CEO to explain her reservations, but make it clear that the decision stands unless she indicates something that your people cannot have known that effects the decision. You make it abundantly clear that you have absolute faith in the capability and motives of your team and that you only pass down decisions to those best qualified to make them.

Commentary
If both provisos, that it is your decision and that you have absolute faith in your people are met then fine, but make sure that you can really listen to the counter arguments with an open mind. In our psychology of customer behaviour training we have to teach salespeople to listen with the appropriate mindset. The salesperson is motivated by a desire to win and far too often sees the customer as an antagonist who must be beaten. If we are not careful the salesperson mentally prepares his or her own "devastating" counter arguments as they "listen" and misses what the customer is trying to communicate. A little discipline helps. We insist that they:

- Listen actively to put himself or herself genuinely in the place of the customer and really understand what the customer is thinking and feeling even when the customer must subsequently be shown that they are wrong to think and feel as they do – though they, as fallible human beings, have every right to be wrong.

- Prove that they understand by reflecting back to the customer, in different words, either the content or the feelings behind the content. ("Let me be sure that I have understood you, you feel that . . . or . . . you are saying that . . .")

- Show empathy so that the customer that is wrong never feels deprived of the right to make a mistake. ("I'm not surprised at how you feel, a lot of people feel as you do at first.")

- Take responsibility for any misunderstanding. ("It's my fault, I should have explained that . . .")

- Deal with the specific concern that has been raised and *never try to guess what may lie behind what is being said*.

- Let the customer raise further concerns and listen just as carefully and courteously before dealing with them in turn to the satisfaction of the customer.

A similar approach works when overcoming opposition to ideas or concepts. You may wish to try it without allowing it to decline in to a parrot-like formula. Choose your words with care. In spite of the nonsense spouted by some of us psychologists about non-verbal communication words can make a world of difference. Try saying "good morning ladies" or "good morning girls" in a Midwestern office instead of simply "good morning" and you will soon be told what difference a word makes. (Both "ladies" and "girls" are interpreted as attempts to be patronizing that show a high degree of inappropriate sexual prejudice.)

Questions for discussion
1. Where does the leader's principal loyalty lie? To his or her own boss? To the shareholders? To the company? To his or her team? To the desired outcomes? To the shared vision?
2. How do you as leaders manage to demonstrate loyalty to all who demand it of you when the chips are really down?
3. What do you communicate to your subordinates through your behaviour about your attitudes to loyalty?
4. What effects do your personal attitudes have on your people's behaviour?

Situation three

You are the CEO. An opportunity has arisen that will give your firm a considerable short-term advantage over competition. Exploiting it will, however, mean diverting resources from a strategic plan that is on track to deliver your key strategic goals within the planning horizon of three to five years. The effect of such a diversion will be to delay the achievement of the strategy by at least a year. It will, however, produce a substantial extra one-off profit this year and the shareholders, who at last year's AGM vociferously demanded a quick return on their investment, will be happy.

Choice 1
Your responsibility as a chief executive is to the shareholders. Exploit the short-term opportunity. Keep the shareholders off the board's back in the short term and try to conserve enough of the extra profit to bring in additional resources to accelerate progress toward the strategic goals next year and thereafter.

Research indicates that excessive short-term thinking is one of the key reasons why leaders fail. The leader needs to exercise considerable skill in balancing short-term and long-term needs. Just as it is essential to ensure that short-term needs are satisfied for a business to survive into the golden future of the vision, it is equally necessary to retain focus on the effect that decisions made today will have in the longer term. Where stakeholders in the business are concerned it is also necessary to think through the expectations that are being created by decisions made today whether they are aimed at the present or the future. Shareholders who are enjoying a massive return on their investment today do not suddenly become patient if the going becomes tough tomorrow due to lack of investment or an unwise distribution of profits. Arie de Geus (Harvard) in his research into long-lived companies and corporations identifies "frugality with resources in order to be able to invest in the long term" as a common factor in long-term business prosperity.

At the decisive battle of Gettysberg a majority of the Confederate leaders confidently anticipated an easy victory. One, General Longstreet, saw no serious reason to fight. The South could gain little more than a morale boost and some celebration by the "good ole boys" back home while, in the relatively unlikely event of a Northern victory the whole of the Southern States would become effectively defenceless. Longstreet was listened to briefly and then ignored. His colleagues wanted short-term glory regardless of the risk. The unlikely happened and as a result the South was smashed. Longstreet argued throughout his military career that decisions in the short term should be founded on the effect that the result was likely to have on the long-term outcome and that short-term thinking was a dangerous lure. Should a CEO not have a similar strategy?

Charismatic leaders are seen to fail when they choose to pocket short-term benefits at the cost of long-term prosperity. For example, business process re-engineering (BPR) has too often degenerated into a head-cutting tactic that is seen to fail to deliver in at least 70 per cent of cases. In the short term it may deliver reduced costs and, with a little creative accounting (or even false accounting in at least one notorious case), what appears to be a considerable short-term growth in profits. In the longer term, however, evidence has been produced that indicates that those firms that either ignore BPR or use it strictly to improve processes leading to better customer service at lower cost make, on average six times the profits of those "headcount-cutters" that survive in the same sector. This is why, particularly in the United States, the early popularity of BPR created a breed of peripatetic "axe men" who chopped away and moved on after eighteen months to sell their options and leave the corporation haemorrhaging in their wake. The company that had real leadership left to staunch the flow was fortunate in the extreme. Charismatic leadership and defection have nothing in common and the charismatic leader keeps his or her eye on the important long-term survival and prosperity.

Questions for discussion
1. How do we ensure that all decision-makers have the skills and the motivation to consistently balance the short- and long-term needs of the business?
2. Have we communicated the long-term goals convincingly and inspirationally enough so that those who will have to make the effort to achieve them are willing to make personal sacrifices when necessary in the short term?
3. What additional pressures and demands on the top team will a balanced focus bring about in the short term?
4. What can we do today to reduce or eliminate such pressures and demands?

Choice 2
Keep your focus on the strategy. Avoid anything that diverts attention from the mission.

Commentary
A great choice, if and only if, when making it you have checked to ensure

that everything necessary is being done right now to ensure survival and growth into the future. Charismatic leaders are constantly considering:

- How can we use our current strengths, competencies and knowledge more effectively to strengthen our position in the most worthwhile markets today?
- How can we use those same advantages to enter the most promising markets of the future?
- What new competencies, strengths and capabilities do we need to acquire or build to better exploit the best opportunities in today's markets?
- What new competencies, strengths, capabilities and knowledge do we need to build or acquire in order to dominate the best markets of the future?

There is nothing to be gained from being future-focused if you fail to survive long enough to get there, just as there is no value in short-term success that robs you of your future. The charismatic leader and the pragmatic leader both go for balance as described above.

Questions for discussion
1. Do you really have a mission or do you have a mishmash of fancy words that mean nothing to those who need to use it as a tool to get from where you are to where you need to be?
2. To what degree do your training and development operations offer a range of generic programmes rather than building the skills, competencies and capabilities that have been clearly identified as being necessary to achieve corporate goals?
3. How successful are you as a corporation in attracting and retaining the very best people in your business sector?
4. What would make them want to join you and what will make them want to stay?
5. How do the very best people expect to be led?

Choice 3
Put the dilemma before the Board. Try to get consensus and go with whatever decision the Board makes.

Commentary
Fine, that is what the Board is for, to agree actions and strategies, but remember that consensus takes time to reach because as long as there is a single board member who feels that he or she has lost the battle, but still believes that they are right you do not have genuine consensus. You might also like to bear in mind that if you have an expert in the group they may be "outvoted" and the decision may be more expensive than the mere cost of the time that has been used.

Questions for discussion
1. Do we use consensus in the right circumstances (where we are unsure where the expertise may lie) rather than as a "political" dogma?
2. Do we pursue consensus until no individual feels that they are on the "losing side"?
3. How valuable is the time of members of the Board?
   (Bob Townsend, instead of paying director's fees for attendance at board meetings, introduced charges for the time and resources used and reduced the length of meetings without adversely affecting any outcomes or receiving any resignations. Synectics Corporation introduced strict time limits for discussion and not one piece of "unfinished business" was ever raised at a subsequent meeting.)

Situation four

You are marketing director. Your advertising agency has developed a plan that will take you head to head against a bigger competitor. If it is successful the plan will deliver a massive increase in sales and revenues, but given the much greater resources of the competitor it is a high-risk tactic.

Choice 1
Go for it! Business is about risk.

Commentary
A major misconception about charisma is that it is dependent upon having a swashbuckling approach to risk. Of course risks must be taken in business, but only after the most careful assessment not merely of the level of risk and value of the outcome, but of the alternative actions.

A marketing director should be familiar with PEST+ analysis. To assess the level of risk they should look in sufficient detail at the political, economic, social, technological and legal restraints of any market that they plan to enter. Any risk should be analyzed in at least equal detail and I would expect any professional to test with great diligence the degree to which "creatives" are likely to have carried out reliable research.

To take worthwhile business from a bigger competitor needs detailed assessment of:

- Who are the worthwhile customers who consistently deliver profits that greatly outweigh the cost of serving them?
- What similar worthwhile customers (by name) does the competitor serve?
- What do they want from a supplier?
- Of their wants, which are the most important to the customers now?
- Which will become the most important in the foreseeable future?

- Where do we have a clear competitive edge in servicing those wants?
- How can we best communicate our advantage to those specific customers?
- How will we avoid picking up dross that are more hassle to serve than they are worth?
- How can we shed our nuisance customers so that they become a burden to competition?
- Do we have strategic allies that can support us in this initiative?

If you or your advertising agency have this information the risk has been properly minimized.

Questions for discussion
1. What is our attitude to risk?
2. Are we content to be followers or do we choose to be innovators?
3. How does our decision on the above influence our approach to leadership?

Choice 2
Carefully assess your own competitive strengths and weaknesses and develop a series of comprehensive marketing and sales campaigns to pick off weaker competitors one by one, pitting your known strengths against their identified weaknesses, strengthening the company with worthwhile extra revenues and profits until it is ready to take on the giants.

Commentary
If you add to this only a clear strategy to identify and shed those customers who are more trouble than they are worth, you are showing real charismatic leadership. In spite of claims by Tom Peters and the like that the business cycle now spins too quickly for considered action, research shows that successful leaders, whether charismatic or pragmatic, respond by collecting data more quickly and thinking faster rather than by "flying by the seat of the pants". Volatile conditions require more rather than less thought, but as with great military leaders the great leaders of business and commerce are shown by research to have the ability to think and act quickly and effectively. Leaders are made, not born, and they are made great by constant learning and applying what they learn. Back in the 1970s, Tannenbaum and Schmidt completed research that showed that the expectation that others had of leaders was that they would be simultaneously "flexible" and "consistent". What they meant by that was that leaders should be fast on their feet, free of the constraints of past success and consistently right in their actions. These capabilities flourish with education and practice. Hopefully this short instrument has provided a few guidelines to effective action in complex situations.

Questions for discussion

1. How much detailed knowledge does our top team have about our customers?
2. Do we have any mechanism to indicate which customers are worthwhile and which simply cost us money to serve?
3. How could we find such information?
4. How can we divest ourselves of the nuisances?
5. How can we influence our best customers to buy more?

(There are only three basic ways to increase sales without building the customer base:

1. Customers are encouraged to place larger initial orders usually through reversing or reducing any perceived risk in making the purchase.
2. More frequent replacement orders are won usually through co-operatively supporting onward sales – or increasing brand awareness if the customer is a distributor.
3. Customers are persuaded to place larger replacement orders through discounting prices or offering more attractive settlement terms.

(In all cases it is essential to find strategies that actually increase sales rather than pre-buying business that would have been available in any case. It is, of course, essential to assess carefully the effect on cash flow of any increase of business.)

6. How can we identify and attract new customers similar to those who are most profitable from competition?
7. Are our sales policies and reward structures appropriate to a need to attract quality rather than quantity when it comes to customer acquisition?

A leadership game plan

Stage one and Stage five

In any situation where there is novelty, a new team, a new task or a new leader it is wise for the leader to assume control and to concentrate only on achieving the task until the team has begun to develop a track record of success.

- Establishing goals.
- Establishing standards of performance.
- Providing direction.
- Maintaining discipline.
- Communicating norms of behaviour.
- Formal training as required for accomplishing the current task with maximum efficiency.

Stage two

Once the team has begun to enjoy a significant degree of achievement the leader can begin increasingly to introduce "social" leadership as long as this is done without relaxing the task leadership. It is essential that the team is not allowed to form the belief that they "have the formula for success in all situations" or that they fail to recognize changing circumstances. Discipline and direction must be retained or the team will begin to demonstrate that, given earlier success, their confidence is beginning to outrun their competence.

Continue the above and begin to introduce:

- Team building.
- Social problem solving.
- Individual and team coaching and counselling.
- Individual and team development activities and training.
- Knowledge management.
- Culture building.
- Peer coaching.

Stage three

Over time the team actually doing the job will know more about performing the task effectively than the leader can. When this stage is reached the leader can relax control and become a full-time social leader concentrating on the team's needs for:

- Job satisfaction.
- Motivation.
- Inter-team and intra-team relationships.
- Resolving conflict.
- Developing consensus.
- Encouraging creativity.
- Building empowerment within a mutually agreed framework of norms, values and standards.
- Succession planning.
- Self-regulating learning community.

Stage four

The final stage of leadership occurs when the leader is aware that the team can handle all of their task and social needs without requiring intervention from the leader. At this stage the wise leader lets go of the reins and plans the next cycle of growth by identifying new challenges for the team and beginning the cycle again to create a spiral of growing competence in a rapidly changing business environment.

- Enhanced vision.
- More challenging mission.
- Superordinate goals.

Part two

Score: 100–120   You are a remarkably charismatic leader. Are you sure that you are balancing charisma with intelligent pragmatism that ensures that those whom you lead with such enthusiasm are consistently doing the right thing in the right way at the right time?

Score: 80–99   You have charisma, but is there a danger that those who follow you will seek to become clones of your style when it is no longer appropriate to the company's needs?

Score 50–79   You appear to show a balanced style in which a little charisma is enough to inspire your people while a good deal of common sense leads to consistently making the right decision.

Score 49 or under   Bear in mind that there are at least as many successful leaders who are perceived as lacking charisma as there are those that have it by the bucketful, but please go back over the two sets of answers to ensure that either you have the key skills that are essential to any and all leaders or you know how to acquire them.

The essentials of leadership are not really charisma or otherwise. The nuts and bolts that hold a team together while bringing out more than the best of which they are capable are a matter of getting your behaviour right for the immediate and long-term needs of your people. Leadership demands consistency as does marketing and, like marketing it needs more than one form of consistency. Effective leadership requires consistency – leadership style and behaviour must be consistent with the needs of the task to be done, the people that are being led and the situation in which the action is taken. Yet that is not enough. If you want leadership to be effective you must develop in your people the belief that in any situation they know what you would do so that they can get on with it when you are not around. In short, your behaviour must always appear to be consistent. But in the real world things change. Not only is the business cycle still spinning, it shows every sign of spinning faster and faster. Meanwhile a team's attitudes, beliefs, expectations, ambitions and ability are changing too. In a changing world with a changing team the job to be done is certain to change. Everything is in a state of flux. As everything changes the leader is expected to provide the stability and continuity that people crave. This is the great leadership paradox: if you are to be a successful leader you have no choice other than to be consistent and flexible at the same time. There is only one way to do that. It is more than a matter of style. It is a matter of judgement. The leader who is able to build and sustain success is the leader who is consistently right in all rapidly changing situations.

Before making a decision, ask yourself:

Since I last thought about this what has changed about the people involved?

- To what degree have they developed new skills and abilities?
- To what degree have their attitudes, beliefs and expectations developed?
- To what degree have their personal, economic and team circumstances changed and to what degree are their personal feelings relevant to the situation?
- Do I understand that "feelings" are part of the "facts" of any and all situations involving people?
- How strong is their level of commitment, motivation and morale now compared with how it was?
- What gives them their satisfaction today and how do their sources of satisfaction relate to the present situation?

What has changed about the job to be done?

- How has the advance of technology affected this operation?
- How can we do things better and cheaper?

How has the situation changed?

- Is the decision more or less risky than it would have been earlier?
- What is the general economic situation?
- What is the situation in respect of our industry?
- How exactly have things changed?
- What is in our control and what lies beyond my power to act?
- What are our competitors doing?
- How can we do better?
- What are our customers demanding?
- How can we give them more than they demand at lower cost and with higher quality?

Should I make this decision alone or seek consensus? (For detailed information on when to use consensus – and when not to – see *Key Management Solutions*.)

- Is this a similar situation to those in which I have been successful before or do the changes make this a whole new ball game?
- Where in the total team, myself included, does the real expertise lie?
- What specifically are the risks associated with this decision?

- How will I measure the success of this decision?
- What would be my ideal outcome regardless of the situation?
- How can I get as close as possible to that outcome given the present realities?

Summary

Whether you are a charismatic or pragmatic leader has little to do with the price of fish other than to create a need for you to understand what your leadership strengths are and to apply those strengths effectively to getting things done. David McClelland's research made it clear that the most successful leaders are motivated by a wish to use their power to get things done. Your style is part of your power to succeed if you understand it and use it wisely.

Leadership is often the difference that counts between firms, but it is not really the Jack Welch or Jack Smith that makes the difference. It is the quality of leadership that is shown throughout the business. Those organizations that depend too heavily on a single charismatic leader often find that in a volatile business environment they perpetuate the weaknesses of that leader to the point of disaster. Whatever your position in the business you have three questions that you should always keep in the forefront of your mind.

- What is my leadership style?
- How relevant is it to today's conditions?
- How flexible can I be without giving the impression that I am a "flavour of the month" type of leader without clear values?

5

Forget your problem – give me your solution

questions of finding and fixing business problems

A man of genius makes no mistakes. His errors are the portals of discovery.
James Joyce

- Questions to analyze any problem and develop the best solutions.
- Questions to pre-empt potential problems and keep the plan on track.
- Questions that will get your people eager to be problem solvers.
- Questions that give you the advantages and protect you from the pitfalls of consensus.
- Questions that raise creativity.

What you will gain from this chapter

- An ability to stop problems from arising in the first place.
- An understanding that problems come in well-defined types needing different tools for the best solutions.
- A quick and reliable indicator that saves you from applying the wrong techniques.
- Tools, techniques and information on where to look for more detail if necessary.

Facts you may need to elicit

☑ What percentage of your time is spent attempting to solve problems?

☑ What percentage of your team's time is spent seeking solutions to problems?

☑ What percentage of solutions work first time?

☑ By how much have costs reduced in the past year?

☑ How much cash have we saved through effective problem solving in the last twelve months?

Nothing is perfect

In a perfect world problems would never arise. This is not a perfect world, of course, but there are things that we can do that reduce the incidence and severity of problems and ensure that what ought to be done is done. The following case study shows how one corporation ensure that with new initiatives at least, things work as they should first time and every time.

---

mini case study

The FedEx way of introducing change

Problems routinely arise whenever we try to do something new or do something that we have been doing for years in a new way. We try to anticipate the unexpected and because it is unexpected, we often fail. In strategic planning, for example, we consistently go beyond the mere identification of "threats". We try to establish in advance those that can be avoided by taking action now and we make certain that the prescribed actions are an important part of our tactical plan. We look at those that may sneak up and take us by surprise and we develop contingency plans as part of our strategy. We do all that we can to avoid or manage problems – or do we?

Some key thinkers in Federal Express might argue that we are in real danger of doing too little much too late. Recognizing that the majority of problems arise in situations where something is changed (see comments on Kepner/Tregoe below), FedEx has developed an approach to the introduction of change that is well worth considering in more detail.

In the corporation the solving of problems or the exploitation of opportunities has become a team business so the sequence of events goes like this:

Any idea from management or elsewhere is presented as a rough idea. This ensures that every member of the team understands that they have a role to play in producing the best possible solution. Every team member is expected and encouraged to play a full part both in identifying the best solution and in making that solution work. Nobody has any reason to feel that change is being imposed. They have the opportunity to play a role in developing the idea and it does not stop there.

The team identify and develop "what is in it for them" when they make the idea work. Altruism is no doubt a wonderful thing, but for most of us, much of the time, enlightened self-interest is a better motivator. So the whole team make an exhaustive list of what stands to be gained through their efforts. In this way not only are they committed to making things work, they are *personally* involved. There may be individual differences in motives and ideas, but everybody examines each idea and identifies all that they have to gain from making it work. Gains may include such things as increased job interest and enjoyment, better job security, less hassle or they may be far more detailed and idiosyncratic, but the key point is that individuals and teams identify all the potential benefits. They are clear what the advantages are to them and, as most of those advantages come as a result of having mutuality of interest with the company, the company's interests and their own are clearly seen to be aligned and from day one they are eager to make the idea work.

Problems that have to be solved are identified. Now that the whole team is committed and can clearly identify with making the idea work they look specifically for those problems, and only those problems that could get in the way of implementation. They are the problems that could deny people the benefits that they have identified. Within the culture attitudes to problems have developed so that they are invariably addressed unemotionally as "something to be solved". They are not wallowed in or exaggerated as grievances. There is little temptation to raise old grievances or retell ancient "war stories", but if any individual seeks to work out a hidden agenda, peer pressures handles the situation. The success of FedEx has been highly contingent on this attitude to problem solving rather than blame fixing. Problem solving always addresses the needs of the customer because people have learned to realize that only those problems that are a barrier to customer satisfaction are a priority. Otherwise you consistently play to, and leverage, your strengths.

Problem-solving teams self-select to find solutions to the barriers to successful implementation. By self-selecting those with the best likelihood of success, whether based on knowledge and experience or motivation, they work on the potential problems with creativity, energy and determination.

The remainder of the team continue to work on refining the basic idea. The importance and urgency of the idea to be implemented is underlined by continuity of effort. At no time is the impression given that this can be set aside while we do something else. The idea has been shown to have major benefits to the organization and to its people. It is therefore important. It is a sad fact of business life that what is important, but not perceived as urgent, is regularly put aside for what is urgent whether or not it is important, so continuity of effort counts. In FedEx whatever is important is always treated as urgent. That's how you get things done. Meanwhile those that have assumed the task of problem solving are happy to delegate to let their colleagues get on with the job in hand. Nobody sees any need to be in two places at once. Each member of the team is making a contribution where they think that they can deliver the best result. Few approaches can be more motivational than having people volunteer to do what they know they will do best. In our company and with our clients we try to ensure the best use of the best people as the cornerstone of our and their business growth.

Problem solutions are presented, improved where necessary, approved and implementation is begun at once. By starting the process of implementation by whatever means it is made clear that the process will be fully in place and that subsequent implementation of the idea will meet only with minor problems, if any, that will be easily overcome. As a result the team further build the psychological groundwork for success.

The "rough" idea is refined, agreed and the implementation process is planned. Enthusiasm, motivation and confidence are all at their height. The chances of successful implementation are enormously enhanced. All that needs to be done is to establish the time frame, authority levels, responsibilities for specific outcomes, support requirements from beyond the group, the communication process and audience(s) and the idea is a virtually trouble-free reality.

- Do we involve people intelligently in ideas or do we either work purely top down?
  - Conversely do we have an unstructured "let my people go" attitude to empowerment?
  - Why do we act as we do?
  - Is it the best way, not merely to get things done, but to get things done well?
- Could we adapt and adopt the FedEx approach in part or in its entirety?
  - Should we?
  - Is there a better way, more appropriate to our people, that allows the task to be done in the business situation we are in right now – after all, we are not FedEx?
- Should we be building toward a better approach for the future?
- How will we introduce change while respecting our people's aspirations, our customers' needs and desires, our current and attainable technology, the economic and business situation, competitive activity and the expectation of all our stakeholders?
- What would be the cost saving in making new ideas work first time most times?

The three key problem-solving tools

There are many problem-solving tools. Some have withstood the course of time and have given great service in a wide range of conditions. Some have become so favoured that some of us try to squeeze every problem into the mould of our particular favourite. Problems fall into three basic categories and trouble usually arises only if we take a tool designed for one type of problem and use it with another. The three key problem-solving tools, rational process, creative problem solving and morphological analysis (which includes reverse engineering) are described in *Key Management Solutions*. To decide which tool to use you need to ask a few very simple questions.

- Has something gone wrong with something that normally works well? (If so you have a deviation from norm and you need to apply a form of rational process to identify and correct the fault. The most successful form of rational process is almost certainly that devised by Kepner and Tregoe which is still successfully promoted under their names thrity years after the initial work was developed.)

- Has something always been wrong, no matter what we have tried to put it right?

- Is the problem so new that nobody has experience that could be useful in putting things right?

- Are we looking for a way to achieve a new ideal situation? (If any of these three is true of your problem you need to apply a creative technique such as Synectics.)

Just to clarify a little, bear with me while I repeat my favourite, most simple example of the difference. I have an important meeting many miles from home. I go out to start my trusty Toyota and for the first time ever it lets me down. It fails to start. Now I have a choice. I can treat the problem as a deviation from norm. The car should start, but it doesn't. So I ask myself some key questions.

- What exactly is happening here?
- What is not happening?
- What is the key difference between what is and what is not happening?
- Where is the problem occurring – electrics, starter motor?
- What's my evidence that the fault lies where I think it does?
  - Do the lights work?
  - Is there a spark?
  - Does the starter turn over?
- What are the conditions under which it is happening?
- What is different today from other days?
  - What effect could any difference have?
- Have I changed or amended anything that could have an effect on this problem?
- What is the significance of any change that I have made?

By answering these questions and by testing the solution I may, if I have the technical skills, identify and cure the fault. That would be a rather simplistic example of rational process in action.

However, I lack any technical skills. I would not recognize the difference between an alternator and its alternative. So I have a different problem and one that does not lend itself easily to rational process. I live in a village that lacks public transport. We don't even boast a taxi firm. So, given that it will take hours for a mechanic to come, retrieve and repair my car, how am I to get to my important meeting and maintain my reputation for punctuality? Better yet how can I hold the meeting without travelling anywhere? That is a problem requiring a creative answer and when I need a creative answer I turn to Synectics. (There are excellent books: *Synectics* (Prince and Gordon) and *The New Rational Manager* (Charles Kepner and Ben Tregoe) are examples that provide exhaustive details of each approach. My *Key Management Solutions* offers a simple game plan for each.)

I may ask myself:

- What is the problem as I see it?
- Why specifically is it a problem to me?
- Why is it an important problem to me right now?
- What is my ideal solution?
- What apparently irrelevant thoughts slip unbidden into my mind when I think about this problem?
- Which "feel" as if it would be fun to pursue them?
- What ideas do they raise?
- What ideas appeal to me?
- How would I develop this idea?
- Having developed them which appeals?
- Is my favourite idea feasible, attractive and novel? (If it is then I know it can be done, I will enjoy doing it and I am creating a new approach that may serve me well in the future – I am probably on to a winner!)

Morphological analysis and reverse engineering

I have a very beautiful wallet made of the softest leather and designed to hold the maximum using the least space. It was given to me by a consultant friend, Swee Lip Quek some years ago and I cannot quite remember whether it is an example of the most expensive piece of leatherwork of its type that was made at the time or a Czech low cost, improvement. If you have visited the Czech Republic you will know that the Czech people make very high quality leather goods at what seem to an inhabitant of Britain and even America, where things generally are much cheaper, ridiculously low prices. After the fall of Communism in 1989 my colleague was invited to help to revive the Czech economy. He worked mainly on a major strategy for privatization, but as a key side issue he looked for ways in which Czech firms might exploit existing skills quickly in global markets. He therefore bought at an international airport the most expensive leather items that he could find so that Czech craftsmen could consider them, improve on their design and manufacture goods that would be "better than the best" at lower prices. When the planning was finished they no longer needed my wallet so I got it. What has this to do with problem solving? Plenty.

The "product life cycle" ensures that sooner or later even the best of products loses its appeal to the mass of buyers. Designers and marketers share an unending need to prolong that life cycle or costs will spiral out of control and the benefits of mass production and mass marketing would be lost. One technique that is often used to alleviate the problem of consumer fickleness is morphological analysis. At its most simple the designer "takes apart" the product and rebuilds it with improvements to attract more buyers while the marketer ensures that the improvements made are appropriate to existing or emergent customer needs or desires, or to needs or desires that are dormant, but which could be aroused by the existence of a "new" product offering. Marketers and designers should co-operate in sharing information that will answer the following questions.

- Has the peak of buying activity for this product been reached or passed?
- Do the needs and desires that led to its market success still exist?
- Are needs and desires evolving in such a way that some simple, or even major, improvements to the product will satisfy them?
- Would customers prefer to continue to have the old product at lower cost?
- Will customers buy a new and improved product if the improvements lead to a higher price?
- Can we make "new and improved" really mean what they say? (In the USA a few years ago Lufthansa had a very successful marketing campaign based on the idea of "when we say 'new and improved' things are new and improved – surprised?")
- Can we create a perceived need for a new and improved product?
- Can we do all this and still lower costs?

If the answer is positive then there is a case for morphological analysis to create a "new" product that will revitalize the market.

General questions that work in helping to solve problems

- Do we understand what kind of problem it is and what approach is likely to enable us to solve it?
- Do we have the range of techniques at our disposal?
- Are we making any assumptions based on our desire for them to be true?
- Do the people nearest to the problem have any ideas?
- Are there related problems that we thought that we had fixed?
- Do we need to find a different approach?

Involving others who may be closer to the problem

- Can you tell me exactly what happened?
- How significant is the problem?
- Who and what are affected?
- Are external customers affected?
- Has something like this happened before?
  - How many times has it happened?
  - How did you deal with it then?
  - Is there any reason why the same approach will not work this time?
  - Why has the solution not been permanent?
- Was this problem expected?
- When did the problem arise – at what time stage of the process?
  - When does it not happen?
- Where does it happen – location, stage of the process?
  - Where does it not happen?
- How widespread is the problem?
- Have you any ideas as to why it occurs at certain times or stages of the process?
- Have you any ideas as to why it occurs where it does?
- Has anything changed recently?
- Could the change have any bearing on the problem?

A question of creativity

Too many people believe that they to have shortcomings when it comes to creative thinking. It is often said: "I'm not creative", as if creativity were a gift from God that has been bestowed only on the most fortunate. Of course there are unusually creative people. Training is not going to turn me into a Mozart or a da Vinci, but we all have more neural connections than there are atoms in the universe and we are all capable, although not necessarily equally capable, of being creative. Much has been claimed by the "let my people go" school of empowerment about the "wellspring of creativity that is released when you take off the shackles". Such claims are not without foundation for some, although the experienced businessperson might question where that newfound creativity is directed in the real world. Creativity without direction is anarchy. So the serious executive needs to find ways to encourage creative thinking in everyone without giving licence to some while paralyzing others.

- Do we need more creativity?
- Can we afford a little chaos now and again?
- Do we have the information, resources and time to be creative?
- Are we on target to achieve all our most stretching goals?
- Are our markets static or changing?
  - Are they growing, declining or stable?
  - Are we hurting the competition or are they hurting us?
- Do customers beat a path to our door?
  - Do those customers that come to us stay with us?
  - Are the customers who stay with us worth serving?
- Are most of our problems deviations from norm or are they new?
- Do we encourage people to recognize that, in a changing world "similar to" is not the "same as"?
- Are we training our people to use proven techniques to increase creativity?
  - Do we, through peer coaching and supervisor coaching, encourage people to use those techniques?
- How can we enable our people to relax more without slacking?
- Is there a non-bureaucratic mechanism through which the good ideas of people can be assessed and developed?
- Are we able to rise to Tom Peters' challenge that we must learn to "manage our people's imaginations"?
- What can we do today to re-assure people that we don't expect them to "leave their brains in their lockers" when they come into work?

When you want people to be creative ask them:

- Why is this a problem to you personally?
- In an ideal world how would you like the solution to look?
- What would you do if this were a life or death situation?
- If money, time and resources were no object, how would you proceed?
- What limits your power to act?
- What assumptions need challenging?
- What metaphors spring to mind when you think about this problem?
- If the people involved were say, animals, what animals would they be?
  - Why those particular animals?
- If you made up a story around this what would it be?
- Who do you need to carry with you to make your preferred solution work?
  - How can I help to get the important people on board?
- Have you tried to just stop thinking actively about this problem and let your unconscious mind deliver a solution when it is ready?
  - Have you thought about leaving it to your unconscious, but asking for a solution by a certain day or time? (Research shows that with the common "tip of the tongue" memory lapse if you put the problem of remembering to one side, but specify a time by which you want your brain to deliver, you will find that your mind easily achieves the stated deadline. You remember on schedule, quickly and without effort.)
- Why not just relax and let go for an hour or two and see what happens?
- Did you know that when top people in creativity find themselves wrestling with a problem, like Edward de Bono, they just put the problem to one side and go for a stroll? De Bono goes to the toyshop in the mall. (The toyshop is a wonderful place to get great ideas about anything to do with engineering from new medical equipment to a major civil engineering project. Toyshops are not the only source of ideas. The bubble chamber that was used to follow and identify sub-atomic particles resulted from dreaming over a glass of Bud!)
- Where do you think you might be inspired if you went there in a relaxed state of mind?
  - What is stopping you from going?

If you want to direct creativity to improving what already exists:

- If we listed the strengths and weaknesses on one page what three things would you change to make it better?
  - Why are they the important things?
- What is the stupidest way that you can think of to do this?
- If you were given a modest budget what would you do to improve things?
  - What could be done without involving costs?
- If we were starting up as a competitor to this company what would we have to do to attract customers from this business? From our competitors?
- When you think of the way that we do things around here what animals come to mind?
  - Why?
- What would be the most fun to do?
- If we reversed everything how would things be in this case? (Adrian Furnham has written and self-published a delightful book in which he reverses management theories and, on well-proven psychological research shows what the effects would be of say, "disempowering" people, or having teams appraise the work of their bosses. In many cases things might well be better.)

Final analysis

Creative thinking and particularly creative problem solving is a matter of:

- **Visioning** – having the "big picture of where we want to be rather than merely where we could be".
- **Exploring** – playing with ideas to see what could be achieved in theory and then in reality.
- **Asking** – Why not?
- **Experimenting** – combining the known with the untried or simply combining existing elements in new ways.
- **Modifying** – taking the best ideas that we can find and instead of copying them, improving them.
- **Communicating** – getting other minds in on the act.
- **Influencing** – getting the needful others on board.

The important thing is to remember that we *can* all do these things. The more that we do them the better, the more skilful, the more creative, we become.

When your people have the habit of effective problem solving, for real or potential problems, regardless of the type or technique that is used, you need to get them into the habit of asking themselves or others:

- Are we sure that we have a "customer", internal or external, who wants this idea?
- Is this the time to try this?
- Will it make us more competitive?
- Will it pay for itself in a reasonable time?
- Whose co-operation do we need?
- Can we explain our idea in terms that will be readily understood and that will build enthusiasm?
- What is in it for them?
- How can we test this idea?
- How can we minimize risk?
- Is there a small experiment that we can perform?
- How can we minimize disruption?
- What would be the evidence that this idea works?
- If it works how can we extend it into other meaningful applications?

And as current advertising for Accenture points out, an idea is literally nothing until someone is using it and benefiting from it – so ensure that your thinkers remain effective doers.

Summary

The keys to effective problem solving are simple. All that you need is thoughtful potential problem analysis so that many problems are avoided and you are as ready as you ever can be to deal with the unexpected, followed by careful identification of the problem type and using the correct technique to find the solution.

After careful assimilation of all appropriate information, being prepared to relax and let your unconscious mind do the work rather than get stuck is a key strategy for creative problem solving – and it can help in other situations as well.

6

Decisions, decisions

questions of choice

A man may be ruined by drink, gambling, women or business. My father chose the least interesting road to ruin. Attributed to Pope John XXIII

- Questions that lead to speedy and effective decision-making.
- In a world in which the business cycle spins ever-faster, fast and efficient thinking is the key difference between success and failure.
- This chapter provides the questions to speed decision-making in the real world.

What you will gain from this chapter

The questions that enable you to apply the most proven and time- and money-saving techniques.

Factual questions that are worth asking

- ☑ How much have we saved or made through effective decision-making in this year?
  - What did we save or make last year?
- ☑ How do we measure the quality of our decision-making?
- ☑ Is our decision-making getting better?
  - What's our evidence for improvements?

Ancient history

Ever since the dark and distant days when I was an executive with GM I have been a fan of Chuck Kepner and Ben Tregoe. Not only is their approach to rational problem solving second to none, their decision-making matrix can save hours of work and potentially millions of dollars for companies that choose to use it. Yet the approach is simplicity itself. It is common sense written down and used, and used successfully by top decision-makers for more than thirty years.

In General Motors we were careful to record all the savings that we made through effective problem solving and decision-making. Those savings, which were publicized through a regular newsletter that was sent to all managers and executives swelled the numbers of those who were sent for training in problem-solving and decision-making techniques leading to further multi-million dollar savings for the corporation.

If you have a major decision to make, before you consider the alternatives, try asking and answering the following questions.

What are the "musts" that a decision has to deliver?

- What are the essentials that I am not prepared to do without?
- What is the absolute maximum amount that I am prepared to spend?
- What is the maximum time frame in which I must start to receive the benefits?
- What are the essential benefits that I must enjoy?
- What are the key features that my choice must have?

Make sure that whatever you list as a "must" really is an essential and not merely desirable (we come to them later), because any alternative that fails to satisfy any must is automatically rejected. That is the first big time saver. You do not waste time poring over the merits of any alternative that fails to deliver all the essentials that you are looking for. If you are buying a car and the maximum that you are prepared to spend is £15,000 you don't waste time looking at the latest BMW 700 series. If you must have new equipment up and running in three months you do not bother with the potential virtues of a machine that is still in the development stage.

If you choose to ignore your own musts, why did you list them as essential in the first place? Musts are musts, not maybes. Deciding that something is essential then ignoring it is analogous to using a well-constructed psychometric test and then rejecting the results. If you do not like the results you can only question why you gave the answers on which those results are based. If you write that your new car must cost less than $15,000 and then choose, or even consider the new BMW that means that you simply were not serious or that you were doing some wildly creative problem solving. How do I get the new BMW for less than fifteen grand? In that case the decision is made. Good luck with the problem solving.

What are the "desirables" that you hope to experience?

- What benefits do you want to get from this decision?
- What problems do you hope to eliminate that are not covered by your "musts"?

Having listed benefits and solutions give each a score between 1 and 10 so that the really important things are scored at or near to 10 and the "nice to have", but not really that important are scored close to or at 1. Be careful not to score everything at 10. You are going to use this information, so it needs to be your best assessment of your priorities and a listing built on real value not wishful thinking.

What is the potential downside?

What are the problems, pitfalls or losses that any alternative may carry in its wake? Again score these carefully. Give 10 to the most serious potential drawback and 1 to the gnat's bite that can readily be tolerated.

Now consider all the alternatives

Discard without further thought all that fail to deliver your "musts". If you have thought through your musts effectively then if the price is too high you cannot afford it. If it is too big, too small, too old-fashioned, too technologically advanced, if your people cannot work it – whatever you decided was essential must be deliverable from all the alternatives that you consider in detail. Take what you have left and assuming that there is more than one alternative remaining score each alternative on how well it satisfies your list of desirables. Quickly multiply the alternatives score for its capability to deliver each desirable by its "desirability" score and add them for each alternative. With luck you now have an alternative that is clearly better than the others and which satisfies all your "musts". Now that you have one or more alternatives with scores that indicate that most of what you want and all of what you need will be satisfied, you may wish to double check by scoring each with the score that you gave to the possible pitfalls to signify their seriousness multiplied by your best estimate of the chances that the loss will occur. Add these and take from them the score of each alternative that you have left. Now you should have a clear "winner" that should give you all that you want and need with the minimum of drawbacks.

It really is as simple as that. Hours of agonizing over decisions are usually unnecessary if you ask – and answer – that right question.

General questions for decision-makers

- How are we doing?
- Is making this decision the best use of my time just now?
- What would happen if I did nothing?
- Should I be making the decision or should I delegate it?
- If I delegate it am I prepared to live with the result?
- Why is the decision necessary just now?
- Is this a unique decision or will it have to be made periodically?
- Should I be teaching others the basis of my decision-making in order to be able to delegate in future?
- What benefits should the organization get from this decision?
- How does this decision fit with the values expressed in the mission?
- What are the undesirable consequences that I need to guard against?
- What will it cost?
- What are the alternatives?
- What will each cost?
- What is the most important consequence that I am seeking?
- How should this decision affect all stakeholders? (Employees, suppliers, distributors, customers, stockholders and the society in which we operate.)
- How do I feel about this?
- What is my gut telling me?

Effective decision-making is easy if, and only if, you know what you want. There is some wisdom in using a technique that implies that you spend your time thinking about what you want, the alternatives that could give you what you want and then make the actual decision virtually automatic. That way you consistently get most of what you want with the minimum of effort.

7

Knowing the numbers

questions of finance and performance

Profit is not a proper objective of a business. It is an essential prerequisite for being in business. Peter Drucker

Few have heard of Fra Luca Pacioli, the inventor of double-entry bookkeeping; but he has probably had more influence on human life than has Dante or Michelangelo. Herbert Muller

- Questions that enable the non-specialist to easily understand the world of finance.
- Questions that build revenues and profits.
- Questions that ensure that financial resources are applied effectively and frugally.
- Questions that ensure that when you need to spend you spend to best effect.

What you will gain from this chapter

- Why bean counters actually deliver a vital service to business.
- How to bluff your way in finance.
- How every manager can increase his or her understanding of the key ratios.

Some figures that should be close to everybody's heart

- ☑ What – in pounds or dollars – are our sales revenues this year to date?
- ☑ How do they compare with the same period last year?
- ☑ What is the percentage increase or decrease?
- ☑ What share of the market do they represent?
- ☑ What is our gross profit level?
- ☑ How did we do in terms of gross profit during the same period last year?
- ☑ What is our net profit this year to date?
- ☑ How were we doing this time last year?
- ☑ What is our return on capital employed?
- ☑ Are our costs higher or lower than last year?
- ☑ By how much – in pounds or dollars – have they risen or declined?
- ☑ Are we bringing in more cash each month than is going out?
- ☑ What is the level of positive cash flow?

If you are not certain how to work out simple financial ratios do not be concerned. Easy formulae for the essentials are given below. The subtle and complex stuff can be left to the specialist financial experts.

All businesses are cash businesses

Finance is an essential area of interest for all well-rounded managers. Years ago in my GM days a training programme with the rather unexciting title of "Finance for Non-Financial Managers" was mandated for all. Frankly for most people it was as tedious as the title makes it sound. I replaced it with a seminar that I called "Finance Can Be Fun" – a title that, despite my best efforts should have got me hauled before the trades descriptions people. But finance is important. In the simplest of simplistic terms a business is an organization that uses money to make more money. Profit, in Peter Drucker's phrase is not an objective of the business; it is an essential pre-requisite of being in business. Profit is certainly essential to staying in business in the long term as some of the daft dot coms and their sometimes even dafter investors have finally discovered. And to steal from Drucker again, the key aim of a company is to perpetuate itself.

In his research into long-lived companies de Geus identified two things that are important to this chapter. The business cycle is accelerating with sometimes devastating effect. Companies that could easily have survived for decades can now topple in what appears to be an instant. You have only to consider Enron to be convinced of this. The business cycle spins at such a rate that the average life expectancy of a mature company has reduced from sixty years to about a dozen years. When disaster strikes it strikes suddenly and hard, so all managers at every level should have an understanding of the financial effects of their actions.

The second finding of the Harvard research is that companies that survive are those that are frugal with their resources, particularly their financial resources. Survival is often a matter of timely change and this demands an approach to money that ensures that when the time comes to make such a change the cash is there to finance the resources that are needed.

A few definitions

A business needs cash to get going and it surely needs more cash to keep going. A very small company is often started on no more capital than the owner's savings and an overdraft facility. The problem with that is that the overdraft facility is short-term and can be called in any time and the owner's savings are rarely enough to sustain a business through the often difficult and always expensive early days.

The corporation or limited company is a legal entity separate from the owners. What it owns it owns, what it owes it owes. Owner's *equity* is what is left of the assets (what the business owns) of a business after lenders and creditors have been paid what the business owes them. *Long-term debt*, as opposed to the overdraft facility is the investment provided, if you are large or lucky. Long-term finance may be provided through loans from banks, direct investment by venture capitalists or if you are very large, by *debenture stock* usually guaranteed against a major asset. *Mortgages* are another form of long-term capital. All of these need an actively profitable business to sustain them. Interest accrues and has to be paid out of profits and venture capitalists demand a return on their investment.

As a rule of thumb, it is only when additional profits made are more than sufficient to meet the cost of servicing the loan that borrowing is justified. In business, loans should only be sought where there is a realistic chance of increasing profits as a direct result of borrowing.

Gearing is the relationship between the equity capital and long-term debt. In general the two are kept in balance by the simple mechanism that lenders usually will not provide more money than the owners have put into the business. Where the potential is seen to be great, however, lenders sometimes lose their natural caution and we have the current problems of a telecommunications industry that is saddled with debts that, in many cases, it has no practical hope of servicing or of ever repaying other than through a money-go-round of the sale of assets at inflated prices. Business owners often wrestle with questions such as these.

- Do we have enough resources to exploit market opportunities?
  - Are the opportunities worthwhile?
  - What will be the effect on our cash flow if we pursue this opportunity?
  - Are our major needs for investment or working capital? (Another rough rule of thumb is that long-term loans are needed for long-term capital needs and short-term money is required for working capital. This rule of thumb is often ignored when investment capital is sought – not invariably with satisfactory results.)
  - Will the revenue and profit flows from exploiting opportunities be sustainable over the life of any loan or investment?
- Can we reasonably expect relatively speedy growth if we borrow or seek investment?
- Are we prepared to water down our equity in order to build funds?
- Is our gearing reasonably in balance? (Gearing is the relationship that exists between the owner's equity in the business and loan capital. In the old days when accountants and finance directors based Return on Investment calculations on owned investment alone, many firms opted to increase loan capital as much as possible. If they could service the loans through additional profits, that alone was seen as being enough to justify borrowings. Today the realization has finally dawned that if you have too high a gearing, you no longer own your own business. Even mighty firms like British Telecom now struggles to bring down excessive debts that at one time would have been seen as indicating fiscal strength.)
- Can we afford the burden of interest?
- Can we afford it up to the point where cash flow is positive?
- Should we take professional advice before we commit to long-term debt? (The answer is yes, we should.)

Working capital

A major reason that a business needs money is that it turns that money into goods or services that it sells for more money. In short we all need working capital. The key thought here is that money has to work. "Money in the bank" is a misleading expression. It sounds wonderful, but money that is sitting in a bank account and doing nothing is only making more money for the bank. Every firm, large or small, needs to have a treasury function even if it does not have a treasury department. The treasury function ensures that the money that you earn earns you more money.

- How can we persuade our creditors to help finance our business by waiting a little longer for their money?

- How can we shave a little, or better a lot, off the time it takes for us to get what is coming to us from our debtors?

- How can we reduce inventories without affecting our levels of service?

- Do we have bank accounts with idle credit balances?

- Do we understand the bank charges and shop around for the best deal?

- Do we use the right bank for each aspect of the business?

- Do we understand all the borrowing and deposit instruments that are currently available? (A client of mine, some years ago, when on holiday in the Caribbean, chatted idly to a local banker in the bar. The banker mentioned that his bank was able to offer businesses loans at 3 per cent. My client, who was at that time borrowing to finance the business at double digit interest rates, set-up a small office on the island and not only re-financed his business, but became a very profitable lender of first resort for other UK businesses. A high-risk strategy in the long term, but as he said: "profits and risk are bosom buddies". In the short term at least he made enough money to lose all interest in running his car dealerships.)

- Does the company monitor any currency exposure to keep the risk as low as possible? (Volatility of foreign exchange markets driven by something that they like to call sentiment, can increase the risk of overseas trading. On a personal note I love South Africa, but when working there in recent years it has been an interesting experience to see my income, paid in local currency, decline literally as I speak.)

- Do we cover risk at the lowest possible cost?

Cash flow

It is a basic premise of business finance that more companies fail through adverse cash flow than fail through lack of profits. In simple terms it too often takes longer to get your money in than it does to spend it. Expansion is fraught with danger for many under-capitalized companies. Because of the time lag that always exists between spending and collecting money, doing more business can drive a company into the ground.

- Do we have enough money to finance the gap between using our working capital and receiving what is due to us?
    - Where will the money that we need come from?

- How can we reduce the gap between spending and collecting?
    - Can we use our creditors' money for a little longer without damaging our creditworthiness?
    - Can we sell and make rather than make and sell?
    - How can we maintain service levels by reducing stocks and inventories?
- What level of service do our customers really want?
    - Are we offering far more than the market wants or expects?
- Are those customers who demand the highest levels of service worth the cost of serving them?
- How do we stack up against the competition?

Profit and loss

A brief reminder if I may: *profit is an essential prerequisite to staying in business*. It should not be over-exploited at the risk of destroying competitiveness, but the businessperson should always be considering how to make more money without hurting the potential of the business. Productivity is vital to business and national economic success. By making more to sell at lower cost, profits can be increased. Profits provide not only the "wages" of the providers of capital, they create the reserves that fund future growth. Profits keep people in jobs, provide for our retirement and help to swell the national treasure chest to provide public services.

- How can we increase profits without increasing the prices to our customers?
    - How can we reduce the cost of making our product or of delivering our service?
    - How can we increase productivity?
    - How can we reduce the cost of making the sale?
- Should we consider something new such as affinity marketing? (See my *Big Book of E-Commerce Answers* for details.)
- Should we reconsider our pricing policy?
- How do we ensure the loyalty of our worthwhile customers?
- How do we make our valued customers into advocates for our business?
- How do we win the most worthwhile customers from our competitors?
- How do we build customer loyalty? (Research by Bain and Company clearly shows that the loyal customer is the most

profitable customer. If you can retain 90 per cent of your worthwhile customers for an average of ten years you will far outperform your competition in terms of profitability.)

- Are we serving customers who cost more to service that they deliver in profits?

- How do we offload such customers without damaging our reputation?

- How do we challenge our people to achieve more using less resources?

The balance sheet and some important ratios

The balance sheet is usually described as a "snapshot" of the company taken at a single point in time that is true only for the brief moment at which it is taken. Even that modest assertion is claiming a little too much – a balance sheet often gives a very inaccurate indication of the current market value of fixed assets. It is a somewhat loose statement of what the company owns, what it owes and what would be left for the owners if what it owns were to be sold and what it owes was paid off out of the proceeds. It also allows us to answer some key questions by using *ratios*. (For detailed information the interested reader may wish to read *Key Management Ratios* by Ciaran Walsh.)

- Can the company survive in the short term? (If the *current ratio*, current assets divided by current liabilities, comes to one or more you know that the company could, if it had to, pay its way for the present. The *quick ratio*, current assets less stocks divided by current liabilities is often useful because although stocks are assets, not all stocks are of value. In some companies there is an accumulation of obsolete and unsaleable bits and pieces that may look good on the balance sheet, but which serve no useful purpose beyond that.)

- Are we moving our stocks quickly enough? (*Stock turnover ratio*, sales divided by stocks, is a useful measure of the activity or otherwise of a business. As a general rule of thumb, the lower the stock turnover ratio the higher the profit needs to be to deliver an adequate return on investment, for example the margin on daily papers can be low as a percentage of cost, but the percentage profit on high quality jewellery is always going to be several times the actual cost of the materials and labour.)

- Are we getting in our money efficiently? (*Average collection period*: Debtors divided by Sales per Day, shows how effective you are at getting what is owed to you. The skilled finance manager delights in screwing down the average collection period while simultaneously taking as long as possible to pay creditors. Effectively, he or she is making your suppliers fund your business.)

- Are we profitable enough? (*Profit margin*: Profit before taxes divided by Sales is the most simple measure, but accountants like to dig a little deeper. *Return on total assets*: Profit before tax divided by Total Assets is one of the measures that they use.)

- Should we even be in this business?

- Perhaps we ought to cash it all in and stick it in a building society? (*Return on capital employed*, Net Profit multiplied by Capital Turnover (Total Revenues divided by Total Capital) will usually show that the small businessman's constant moan of "I'd be better off if I just stuck it all in the building society" is unjustified.)

Budgets and budgeting

As a committed believer in David Myddleton's adage that any form of forecasting is little more than an educated guess at what might have happened if what actually does happen doesn't happen, I always hated developing my budgets. They have, however, an important value to managers in major corporations that the bean counters (Gary Wallace of GM being an honourable exception) rarely recognize. When times are hard and the finance people are insisting that cutting all budgets by x per cent is the only route to salvation, it is useful to remember that a budget is simply a business plan stated in financial terms. So when the going gets tough the manager ought to approach the hated budget before agreeing to any cuts with this train of thought in mind. Our objectives were worthwhile and realistic when we set them. Presumably therefore they are still worthwhile, but are not necessarily realistic in today's climate. So assuming that they are still worthwhile, how much more would it cost to achieve them today? Are they still worthwhile? If the answer is "yes" you at least have an argument against the (almost always damaging) general bloodletting preferred by those too lazy to test what ought to be cut and what it is worth going after with as much precious resource as it takes. It really is very difficult to save your way into a profit unless you are simultaneously looking for profitable growth.

- Were our objectives really worthwhile to the company when we set them?
  - Are they still worthwhile today?
  - Would they cost more to achieve today?
  - How much more?
- At that cost would achieving the objectives still be worthwhile?
  - Am I deluding myself because I want to escape any cuts?

- Could I really achieve my objectives with that additional investment if I was creative enough?
- What might I do differently to achieve them without extra costs?
- If I really need extra investment, can the investment be found?
  - Is this worth fighting for?

The advantages of budgets

- Properly done the budgeting process can increase motivation and commitment.
- The objectives are clearly defined at every level.
- Key actions are frequently highlighted.
- Responsibilities and yardsticks are clarified.
- Combined, they provide an overview of the companies activities.
- Decisions concerning the allocation of resources are easier and more logical.
- Inter-departmental conflict can be reduced or eliminated by intelligent budgeting.
- Early warning of problems is facilitated.

Using the budget

To use a budget successfully:

- Build a robust strategic plan.
- Identify corporate objectives.
- Break down to departmental and divisional objectives.
- Develop tactical plans to achieve the strategy.
- Prepare budgets that reflect the plans.
- Measure actuals.
- Identify variances.
- Take corrective action.
- Create feedback for next planning session.
- Build a robust strategic plan.

Try as I might I have never been able to convince myself that finance is fun. It is, however, essential that businesspeople recognize that business is about money. Profit is sooner or later essential and cash flow makes the difference between survival and failure. Decisions about money should not be taken in isolation. Conversely, however, few decisions can be taken without considering their financial effects. If you want the company that pays your salary to survive and prosper, learn to practise frugality until the market clearly tells you that this is the time to invest.

8

You can buck the market!

questions of markets and marketeers

The only valid purpose of a business is to create and keep a customer.
Charles Revlon

Being good in business is the most fascinating kind of art. Andy Warhol

- Key questions that will enable you to exploit market opportunities at home and abroad.
- Essential questions for when there is a downturn.
- Questions that enable you to identify growth and exploit opportunity.
- Questions that ensure that your market-spend gets results.
- Questions that help you decide when to stop spending and start winning.
- Questions that enable you to turn the competition into "also rans".

What you will gain from this chapter

- A market strategy that will enable you to set the rules by which others have to play.
- How to work towards a position of market dominance.
- How to prosper in the key markets of the future.
- How to exploit the most valuable market opportunities of the present.

Essential factual questions

- ☑ Who are the 20 per cent of customers whose business delivers 80 per cent of our profits?

- ☑ Who are the customers who are served by our competition who have a need profile most similar to our best?

- ☑ What do those customers want from their suppliers that we can deliver better than our competitors?

- ☑ Which customers cause us the highest costs as we try to serve them?

- ☑ How much profit do they deliver?

Mrs Thatcher may have been wrong

Business shows that for some risk-takers bucking the market may be fun, wildly exciting and highly profitable. Most forward-looking firms, recognizing the complexity and volatility of the market and the speed with which the business and economic cycle spin, prefer to manage the market. That can be fun too, especially if you manage the market by making your competitors dance to your tune.

Market dominance, creating the rules by which your competition has to play, is probably the most fun that you can have in business as well as being the only logical way to approach the market. When working in the USA I found that American corporations would leap at the chance to dominate their markets, force the competition to spend their resources playing catch-up, lower competitors' profits and eventually force them to lose money and withdraw. Or as they might express: "kick ass". I had great fun in this area too. By the very nature of things competition never stands still, particularly if you are coming from behind. If you start off by being smaller and weaker you are wise to give no inkling to the currently big and powerful of what you are up to, so I had all the extra fun of being involved in a "cloak and dagger" activity. But make no mistake about it, in Jack Welch's words "if you don't control your destiny someone else will". In business terms that means that either you create the rules for your industry or someone else will and "me too" rarely leads to worthwhile market share.

The maxim "first know yourself" makes absolute sense so the first set of questions that you may wish to ask are directed at you and your peers.

- ■ Is there consensus at board level that we share a burning determination to become and remain the best of the best? (Unless the answer to this question is an unequivocal "yes", you can forget the rest. Someone, somewhere out there is going to steal your business from you.)

- If we are going to be the best, how can we do so at the lowest possible cost?

■ Is our passion communicated to, and shared by, all our employees?

- How should we communicate our vision so that everyone shares it today and continues to work for it when the going gets tough? (Never repeat a communications strategy that was used and failed in the past. Nothing makes it easier to ignore what is being said than the thought: "here we go again".)

■ Do we have a robust strategy in place that will enable us grow rapidly in the market?

- Do we have the financial, technological and human resources to achieve that strategy?

■ Have we developed a realistic tactical plan to enable us to build a secure platform from which to grow?

- Can we cope with rapid growth?

■ Do we have loyal and worthwhile customers who delight in doing business with us?

■ Are we prepared to analyze global best practice not merely to copy it, but to improve on it?

■ Do we leave our customers or clients delighted at the end of every transaction?

You need to know your customer from their point of view. One of the key findings of Frederick Reichheld's research into the effects of customer loyalty on a business is that it is possible to increase profits massively by building customer loyalty because your people can identify and predict trends in the worthwhile market sectors and beat competition to the punch by finding ways to satisfy emerging customer needs at the lowest possible cost.

■ Who is my best type of customer?

- What do they need?

- What do they want as opposed to need? (WOMAN – wants overcome (lack of) money and needs)

- Are there others of a similar type with similar desires and needs that I don't serve yet?

■ Where do I outperform competition in satisfying the important customer needs and wants?

- What motivates them to buy?

- What motivates them to buy from a specific supplier?

- How can we direct our salespeople to those customers with a clear statement of our competitive advantage? (*Key*

Management Solutions includes a simple tool that makes this child's play, pages 172–174.)

- How can I give the most worthwhile customers more of what they like?
- How are their interests, needs and desires changing?
- If they want "A" today could they be persuaded to want "B" tomorrow?

■ What is the average time that a customer stays with us?

- How can we prolong it?

■ What is the lifetime value of a customer?

- How much can I afford to spend to attract the right customer?

■ How will I delight and go on delighting my worthwhile customers?

■ How can I dump those who are more trouble than they are worth without damaging my reputation, credibility and image?

■ How can I make the best, most economical use of emerging technology to delight and go on delighting my customers?

Summary

Any market is no more than the combined desires and value of the customers who comprise it. Understanding those customers is vital. Building on that understanding by creating and satisfying desire delivers massive profits. But it begins and ends with the customer.

It is important to understand that if your sales and marketing people cannot give you both full and accurate answers to the above questions they are working with their hands tied behind their backs. The shame of it is that it is they themselves who tied the cord.

Market dominance planning

The chapter on strategic planning will have helped you to develop an overall plan for the business. I hope that you are already all fired up and determined to dominate your chosen markets whether they are niches, sectors (customer/need driven), or segments (product or service driven). Now you need to look specifically at the contribution marketing and sales can make to dominance. Just one small point if you will.

Marketing is not a departmental matter. *Either every individual in the company is marketing or nobody is.* In my GM days I was so anxious to get this idea across that I proposed that we change the title of every CEO to be

"Marketing Unit Manager". It was not the most popular suggestion that I ever made, but it was among the most meaningful. Marketing has three key elements. It is integrated – everybody has a part to play. It is customer focused – it uses all the resources of the business to identify, create and satisfy customer desires, and it is profitable – marketing should always deliver more than customers, it should deliver profit in everything that it does otherwise it becomes a fancy cost centre.

- Does every employee recognize that they have a personal marketing responsibility?
    - Do they all proactively seek ways to fulfil that function?
    - How can we best clarify the essential contribution that everybody can make to building market intelligence, identifying and attracting customers and delighting the customer?
    - Having involved everybody in the business of getting customers to beat a path to our door, how can we involve them in delivering superior service at lower cost?
    - How should the top team make themselves role models for involvement in proactive marketing?
- How can we ensure that our marketing department identify and use low cost/no cost marketing tactics where these are more effective than expensive advertising?
- How do we keep abreast of customer needs and wants?
- How do we create the need for what we can produce?
- Does our marketing strategy play a key role in keeping profit at the forefront of all our people's thinking?

The marketing strategy

- Do we have the right products at the right price in the right place?
    - Have we got the right people to provide them?
    - If we haven't, how can we make our products and prices desirable to customers in the short term?
- Do we understand all who might need, or better, want our products and services?
- Are we exploiting all our strengths, capabilities and competencies against known market desires?
    - How do we turn our strengths into market offerings quickly and at lowest possible cost?
    - How can we promote our strengths more effectively?

- How can we get closer to our most worthwhile customers?
- How can we enrol all our stakeholders (employees, customers, suppliers, distributors and the community) into our marketing strategy?
- Can we specify where we are better at delivering customer satisfaction than each individual competitor in order to approach their best customers with an offer that is tailored to their unsatisfied needs. (Use the simple Comparative/Competitive Analysis in *Key Management Solutions* and you will be.)
- Are we planning for growth?
  - Should we be?
- Do we propose to develop new products and services, penetrate new markets, win their best customers from competition or diversify?
- Are we ready to change our culture if we need to?
- Have we carefully analyzed the costs of growth – extended resources, possible loss of focus, potential need to do things differently, possible slow return?

The market dominance plan

- Have we completed a clear, comprehensive review of our strengths?
- Have we analyzed customer desires and expectations and identified the best fit between these and our strengths and competencies?
- Have we considered emerging customer needs and expectations and worked out how we will use our present strengths to address these?
- Have we established what strengths we need to build or acquire to dominate our chosen markets?
- Have we established meaningful targets and objectives?
- Do these include key financial objectives as well as marketing objectives? (Turnover, profitability: units of sale, market share.)
- Do we have a realistic product plan? (Existing, improvements, development, invention.)
- Do we have a comprehensive market plan? (Markets – current, extended, new.)
- Do we have a strategic approach to pricing?
- Do we use pricing to attract those customers that we want rather than use either "cost plus", "finger in the wind" or "what are competition doing?" as the basis of pricing policy?

- Do we avoid offering discounts for initial orders that may upset existing loyal customers?
- Do we use pricing to build loyalty?
- Do we have a low cost promotional plan that is consistent in application and consistent with our desired image?
- Do we make the most of "free ink", sponsorship, co-operative programmes, affiliate programmes?
- If we have a website is it easy to find, easy to use and packed with relevant information?
- Do we invite customers to opt-in for further information?
- Do we promote our strengths?
- Is everybody clear about our competitive advantage?
- Is our competitive advantage in those areas where it is most meaningful to the most worthwhile customers?
- Do we use technology effectively to reduce marketing costs?
- Are our direct sales-team well directed and supported with key market intelligence?
- Do we use market testing rather than market research whenever this is a feasible alternative?
- Do we constantly probe for competitor weaknesses?
- Do we have a detailed sales plan including effective, non-bureaucratic reporting?
- Have we an effective people plan in place? (Recruitment and retention, training and development, performance management, incentives and even the organizational structure are all potentially important parts of the marketing strategic and tactical plan.)
- Are our budgets adequate without being over-generous?
- Could we achieve more with less?
- Are our feedback, evaluation, review and re-direction activities integrated into our planning?
- Are we ready to be responsive to what the market is telling us?
- Are we using all sources of information?
- If we have non-executive directors are they expected to keep a watchful eye on the market and ask the tough questions at the right time?

The elements of a marketing plan

The old-fashioned eight-step marketing plan has still many virtues. In today's fast-moving markets, however, we need a little more. We need:

1. **Targets and objectives** – financial and sales/marketing.

2. **A product plan.**

3. **A pricing plan** – strategic pricing aimed at building business and profits.

4. **A market information plan** – including detailed analysis of competitive capability and your competitive advantage.

5. **A sales plan** – direct sales, e-commerce, distributors, affiliates.

6. **A promotional plan** – paid for and free promotional activities.

7. **Structure** – building the organization to do the job.

8. **Staffing** – having the right people with the right skills in the right place with the right behaviours and attitudes.

9. **Budgets** – frugal but realistic.

10. **A competitive plan** – clear identification of the customers to be won from competition with a schedule of which competitors are to be attacked, in order, from weakest to strongest.

11. **Feedback**, **evaluation** and **review** planned in advance.

12. **Contingency planning** with clear action indicators to trigger the plan(s).

13. **An implementation plan** – Who has the responsibility for taking action? What support will they need and who will deliver it? By what date is the support required? What is the deadline for implementation to be completed? Who needs to authorize the activities? Do they need to be co-ordinated? Who needs to be informed of what is happening? Who has the responsibility to ensure effective communication?

Summary

Marketing plans devised by marketing departments often fail because too much depends on expensive advertising and promotional campaigns and not enough understanding of the logistical and financial problems of responding to increased demand. That is why the top team, supported by their people must direct and be fully involved in the planning process.

Business today is under major time pressures. Customers, investors and all other stakeholders are increasingly impatient and looking for quick results. Meanwhile, the business cycle spins ever faster so that the cost of failure is higher and the timeframe in which to recover is shorter. In such circumstances it is essential to ensure that you build a firm platform today on which you can construct tomorrow's growing prosperity. Creating highly profitable operations today is not short-term thinking. It is the only way to ensure survival in the future. So look at today's markets and how you can win more profitable business from them because if you become too "future-minded" you are in danger of having no future to enjoy. Part of our consultancy work is to win those profitable sales today for our clients to fund their future. Our approach is to get in and out quickly. Do the job and leave the client with the tools to do it again and again. Only when today is secure can we turn our minds to tomorrow.

Some performance indicators

- Are our customers consistently expressing delight?
- Are we winning the customers that we are targeting?
- Are our sales rising as forecast?
- Are we coping with the logistics?
- Are we maintaining our margins?
- Are we within budget?
- Are our salespeople bringing in worthwhile customers rather than just going for numbers?
- Is our credit control remaining effective?
- Are our competition showing signs of feeling the pain?
- Are our people committed to achieving more at lower cost?
- Have we avoided the trap of delivering more than the market demands?
- When we last advertised what was the cost of each enquiry?
  - What was the advertising cost of each sale?

Sales reporting

Salespeople hate writing reports, but you must know:

- On whom are they calling?
- Why are they calling?
- What is the result of the call?
- What do the customers want?
- What are they likely to want in the future?
- What action is required after the call?

Promotional activities

- Are we creating greater awareness of our capabilities and particularly our competitive advantage?
- Are we making it easier to buy from us?
- Are we reaching and attracting the right customer?
- Are we building market share?
  - Are we taking enough market share? (Objectives should clearly state the level of market share that is required to dominate the market. This means that you need to have a very clear view of the market segments that you serve.)
- Are we being invited to keep in touch by customers and prospects and to provide further information as it is available?
- Are we building the company image and reputation?
- Are we reducing the cost of selling while increasing sales value?
  - What are our sales costs per pound or dollar in revenues?
  - How much have they changed in the past twelve months?
  - Are we selling or buying business?

Some important further questions

- What is the purchase lifetime of the average customer?
- How frequently does the average customer buy?
- What parts of your range are "cash cows"?
- How are they promoted?
- What parts are "stars"?
- How are they promoted?
- What items are "question marks" at present?
- How are you keeping the costs of market testing them within bounds?
- What do you do to ensure that you can lose "dogs" without losing customers?

(Note: Cash cows are established product lines that generate high revenues without further investment. Stars are high potential product lines that still require considerable investment of money and effort to market, but which are selling well. Question marks are possible future stars which need thorough market testing to justify a high investment of time, creativity and money. Dogs are slow moving, low value lines that probably cost more to supply than they generate in

profit. It is probably a good exercise to look at clients and customers using the same definitions and the same nomenclature – but not in their earshot!)

- What specifically do you do to lengthen the product life cycle of cash cows and accelerate the wide acceptance of stars?
- What is your policy for getting rid of customers who are, and will remain, more hassle than they are worth?
- How often do you communicate with your customers?
- How do you personalize communications?
- Have you checked your letterhead recently?
  - What does it do to promote sales?
  - Does it promote your business?
- What is in your signature file for e-mails?
  - Does it tell the recipient anything about you and your business?
  - Does it build business opportunities?
- How can we make life easier for our best customers?
- If you use them, which host/beneficiary deals are bringing in the most business?
  - Which are bringing in the most profitable business?

    If you are not using them, should you? (See *E-Market Dominance* by Brian Ash and myself for details.)
- Which are competition's most profitable customers?
  - What is your strategy for capturing them?
- What is your unique selling proposition?
- What is your referral *system*?
  - How do you reward referrals?
- If you could improve one key aspect of your marketing at a stroke what would it be?
  - What would be the result?

A brief word about a tricky subject

Howard Shenson used to say that "you may be certain that whatever response marketing people claim for a direct mail initiative, high or low – it is a lie". Direct mail, whether by old-fashioned post or by e-mail is difficult to do and difficult to assess.

- Is the list the best available?
- Is mail the best way to approach this prospective customer?

- Will the message reach the decision-maker?
- Is the timing right for this offer to this customer?
- Will he or she read it?
- Is the opening compelling?
- Is the offer right?
- Is the letter creative without being gimmicky?
- Is there clear evidence that we can deliver all that we promise?
- Is the response mechanism easy to use?
- Is it easy to buy?
- Are all contact details in place and accurate?

Case studies and research

Research has shown that there are ways to raise low response rates to direct mail as direct mail, whether dispatched electronically or in an envelope remains important to most businesses. Post-September 11 and the "anthrax through the mail" scares that followed, e-mail marketing has grown in the USA by more than 60 per cent a month. Where the USA is today the rest of the world will be tomorrow, for the simple competitive reason that if the USA gains savings the rest of the world is forced to try to do as much if not more. So we will all have to look with a new eye at what has been achieved in the past. We will not only have to draw lessons from what is, but raise the question of what may be, for the probability is that what may be will be.

Take a look at the case study and research findings outlined below to identify the key questions that, given your business realities and the markets in which you operate, will deliver a higher level of more profitable business most quickly and most economically.

---

mini case study

research – the American Marketing Association

The American Marketing Association conducted an experiment some years ago. Identical mailings were sent to carefully targeted groups that were equal in size and potential experimental and control groups. The control group received the mailing in the normal way. The experimental group was sent the same promotional material but it was preceded by a telephone call to the recipient with the objective of persuading him/her to look out for it. (The call was generally made by a member of the opposite sex from that of the recipient. The near compulsion of keeping a promise to a member of the opposite sex is strong in most of us.)

After the mailing was received a follow-up telephone call was made to establish the recipient's response to what they had read.

The control group response rate was a little under 1 per cent.

The experimental group buying rate was a little over 15 per cent.

Consider just what happened in this case. Like most of us the experimental group probably disliked junk mail. Their usual response to it was probably to bin it without even opening it, or to glance at it and decide that it held no interest for them. But that telephone call had persuaded them to look out for this mailing and the vast majority of us keep our word especially if doing so is neither too onerous nor too expensive. So for starters it is almost certain that more people read the message, but there is more to it than that. Psychology teaches us that when we do something out of the ordinary we justify the changed behaviour to ourselves any way than we can. More people read the mailing, but more importantly they read it with the intention of finding something worthwhile in it. In short, they sold themselves on the message.

This three-pronged approach costs a little more but, unless you can afford massive mailings, a 15 to 1 response ratio is almost certainly worth the additional cost. This is particularly true for those who take our advice and test their marketing initiatives with small numbers. A few thousand telephone calls will stretch the budget of all but the biggest spender, but a couple of hundred brief calls, even if repeated, can be carried out relatively quickly and cheaply.

mini case study

The bane of the mailing expert's existence is the gatekeeper or dragon. The personal assistant who dumps unsolicited mail in the bin rather than bother a busy boss with it. If, and only if, you can get your message past the gatekeeper and into the hands of the intended recipient can you make a sale. This innovative approach went like this:

- Most PAs in this sexually unequal world are still women.

- Most women like flowers and regard red roses as particularly romantic.

- Romance and mystery go together and are great, though harmless, fun.

This mailing was aimed at chief executives with the intention of getting them to a meeting to assess a new and exciting concept. The whole campaign went like this:

Step one
A single long-stemmed red rose was mailed to each gatekeeper. It had a gold-edged card attached bearing no message, only the lady's given name. The card was attached by a green ribbon.

Step two
Three days later a gold-edged envelope with an identical ribbon and addressed to the chief executive arrived in the mail. Inside was an invitation card that matched that which had been attached to the rose in every way except that it bore details of the proposed meeting and was therefore larger. The PAs, in the main, went further than

simply passing the invitation to the boss. They drew his/her attention to it and treated it as if it was very special. The response rate for attending the meeting was 78 out of 100. Putting that another way, 78 busy business opinion leaders attended the meeting, assessed the concept and bought into the idea. More importantly, they became advocates who praised the idea to their business contacts which led to many more unsolicited sales.

The firm with the idea to sell was a marketing consultancy, but every entrepreneur should think through successful approaches with the intention of building their own creativity.

Consultants are better than most . . . but they must do better – trust me I'm a consultant!

In 1997 the Direct Mail Information Service researched thirty-eight mailings from different consultants. If consultants offer anything worth buying to their clients they ought to be able to do better than most in promoting their wares. Fortunately their results were an improvement on the 0.5 per cent to 2 per cent that we have learned to expect. They scored on average a response rate of 5.3 per cent. Of course, consultants seldom use mailings to sell a product or service. They sell a meeting with the potential client so you would expect a higher response rate than the norm on two accounts:

- It is an easier sale if all that you are selling is the "no obligation" appointment.
- Consultants should be good at doing what they teach others to do.

Advertising

Recently I read an article by a highly respected business editor who advised that when nobody wants to buy your product or service you should advertise heavily. I could not agree less. The demise of the more stupid dot com ideas has been largely a direct result of trying to advertise the company's way out of trouble when nobody wanted what they had to sell. It is, of course the responsibility of marketing to create desire for products and services, but advertising is not the best way to do this without far less expensive groundwork. A virtually cost-free PR campaign followed by advertising when the market has been "warmed up" sometimes makes sense, but unless you know who the potential buyers for your offering are, advertising may be a very expensive way of saying the wrong things to the wrong people just when they have no wish to hear it.

Advertising also has the disadvantage of being plagued by what I call the Mandy Rice-Davies syndrome. Unless their minds are previously disposed toward the offering people, if they read the advertisement at all, read it with the attitude "they would say that, wouldn't they?" Only those who are predisposed to take a positive view swallow advertising puff wholesale.

A business needs to communicate. It needs to tell all those people who might buy the goods or services that it offers, what they are and what they will do for the customer. Sometimes the way to do this is through advertising and sometimes not. Let us lay down some ground rules.

Only use paid advertising when there is clearly no better alternative

Press releases, direct mail, word of mouth, seminars, conference presentations, point of sale promotions, articles in trade journals, letters to the editor or networking may be better and will certainly be cheaper.

If you must advertise make sure that a high percentage of those who will see your message are interested in what you offer

Avoid being seduced by the agency view of reach. "Reach" has to mean that you place your advertisement only where it will be seen by a large number of potential customers rather than getting the idle attention of uninterested passers by. Media are comprehensively listed in *BRAD* (*SRDS* in the USA) and *Willings Press Guide*. If you have designed the proverbial better mousetrap these publications will guide you to *The Mouse Haters Gazette* – if there is such a recondite publication.

Design advertisements that lead the customer to take action

Haemorrhoids are undoubtedly unpleasant, but given the unenviable choice between haemorrhoids or a tombstone, I think that I might learn to live with haemorrhoids.

The key steps toward successful sensible budget advertising

Choose your medium with care

Having identified the probable media from *Willings, BRAD* or *SRDS*, contact them and ask for a "media pack". This will answer important questions for you:

- What is the demographic breakdown of the readership or audience?
- How many readers buy the magazine or service?

- How many read, watch or listen to the publication or service? (For every buyer of a publication there are one or more extra readers. You take home a newspaper and the family read those parts that interest them. Magazines are passed round and often end up in waiting rooms.)
- What are those readers, listeners or viewers interested in right now in terms of editorial material?
- What are they arguing about on the "letters" page or elsewhere?
- What is likely to excite the editor or production team by helping to raise new issues – contentious or otherwise? (Though they generally prefer contentious, properly handled discord sells newspapers and periodicals. When the editor of the *Daily Bugle* makes personal attacks on the editor of *The Scandal* it is less to vent spite than to sell newspapers by forcing readers to demonstrate their "loyalty".)

With this information you can make an informed decision.

- Is this the right medium for you?
- Might a cheaper approach than advertising get better results?
- Could paid advertising and editorial work in tandem?
- Should you become a radio or television personality?
- Might you usefully offer the editor a regular column or an "agony aunt" piece that may turn you into the world's first "mousetrap guru"?

So you decide to advertise

Design your advertisement with care.

- Create a heading or headline which will get the attention of every reader, listener or viewer who is in the market for your product or service. *"Do You Hate Mice?"* Make sure that you speak to your potential customers personally. Remember that the word **"you"** is the strongest word in the advertising lexicon. Speak to your customer as if in a one-to-one conversation and grab their attention quickly. They haven't a lot of time to spare.
- Make a promise. **"The new Acme Mousetrap will rid your home of mice more quickly, cleanly and cheaply than any competitive product."** "New" is a powerful word, but it must mean what it says. We are all a little tired of "new and improved" meaning the same old stuff in a different box.
- Provide credible evidence that your promise will be fulfilled. **"Professor Felix Kattzenpuss of the Vienna Institute of**

Mouse Annihilation says 'in tests nine out of ten mouzes preverred zis method of execution'."

- Tell the customer precisely how to get the benefit of your product or service while they remain excited by it. **"Ring toll free 800 Mouse today while limited stocks last."**

- You may wish to provide an incentive to call immediately. People are greedy, selfish and short of time. (Much more about this later when I discuss direct sales.) **"The first one hundred purchasers will receive, completely free of charge, the Acme patented mouse interment shovel."**

Remember that any advertisement must generate at least enough additional profit to pay for itself and for the next advertisement

If that is all it does, it is a failure. If it produces less it is an abject failure that has helped to destroy companies. In today's volatile markets the penalty for a wrong decision may be swift and terrible.

How do consultants help with market dominance?

As a consultant and manager of consulting firms on both sides of the Atlantic it has often been my pleasure to help corporations to develop their dominance marketing strategy. Over the years I have developed a set of questions that enable us to see very clearly where we are starting from and where we might give help without re-inventing any wheels. You might find it both useful and interesting to play the role of consultant in your own company and ask the questions that we might ask. Your great advantage in having detailed knowledge of your company operations may well lead you to even more useful supplementary questions and deeper and more detailed answers.

Summary

Low cost/no cost marketing techniques have the considerable advantage that, unlike advertising they are most readily believed, that is why they have been consistently used by consultants and other professionals, to whom credibility is important, for more than twenty years. All businesspeople should be looking to develop a judicious blend of no cost marketing allied to effective paid promotion. (For some proven no cost ideas the interested reader may wish to glance at my *High Income Consulting*.)

The following is a tool that my colleagues have found to be of great value in identifying whether clients are ready for the development of a market dominance strategy. In simple terms the client is ready if, and only if, there is a robust tactical and strategic plan in place to provide a secure platform for building dominance. I keep saying it, but it is vital: to have a worthwhile strategy you need to be as certain as you can be in a volatile business environment that you can go beyond survival. You need to have a tactical plan that will deliver all the resources, financial and more that you need when you need them.

The Lambert Dominance Marketing Strategy Audit

Does the client fully understand the market?

Before completing a full audit, we will look at a few simple questions and identify how much help, if any, the client needs on the basis of the answers provided. It is essential that the client is asked carefully thought out supplementary questions to help to widen and deepen the understanding of marketing in general and dominance strategies in particular. The examples given are no more than guides. The actual questions used should arise as naturally as possible from the conversation. All answers should be fully recorded.

The key to this instrument is to help the client to think more deeply about marketing. It is essential therefore that the consultant maintains a professional degree of detachment and avoids challenging the client thinking at this stage. The client should not be put under pressure. The subsequent verbal and written reports will provide every opportunity to "educate" the client should this prove necessary. Try not to let the client become distracted by your notes. Keep them as brief as possible and always ask permission to make notes before starting to write.

- Does the firm really understand the marketing concept? (*Example of a supplementary: How is marketing defined in this company? If you say the word "marketing" to your colleagues what is it that they think about? Advertising? Selling? Something more complex?*)

- Do all your people understand that every employee should be actively seeking to make a contribution to the marketing effort? (*Examples of supplementary questions: Have they been given guidance or training on what contribution they can make? Does any contribution by an employee stick in your mind as having been particularly useful?*)

- Do they know that marketing requires them to seek to create as well as identify and satisfy customer need? (*Example of a supplementary: How are developing customer desires and expectations fed back into the marketing strategy? Does an individual member of the top team have personal responsibility for receiving ideas and assessing their value? How are employees rewarded for ideas and intelligence fed into the company?)*

- Do they recognize that profit is a marketing responsibility? *(Supplementary: How do staff members demonstrate their commitment to reducing costs and increasing productivity while improving service and quality?)*

- Are they aware that the only appropriate head of marketing is the CEO and that he/she is responsible for a marketing unit? *(Supplementary: Do you agree that since innovation and marketing are ultimately the only sources of profit you are the strategic head of both activities?)*

- Is there a written market plan? *(Supplementary: How are feedback, evaluation and review managed at top team level? How are results communicated to those responsible? How often do the board review and challenge the current marketing plan? How flexible is their thinking?)*

- What kind of intelligence is being collected about customers?

- Who collects it? *(Supplementary (if intelligence gathering is limited to sales people): How is the accuracy of information tested? How often do you meet customers face to face?)*

- What is the quality and reliability of the intelligence collected? *(Supplementary: How is its reliability tested before potentially expensive steps are taken?)*

- In general how reliable is it?

- How much of it is used?

- By whom is it used?

- To what degree was there consensus within the senior team about the marketing plan that is being implemented? *(Supplementary: Is every member of the top team consistently "walking the talk" of dominating your selected markets? Does each member of your top team give everybody the feeling that you are absolutely determined to be the best of the best in your chosen markets?)*

- Were the right customers targeted? *(Supplementary: What percentage of your customers are more trouble to serve than they are worth? How do you get rid of the nuisance customer?)*

- Do you feel that the products/services were positioned correctly? *(Supplementary: What segments, sectors or niches did you target? On what considerations did you base your pricing strategy?)*

- Was the product well designed? *(Supplementary: How are customer complaints recorded? Who reviews them? What actions are typically taken? What is the percentage of errors in quality or shipping?)*

- Does the product and the competencies and resources that go into creating it suggest that life extension is a realistic possibility? (*Supplementary: Are your people familiar with the concept of the product life cycle? Do your team actively seek to increase the life cycle of all cash cows?* Note: You may need to explain Porter's concept of Cash Cows, Stars, Question Marks (Wild Cards) and Dogs as a useful way to assess the position on the life cycle of products to the client. Avoid explicit or implicit criticisms of the client business, but provide any information that will facilitate answering of later questions or will deepen and broaden client thinking.)
- Are you actively considering other markets, segments, sectors, niches or customers who may have needs that the firm has the competencies and resources to satisfy? (*Supplementary: Could you please give me an example of what is in the pipeline?*)
- Are there sufficient new products in the pipeline to build revenues and discourage customers from defecting to other suppliers? (*Supplementary: How do you communicate new products or services to the marketplace? How would/do your customers describe your business?*)
- Have you developed plans to lengthen the product life cycle of cash cows?
- Are you taking steps to get rid of "dogs" in terms of customers as well as products?
- How do you evaluate "question marks" quickly to avoid over-investing in new products which may turn out to be "dogs" when they hit the market?
- Are steps being taken to reduce the investment needs of "stars" as quickly as possible so that they will become "cash cows"?
- Is your advertising effective? (*Supplementary: Is there a clear linkage between advertising spend, sales volumes and profits?*)
- How is the advertising evaluated?
- By whom is it evaluated?
- When does the evaluation take place?
- Do customers recognize the benefits of your products or services as if they were brands like Coca-Cola or Sony? (*Supplementary: What do your customers tell you about their response to your brands? Why do they say that they buy? What do they like about doing business with you? What are you doing to give them more of what they like?*)
- Does your finance operation work with marketing to assess the value of brand equity? (*Supplementary: How is brand equity value reflected in your financial reports?*)

- How do you decide on appropriate distribution channels? (*Supplementary: Do you have any intellectual property that could be effectively distributed online? Do you understand the tax implications of online distribution?*)

- How effective are trade or retail sales promotions for you?

- Are you convinced that sales promotions led to a real growth in sales and that the company did not pre-buy future business?

- Do you have a consistent company public relations activity? (*Supplementary: Do you do it yourself or use an agency?*)

- How timely and effective is the marketing feedback, evaluation and review process in your opinion? (*Supplementary: Do you have any examples of how a change in direction led to increased revenues, profits or customer retention?*)

- How effective are your sales people? (*Supplementary: In an ideal world where you could really pick and choose how many of them would you keep?*)

- Are individual closing rates of sales people known to their management? (*Supplementary: How is the information used?*)

- What is being done to raise the performance of the less successful? (*Supplementary: What kind of training? In house or external? Who does it? How do you measure the effect?*)

- What is being done to get the more successful in front of more customers or prospects?

- What evidence is there that the return on the marketing investment is adequate? (*Supplementary: As a rough percentage figure how does marketing spend stack up against revenues? If you put a complete bar on marketing spending today what would you lose in terms of revenues and profits?*)

- What is the level of customer retention year on year? (*Supplementary: Have you seen the research on the effect of loyal customers on a business? Do you find it convincing? What is the lifetime value of your average customer?*)

- Are the customers who are retained those the company wishes to retain?

- What percentage of your total customer base is new and profitable? (*Supplementary: What specific steps are in your marketing plan to ensure that you retain the best customers?*)

- Is the size of initial orders static, growing or falling? (*Supplementary: What are you doing to increase the value of initial orders?*)

- Is order frequency growing, static or falling? (*Supplementary: How do your sales and marketing efforts work to increase order frequency and size?*)

- Is the trend for repeat orders to be smaller, larger or is this static?

- When did the company last conduct a professional market research programme? (*Supplementary: How do you feel about the results? Were they reliable? What have you done as a result of the research? What has been the effect?*)

- How do you market test new ideas? (*Supplementary: Do you market test your marketing ideas before plunging into major investment? How do you do that?*)

- How do you keep a calculating eye on emerging trends? (*Supplementary: Have you read the Popcorn report? What do you think of it? Do you use the web for research into trends?*)

- Were all your marketing objectives clearly measurable, realistic, specific and worthwhile in terms of their contribution to the strategic goals and return on investment? (*Supplementary: If you were to produce the plan again today, what would you do differently?*)

- How well was the market plan marketed internally? (*Supplementary: How was it communicated to every employee? Did it achieve wholehearted senior management support from all functions?*)

- How is marketing expenditure allocated? (*Supplementary: By market segment? By product line? As a single overall budget? On an ad hoc, as required, basis?*)

- Can a Boston matrix (cash cows etc.) of current products and services be readily produced?

- Where specifically are sales revenues falling? (*Supplementary: Do you have a clear understanding of why?*)

- Is each part of the plan that fails to meet its objectives carefully scrutinized to establish how it might be done better next time? (*Supplementary: Who does the evaluation? How reliable is it?*)

- Is a comprehensive marketing audit carried out annually with specific recommendations for improving next year's performance?

- What business are you really in? (*Supplementary: What customer needs or wants do you exist to satisfy? What is the big picture of this business in your mind? What business could you be in?*)

- How do you feel about being prepared to abandon what has been successful for a long time if the market changes? (*Supplementary: Are you planning to target the most exciting markets of the future? What will they be in your opinion? What will give you a competitive edge in new markets?*)

- Have you actually listed the most exciting markets that you anticipate five years hence, giving your reasons and specifying any assumptions that you are making? (*Supplementary: Have you evaluated your capability to enter those markets and written plans to win business? Can you state why you are confident that competition will perform less well than you in the appropriate sectors or segments?*)

- What shows you that the exploitation of this market will deliver an appropriate return on the use of people, resources, money and materials?

- What is your timeframe to achieve such a return?

- How do you know that it is a realistic estimate? (*Supplementary: Have you a sufficient financial provision to enable you to enter such a market without excessive borrowing? Could there be a more economical approach? Have you considered the possibilities of an e-commerce strategy for example? Do your people have the required skills? Have they all been trained? What have you done to ensure the transfer of skills from the training room to the workplace?*)

- Have you listed and analyzed the risks of entry into new markets? (*Supplementary: Have the risks been minimized by appropriate research? Who carried it out? How did they do it?*)

- Have you completed an appropriate degree of comparative/ competitive/capability analysis to permit focused action in the short term as well as in the future?

Summary

The more experience that I have of international business the more that I become convinced that market dominance really is "the only game in town". But market dominance is not easy. It begins with a passion to become and remain the number one player whether your market is great or small. It depends on a detailed, accurate and up-to-date understanding of your customers and competitors and of your own capabilities. Asking the right questions is essential and there is limited value in asking them only once. In a volatile business environment asking questions must be constant and you must be committed to acting on the answers.

9

Making the right connections

questions of profitable e-commerce

"Is this a game of chance?" Not the way I play it. W.C. Fields

- Questions that will ensure that you can make money online.
- Questions that will turn your website into a money machine.
- Questions that will enable you to time your entry to new markets to perfection.
- Questions that obviate risk.
- Questions that multiply profit opportunities.
- Questions that turn mere technology into revenues and profits.

What you will gain from this chapter

- A working document that will lead you to turning your e-commerce activity into a money machine. You need to understand that e-commerce is not a fad that has come and gone. It is a totally new way of doing business that, not surprisingly, has had its casualties as new ideas have been tried and some have been found wanting.
- How to get ahead of the competition.
- How to make full use of business building, cost saving opportunities.
- How to win the best of tomorrow's markets today.

New has always been volatile

In spite of press hype to the contrary and the collapse of a number of badly thought through internet enterprises, the New Economy is both new and here to stay. Never has there been a greater opportunity for firms to provide their customers with superlative service at the lowest possible cost. Never has there been a greater opportunity to become global without major investment. With effective online marketing everybody is a winner. My book, *The Big Book of E-Commerce Answers* develops the argument in detail. It also provides the data to help you to answer most or all of the following questions. Meanwhile, please take my word for it, you should be asking yourself:

- How do we make the most of this new opportunity to do global business at minimum cost?
- How do we ensure that our e-commerce activity is a money machine and not a "techies' paradise"?
- How do we attract customers who want to buy our offerings rather than "boy surfers"?
- How do we avoid paying for "clicks" that deliver no business?
- How do we keep abreast of the changing algorithms of the search engines?
- How do we build the brand to the degree that the search engines are irrelevant?
- How do we use our website to bind customers to us and increase customer loyalty?
- How do we make and sell rather than sell and make?
- How do we use the internet to reduce our inventory costs?
- How do we use the internet to reduce our advertising costs?
- How do we use the internet to test offerings at virtually no cost?
- How do we get people to visit our website?
- How do we avoid the stupid costs of mass advertising?
- How do we get buyers to stay and buy?
- How do we get them to contact us and tell us their needs and wants?
- How do we persuade them to give us permission to contact them with further information?
- How do we use the internet to reach new markets at virtually no cost?
- How do we exploit opportunities to develop online products and services that cost almost nothing to provide, but bring in massive revenues and profits?

- How do we persuade people to trust our internet site to handle their money and confidential details properly?
- How do we find partners to help us to sell our products and services?
- How do we create a meaningful online strategy?

To create a meaningful strategy you need to have a clear view of the big picture. What follows has proved useful to many organizations, helping them to clearly define what they want from their website. It has appeared elsewhere, but its proven usefulness is such that I make no apology for offering it again here.

E-business corporate analysis

The following brief, but detailed, survey is designed to enable you to take a fresh look at your e-business strategy as you consider the degree to which you have established and are meeting optimal objectives for your firm. The survey is not exhaustive, but it is sufficiently comprehensive to enable at least one or two "eureka!" thought breakthroughs for most businesses and professional practices.

What key strategic or tactical benefits are you seeking from your e-business initiative? Why have you chosen to go to the expense and trouble of having a website? Please tick each item that you are seeking from an online presence and give the others some thought. Should you widen your thinking about what the internet might deliver for you? Have you set your sights on the right outcomes for today and, more importantly, tomorrow?

- [ ] Sale of online advertising
- [ ] Building brands – existing products/services
- [ ] Opt-in e-mail marketing
- [ ] Customer/market information
- [ ] Access to world markets
- [ ] Affinity (host/beneficiary) marketing
- [ ] Direct B2B sales
- [ ] Direct B2C sales
- [ ] Global presence/visibility
- [ ] Knowledge sharing
- [ ] Online training and development
- [ ] Sale of lists to e-mailers
- [ ] Cost reductions
- [ ] New advertising channel

- [ ] Attracting new customers
- [ ] Improved buying terms
- [ ] Recruitment and retention of staff
- [ ] Shorten supply chain (reduce intermediaries)
- [ ] Personalized customer service
- [ ] Reduced time-to-market
- [ ] 24×7 availability to customers
- [ ] Global business platform
- [ ] Identify new suppliers
- [ ] Enhanced responsiveness to market
- [ ] Online distribution
- [ ] Faster decision-making
- [ ] Low cost entry into new markets

To what degree have you been successful in enjoying the benefits of your e-business strategy? How well is it working for you? Has the web delivered what you planned for? Has it delivered the unexpected? Do you need to revisit your strategy and beef it up a little – or a lot? Please circle the appropriate number using the following guidelines.

0 No success as yet
1 First glimmerings of results
2 Some clear early benefits experienced
3 Considerable benefits
4 A major success

Access to world markets	0 1 2 3 4
Sale of online advertising	0 1 2 3 4
Building brands – existing products/services	0 1 2 3 4
Opt-in e-mail marketing	0 1 2 3 4
Customer/market information	0 1 2 3 4
Customer retention	0 1 2 3 4
Affinity (host/beneficiary) marketing	0 1 2 3 4
Direct B2B sales	0 1 2 3 4
Direct B2C sales	0 1 2 3 4
Global presence/visibility	0 1 2 3 4
Knowledge sharing	0 1 2 3 4
Online training and development	0 1 2 3 4
Sale of lists to e-mailers	0 1 2 3 4

Cost reductions	0 1 2 3 4
New advertising channel	0 1 2 3 4
Attracting new customers	0 1 2 3 4
Improved buying terms	0 1 2 3 4
Recruitment and retention of staff	0 1 2 3 4
Shorten supply chain (reduce intermediaries)	0 1 2 3 4
Personalized customer service	0 1 2 3 4
Reduced time-to-market	0 1 2 3 4
24×7 availability to customers	0 1 2 3 4
Global business platform	0 1 2 3 4
Identify new suppliers	0 1 2 3 4
Enhanced responsiveness to market	0 1 2 3 4
Online distribution	0 1 2 3 4
Faster decision-making	0 1 2 3 4
Low cost entry into new markets	0 1 2 3 4

What are the key performance indicators of your e-business? Please tick the appropriate items. What are the sign posts which will tell you that it is working for you? What are the warning signs that should scream at you: "do something different and do it now"?

- ☐ Increased sales revenues in existing markets
- ☐ Increased share of revenues from new markets
- ☐ Increased profitability
- ☐ Enhanced return on capital employed
- ☐ Investment funds attracted
- ☐ Enhanced market value of company
- ☐ Competencies developed
- ☐ Information flow
- ☐ Cost per transaction
- ☐ Information distribution cost
- ☐ Increased stock turnover
- ☐ Customer retention
- ☐ Customer satisfaction
- ☐ Market share
- ☐ Share of customer
- ☐ Overall cost reduction

- [ ] Staff reductions
- [ ] Sales per staff member
- [ ] Overall productivity
- [ ] Speed to market
- [ ] Number of customers
- [ ] Just-in-time deliveries
- [ ] Number of website visits
- [ ] Number of website transactions
- [ ] Trends recognized
- [ ] Sales per website visitor
- [ ] Number of customer opt-ins
- [ ] Speed of response
- [ ] Service quality
- [ ] Staff retention
- [ ] Customer "churn"
- [ ] Staff "churn"
- [ ] Website downtime
- [ ] Brand recognition
- [ ] Transaction security failures

Having assessed your objectives, the status of your business to date and the key indicators of your online business success, you may well want to reassess or reconsider your initial strategic and tactical considerations. If this small survey has helped you to think again it has achieved its purpose.

Typical thoughts might include:

- Are we attracting enough visitors?
- Do they stay?
- Do they welcome the offer of further information?
- Are we treating our customers as individuals with different needs?
- Do visitors buy online?
- Do they come back to visit again?
- Do we know with certainty what the emerging needs of our customers are?
- How do we compare against our competition when it comes to delighting the customer?
- Do we know our online competition by name and understand each one's unique marketing proposition?
- Does our site add transactional value for buyers?

- Does it give us added value as sellers?
- Does it make it easier than ever to do business with us?
- Is our unique selling proposition emphasized effectively?
- Could we use online activities to sell and make rather than to make and sell?
- Is our site properly integrated with the rest of the business?
- Is our site too clever to be useful to visitors?
- Does our site help build our service standards?
- Are we attracting enough prospects of the right kind to our site?
- Have we entered into the right online strategic alliances?
- Do we make it easy to do business online?
- Is our off-line distribution up to the job?
- Should we find ways to deliver more online?
- Do we really understand how to keep in touch with the ever-changing search engine algorithms?
- Are we treating our site as a technology breakthrough rather than a marketing and sales operation?
- Do we know how to use it as a sales and marketing operation, because that is what it ought to be?
- Have we been persuaded by those with an axe to grind that a website is merely an electronic brand building exercise?
- Have we a comprehensive strategy in place or was our web presence cobbled together by junior "techies" after the chairman returned from the golf course full of web enthusiasm?
- Does our off-line marketing support success online?
- Has our web presence enabled us to cut costs?
- Have we passed some of the advantages we have gained to our customers in the exceptional value and quality of our offering?

Having answered the above questions or having received satisfactory answers to them from your colleagues you are now in a position to do two vital things. You can incorporate your online strategy into your overall strategic plan: bricks and clicks carefully integrated, have a better record of success than either bricks or clicks alone. You can turn that website that cost so much to design and develop into a money machine.

Consultants like me and the new (that is to say "old") economy

In spite of the prognostications of pundits and press barons, business on the internet continues to grow even faster than the demand for consultancy. The demand for consultancy continues to grow at a rate of more than 20 per cent each year. As it is impossible to predict the questions that a consultant might ask about each and every aspect of a business the following is offered as an important example of the kind of questions that you should expect from consultants. Online business has grown, is growing and is unlikely to diminish. Every company, large and small, should be considering how they will exploit the opportunities for rapid growth.

With the highly publicized failure of dot coms and the apparent inability of top companies to use expensive websites effectively, it is at least as important to plan your success on the internet as it is in the "real world". The cost of getting online may be modest, but the opportunities are not, so you owe it to yourself to think things through carefully. These days, when I advise a corporation who are developing a new strategy, the internet is an important feature. I ensure that clients take it very seriously.

The following are some of the questions that I would typically ask to ensure that my clients were planning for online success and not assuming that a web presence is simply part of the old routine or a minor "bolt-on" brand building exercise.

May I suggest that you carefully consider each question? Your additional business and the profits that it will bring will make you glad that you took the time. Even if you do not have a web presence think through each question as if it referred to your "bricks" rather than "clicks" strategy. The New Economy is, in many ways, not as divorced from the old as some pundits would have us believe. The best that can happen is that you are developing detailed plans for your future prosperity. The worst that can happen is that you save my £3,000 ($5,000) a day by not paying me to ask the questions.

- In an ideal world where anything is possible what would you choose to accomplish through your web presence?
- What is your objective for increased sales in the first year?
- How will a website support the achievement of this goal?
- What are your specific cost cutting goals? How do you expect to measure the economies of being online?
- How will your people become more productive?
- How will you enjoy low cost/no cost entry into new markets?
- How will you switch from make and sell to sell and make?
- What products or services can be delivered online?
- What intermediaries can you stop having to pay?

- What are you doing to make your best customers more loyal?
- Some experts believe that online business will take off and will grow at a cumulative rate of at least 30 per cent a year for the next five years. (The last quarter of 2001 showed an increase, year on year, of 74 per cent.) What are you doing to ensure that you can handle the distribution and customer service problems that could arise if your business grew that fast or faster? (At this stage clients grin and say: "That's a problem I would like to have to deal with when it happens." To which I rather bad-temperedly reply: "Never mind the problem. What's your solution?")
- What are your goals for customer service improvements?
- How will you measure your advances in customer service?
- What motivates your best customers to buy?
- What motivates them to buy from you?
- What motivates others with the same or better potential to buy elsewhere?
- Who do your best customers also do business with or get information from on the internet?
- What are your goals for doing joint ventures on the internet?
- Can you list the internet chat rooms, publications, newsgroups that your best customers participate in?
- What do your best customers say about you and your service online and off-line?
- How do your best customers perceive your business?
- What precisely are your competitors doing online and what are you doing to ensure a competitive edge?
- As they change how will you stay ahead of the pack?
- What is the profile of your best customers?
- What future needs of your customers will your online presence enable you to satisfy?
- How do you plan to identify changing customer needs and expectations more quickly than your competition?
- Right now how are you building the competencies that you will need in the most profitable markets of the future?
- What is your online marketing budget?
- What is your advertising policy?
- How many internet PR pieces do you intend to have published each month?
- Who will publish them?

- Why will they publish your stuff?
- What are your growth limitations?
- What about order processing and fulfilment, e-mail capacity, credit card processing and security, distribution and delivery, customer service and customer delight? What concrete steps have you put in place today to ensure your optimal future growth potential?

If you already have a website

- Who, outside the company has checked your website for speed of loading and ease of use?
- Do the headlines on each page sell to the customer as well as to the search engines?
- What are the specific benefits that you use?
- Are all contact details on each page?
- Do you give all potential customers clear and compelling reasons to give you their e-mail addresses for further information?
- If I visited your page for xxxxx what specifically would make me want to permit you to keep in touch?
- How do you measure website traffic?
- How do you measure the sales per visitor?
- What keywords do people use to get to your site?
- What other sites, or newsrooms do they come from?
- How often do you check the search engines to ensure that you are in the top ten?
- How do you make the required changes when you find that you are slipping?
- How many times each day do your people check e-mails?
- How often do you check your auto responder messages to customers to be certain that they are still relevant?
- When was the product or service information that you are currently sending out last updated?
- Where do you display customer testimonials?

Down and dirty online marketing

- How do you capture all customers, prospects, suppliers, distributors, affiliates, prospective affiliate promoters and joint venture partners' e-mail addresses?

- Where would you find a list of, say, potential joint venture partners if you wanted to do it personally in a hurry?
- What is the average purchase per visit?
- What is the purchase lifetime of the average customer?
- How frequently does the average customer buy?
- What parts of your range are "cash cows"?
- How are they promoted?
- What parts are "stars"?
- How are they promoted?
- What items are "question marks" at present?
- How are you keeping the costs of market testing them within bounds?
- What do you do to ensure that you can lose "dogs" without losing customers?

  (*Note: Cash cows are established product lines that generate high revenues without further investment. Stars are high potential product lines that still require considerable investment but which are selling well. Question marks are possible future stars but which, at present need thorough market testing to justify a high investment of time, creativity and money. Dogs are slow moving, low value lines that probably cost more to supply than they generate in profit. It is probably a good exercise to look at clients and customers using the same definitions and the same nomenclature – but not in their earshot!*)

- What specifically do you do to lengthen the product life cycle of cash cows and accelerate the wide acceptance of stars?
- What is your policy for getting rid of customers who are and will remain more hassle than they are worth?
- How often do you communicate with your customers?
- How do you personalize communications?
- What is in your signature file for e-mails?
- Which host/beneficiary deals are bringing in the most business?
- Which are bringing in the most profitable business?
- Which are competition's most profitable customers?
- What is your strategy for capturing them?
- What is your unique selling proposition online?
- What is it in the dirt world?
- What is your referral system?
- How do you reward referrals?

- If you could improve one key aspect of your marketing at a stroke what would it be?

I cannot pretend that this is an exhaustive list of questions that I ask in any specific situation. The answers to good questions always lead to supplementary questions and they often only have relevance in the light of what has already been discussed. Similarly, not all of the questions listed will be the key questions to which your specific situation and strategy demands full and careful answers. They should, however, be of considerable relevance and, at the very worst, they will remind you of the important questions that you ought to be asking yourself.

From a marketer's viewpoint whether you market online or in the local flea market you must always keep in the forefront of your mind:

- Who is my best type of customer?
- What do they need?
- What do they want (WOMAN – wants overcome (lack of) money and needs)?
- What motivates them to buy?
- What motivates them to buy from a specific supplier?
- How can I give them more of what they like?
- How are their interests, needs and desires changing?
- If they want "A" today could they be persuaded to want "B" tomorrow?
- What is the lifetime value of a customer?
- How much can I spend to attract the right customer?
- How will I delight and go on delighting my customers?
- How can I dump those who are more trouble than they are worth without damaging my reputation, credibility and image?
- How can I make the best, most economical use of emerging technology to delight and go on delighting my customers?

Ten tips for the small (and large) business website (and for consultants)

1. Identity – Be clear about who you are and what you offer from the customer's viewpoint.

2. Take a pride in your expertise, but don't try to push what customers don't want.

3. Creativity – be creative, but never cloud the purpose of your business with cleverness for its own sake.

4. Constantly look at what works for others, adapt and adopt the best that your creativity and budget can manage.

5. Build customer loyalty and you will build employee loyalty without effort.

6. Deliver more than you promise.

7. Remember customers online are short on time and attention, not money.

8. Make it easy for people to buy online.

9. Avoid pop up advertising and "get off my site" banners that distract customers from their purpose.

10. Be consistent: market consistently when you're fat, dumb and happy. Ensure that your messages consistently reflect the image that you want. Ensure that the customer is never confused by conflicting messages.

11. Make it easy for customers to contact you.

12. Always deliver more than you promise!

Summary

There really is a new economy. It will, once the dust of stupidity settles, have as much effect on business as did the invention of the steam engine and it will have that effect much more quickly. An example of the speed with which things happen can be taken from relatively recent happenings in the USA. Following the murderous attack on the World Trade Center there was a short-lived, but foul series of mailings that included deadly anthrax spores. Not surprisingly, people began to take less than kindly to unsolicited mail. Businesses that were setup to do this turned instead to e-mail marketing. The increase both in communication and sales was massive and it has been sustained as organizations have discovered that they have an almost cost-free way to give their customers and prospects the information that they desire.

Be ready by asking yourself the key questions today. If you are already up to speed, keep asking the questions to stay ahead of competition and to prosper.

10

The power to influence

questions of sales and success

Influence is a matter of ethics. Anon.

- Questions to turn your sales team into a superior force.
- Questions that build profits by making the best customers yours for life.
- Questions that market and sell your operation internally.
- Questions that make people buy into your ideas.
- Questions to improve products and services.

What you will gain from this chapter

- How people think when assessing a product, service or idea.
- How to use psychological and practical research to sell your products and services.
- How to apply your understanding of the mind to persuade others to accept your good ideas.
- How to succeed where you have no power.
- How to have an ethical approach to making any kind of sale.

It should come as no surprise when I say that everybody in business needs to have a strong grasp of sales skills. If you have a good product someone needs to sell it. If you offer good services they have to be sold. Most importantly, however, if any individual in your business has a good idea they must have some ability to sell that idea or it may be lost forever. If Peters, Nonaka, Tacheuchi and the rest are right, and they most certainly are, the thoughts, hunches and ideas of your committed people are the key source of competitive advantage. You are not, I assume, gifted with the ability to read minds, so they have to be willing and able to describe their ideas to you and to others in a convincing and inspirational way. That too requires sales skills of a high order.

It will come as even less of a surprise when, having written the above, I confirm that professional salespeople apart, most businesspeople baulk at developing sales skills and some actually believe that such skills are beneath them. Engineers have been known to tell me: "if they can't see the merit of that, they are idiots and don't deserve to enjoy the benefits". Some years ago what was then called Personnel and is now rather more grandly spoken of as HR was going through a bad patch. We were just emerging from one of the cyclical business downturns that characterized the "economic miracle" of the 1980s and 1990s. During the tough times many managers had assumed, as an economy measure, the functions and role of personnel. As Bob Townsend would undoubtedly predict they were mightily pleased with the result. They had sought staff as it suited them, recruited in a downturn with ease, interviewed cogently in their own estimation and had attracted people at least as good as those usually provided for interview by the expensive personnel operation. As to most managers recruiting and screening applicants for jobs was all that personnel seemed to do, there seemed little, if any, reason to retain such a department when it appeared obvious that line management could do the job equally well. The result was that in many firms the Personnel Department has been downgraded. Personnel directors lost their seats on boards and the department was fighting, without much success, to regain recognition.

I was invited by the Institute of Personnel Management (soon after my appearance to become the Institute of Personnel and Training) to speak at a conference. I chose as my theme "Marketing the Personnel Function in the Firm". I delivered a brief and, I hope, witty (you can never be sure with HR people), overview of marketing and how to adapt it to promoting an activity internally. After the morning session each speaker was to conduct a workshop in the afternoon. Delegates could choose where to attend. After a pleasant lunch I returned to find that something like 85 per cent of delegates were crammed into my small room. Never put out of countenance I addressed the group.

"Are we agreed that it is essential to market ourselves so that others understand and want to use our expert services?"

Much nodding of heads and even verbal indications of enthusiasm greeted the question. Encouraged I continued.

"So what specifically are we going to do?"

Answer came there none – so I paraphrased the question and repeated it. After a long silence one delegate spoke.

"We are going to set out our stall."

"Great, so what are we going to set out on that stall of ours?"

Silence.

"Let me re-phrase the question. What do we offer our 'customers' that they will want to buy?"

More silence. I paraphrased the question again and again until my powers of language began to desert me.

"Let me try once more. What benefits do we deliver to those who use our services?"

This time the silence was finally broken by a voice from the back of the room.

"I say old boy, don't you realize that I am a professional? You cannot seriously be asking me to act like a f****** salesman?"

I continued the session as a chalk and talk presentation that was received with considerable enthusiasm. I still sometimes wonder why I bothered.

The simple fact is that we tend to undervalue the role and skills of the salesperson. That is where the whole thing began way back in 1931. The world was in deep depression. In the United States one person in four was without a job. Many of those that had jobs were doing pretty well. Price deflation meant that their wages, low as they might be, had more purchasing power with each day that passed. Salespeople were unhappy. They felt, with some justification, that they were the grease that kept at least some wheels turning. If 75 per cent of the population could still put food on the table it was due in no small measure to the skills and determination of salespeople. Yet salespeople received no recognition for their achievements. Lawyers were not trusted, but admired for their learning. Teachers were respected. Doctors were idolized, but admit that you were a salesperson and you would be treated with scant respect. When you are in the business of struggling to save the economy and keep a nation fed, that hurts. Salespeople decided to do something about it. They held a national conference.

The conference decided that what would change things, would be the recognition that being in sales is to be a profession equal in value, if not in status, to other professions. Why was such recognition denied them? It was withheld because they lacked an educational programme and formal accreditation to an institute. They formed such an institute and charged it with developing a comprehensive educational programme. The working salespeople who were elected or dragooned into this task worked with a will. They developed the programme, but since they were not academics they based it entirely on their personal experience of what works. They had little or no knowledge of why it worked, but of one thing they were sure – it worked because it had to work. Their, often considerable, earnings were dependent on consistently doing and saying the right thing. Lack of academic justification continued to rankle, however, so they turned their half-formulated ideas over to the University of Columbia, New York and invited them to assess the value of the material. Thus began an academic and practical research programme that has continued for almost seventy years in all parts of the world. The result has been probably the most detailed understanding of how the mind works as we make the decision to accept another's reasoning combined with practical and proven tools to enable the influencing of the behaviour in others. In a phrase they have developed and tested state of the art, professional and ethical "sales" techniques that should be in the "personal toolkit" of every manager, executive or salesperson.

Using questions intelligently

Effective salespeople constantly analyze and assess their work. They assure me that if they find that they have talked more than say, 40 per cent of the time, they have failed whether they made the sale or not. If they believe in the central importance of the "customer" whether that customer is buying an idea, a service or a product they need to ask questions that are brief and to the point and listen to the answers. This means that the customer must do the bulk of the talking. The salesperson that demonstrates the mere gift of the gab is a salesperson in trouble.

I need to build just a little on the very brief notes on questioning skills that were in the introduction to this book. Effective questioning is essential to you as a manager or executive if you want to have your ideas accepted and implemented, just as it is the crucial tool of the salesperson. To maximize the flow of conversation you must:

Use *open* questions

These cannot be answered by a "yes" or a "no" and cause the other person to express their feelings or opinion:

- How do you feel about the state of the economy at present?
- What did you think of the Mansion House speech last night?
- What did you think of the prospects for economic growth?
- How do you feel about the behaviour of customers these days?
- What are the most significant values that you, as a businessperson, hold?
- What are the issues your industry faces at the moment?
- What would be your ideal solution to the problems that you confront?
- If you could change one important thing about business today what would it be?
  - Why is it important to you to change that?
- What is the effect of the accelerating business and economic cycle on your business strategy?
- What keeps you awake at night?

But, asking open questions is not enough. You must reward the other person for giving you valuable information by:

- **Thanking them** – "That's very interesting, thank you."
- **Praising them** – "You're very generous (kind, brave, helpful, honest, open – or my personal favourite description of other people – gracious), sharing that with me. I appreciate your trust."
- **Smiling** and making direct **eye contact**.
- **Nodding**.
- **Paraphrasing** key ideas to show that you are listening – "So you think that there will be tough times ahead for your industry?"
- **Asking for further information** – "That's very interesting. Could you tell me a little more about that?"
- Maintaining an alert and interested **posture**.
- Ensuring that your **posture, manner and mood** are as close to theirs as possible. (Students of NLP (neurolinguistic programming) or of good old-fashioned social psychology will understand that aligning your posture, mood and manner as closely as you may to that of the other person without risking offensive caricaturing builds an emotional sense of warmth between individuals. My *The Power of Influence* goes into enough detail to enable Richard Donkin of the *Financial Times* to write a delightful skit, by way of a critique that compared some of the advice in the book to the mating dances of grebes or ducks.)
- Asking further **open questions** to enable the other person to expand on other areas that are of importance to them.

Semi-closed/closed questions

Use more focused or *semi-closed* questions to increase your control of the conversation, reduce meandering and garrulousness and clarify your own thinking. These are questions which clearly indicate the area which you want the other to address without demanding a short or "yes-no" answer.

- Why precisely is it a problem that is particularly important to you right now?
  - What other factors make it most pressing today?
- What have you tried within the last year to achieve the outcome that you are looking for?
  - What has worked best for you?
  - Are you still doing that?
- What led you to make a change in strategy (or tactics)?
- What would be your ideal solution? (This is either an open or a

semi-closed question according to context. If you have already identified and discussed a problem area it is moving toward being more closed than open.)

When you have all the information that you need, or are likely to get, turn up the control mechanism another notch by asking genuinely *closed* questions.

- Is the redundancy programme the only area where you want to hear my ideas at the moment?
- Do you have a budget for this?
- Is your key objective to reduce downtime by 20 per cent?
- Are you eager to identify ways to increase sales?

Absolute control comes from asking questions to which the only reasonable answer is "yes" or sometimes "no", but in influence psychology "yes" is always better. The more times I say "yes" to you the less likely that I am to say "no" when you ask for my agreement.

Value/leading questions

Questions that you may expect to lead the other to answer affirmatively may include *value questions* such as:

- As a parent, do you agree that the quality of education will be critical to your child's future?
- Do you agree that we who have so much should do what we can to reduce the suffering of starving children?

or

Leading questions

- Having satisfied you on all the points that you have raised do you think that this is a good idea for you right now? (How could it not be a good idea if I have satisfied the listener on all the points that he or she has raised?)
- Do you see why short-term growth is the right strategy in today's conditions? (Few of us have the courage to say, "no sorry I'm not smart enough to understand".)

To keep your argument on track once you are doing a considerable share of the talking, and to keep the other actively involved use *progress test* questions that place the burden back where it belongs on you the skilled influencer:

- Have I made it clear how the new system will solve your problems?
- Does what I've said (shown you, given you a feel for) sound (look, feel) right to you?

Obstacle handling questions

A piece of personal bias: I dislike the way that some salespeople are trained to always answer a question or complaint with another question. "If I answer that for you will you buy today?" is a blatant example. However, something similar can be done effectively and ethically if, and only if, it is truly in the interests of the customer to hasten the conclusion and get on with implementing the solution. The exact way that you ask the question, however, should always give the listener a way out.

- Yes that does sound difficult, if I can convince you that I can show you how to overcome that will you be prepared to give it a try?
- Is that your only concern?

Influence psychology

More than sixty years of practical, carefully validated and comprehensive research have led to the development of a *cognitive map* of exactly – step by step – how people think when making the decision whether to accept a line of reasoning or not. Each step implies a question. I do not pretend that the questions are phrased in the words that I use, but research has proved beyond a shadow of doubt that if you are able to answer these questions in the structure, sequence and words of your argument, the listener's mind will move comfortably and easily from one set of questions to the next. If the presentation of your product, service or idea is structured so that each question is answered indirectly, but affirmatively in turn, the mind is programmed to reach the decision "YES". Only by inputting ideas at the wrong time or in the wrong sequence do we fail. Get the sequence and timing precisely right every time and you will succeed every time.

A cognitive map of decision-making

I am important – will my importance be recognized?

- Will my needs be treated as imperative?
- Is this person offering me something of value or is he or she simply trying to push me into something?
- Should I listen, or should I simply seek ways of saying "no" politely or otherwise?

I have developed a point of view – will my opinion be respected and understood?

- Will the value that I put on my personal experience be appreciated?
- Does this person recognize that what I believe is in effect a precious part of who I am?

- Does he or she realize that the person who I am today, the position that I hold, my self-image are all the result of the views and values that I have developed through my experience?
- Does he or she understand that if my beliefs are attacked I will treat that attack as if it were an act of aggression aimed at my person? (Defensive communication was researched a number of years ago by Jack Gibb. In essence his research showed that our beliefs are so important to us that if someone attempts, with the utmost of good will, to change our thinking we are likely to respond by defending our, often outdated, beliefs.)

I'm a busy person – should I really listen to this or just think of ways to say "no" quickly while he or she talks?

- Why should I give this idea "time of day"?
- Is there something in this for me?
- Is listening to this a proper use of my valuable time right now?

What is the idea? – What is the detail?

- How does it work?
- Would it work for me?
- Is it safe?
- Is it new?
- Is it attractive?
- What is the evidence that it works?
- Who has tried it?
- What would people that I trust and admire say about it?
- Am I being persuaded to be an innovator and take a major risk?
- Or am I being eased down a well-worn path?

Will this idea help me and give me what I want? – does this person understand what I want?

- Is success guaranteed?
- Do the benefits outweigh the costs?
- Do the benefits logically arise from the idea?
- Will they give me all that I want?
- Will this idea help me to achieve what is important to me right now?

Am I being unduly pressured? – am I genuinely free to make up my own mind or am I in danger of being pushed into something that I will regret?

- Is this person using blatant sales techniques?

- Are they trying to build up the pressure?
- Do I feel comfortable with this?

The sequence for presenting an idea, product or service to lead the listener comfortably through the cognitive map of decision-making

1. Express the listener's most important objective that you can help them to achieve and make it clear that achieving their objective is the sole topic of your conversation.

2. Explain why they may need to change their behaviour to succeed because the world is changing and what has worked in the past is no longer necessarily as effective in helping them to attain their goals as it once was. Ensure that they understand that you are not dismissing their old behaviour as "wrong". You are merely recognizing that because other people's attitudes and behaviours change what once worked so well meets with opposition today. (If this is not true, if their treasured behaviour is still the best way to get the results that they want, you do not have a case. Why would you want anyone to reject something that works unless you have an idea that will work better? And if you have an idea that will work better there simply have to be problems associated with the old approach. You must sensitively show that it is not a matter of fault, it is merely the result of changing circumstances beyond either the listener's or your control.)

3. Suggest one or two benefits that they will get from simply listening to what you have to say. Limit yourself to one, or at most two. If listening will lead to the listener to enjoy even one benefit, then a reasonable person will be prepared to listen. If, however, you go overboard and list a whole series of benefits, no matter how truthful you may be, you will sound over-anxious and tedious as well as giving the listener the impression that you are trying to push him or her into something that is your interest rather than theirs.

4. Explain your idea in detail. What it is. How it is used. Who has used it. What they say about it. What resources the listener already has to make it work for them. What resources you can contribute to help them to succeed. Deliver a total feature presentation so that the listener fully understands that this product, service or idea infallibly delivers the goods that they desire. Be selective, however, in the details that you decide to offer. If I believe myself to be a great innovator, I will not respond positively to the news that hundreds have already tried the idea. If I am averse to risk I am unlikely to be enthused when you tell me that I will be the first to use the approach that you are are suggesting. It comes back, as it always does, to preparation. And the key to preparation is to know your customer. That is why the best, most successful salespeople listen far more than

they talk. This description, however, assumes that you have done your listening and the time has come to present your case.

5. List the important benefits logically to prove that the listener's objective will definitely be achieved. Use "which means" between benefits to test the logic. If "which means" makes sense your case is logical and it will work.

6. Avoid smart closing techniques. In fact forget any closing technique other than asking politely, but confidently for the order or agreement and then stop talking until the listener says something. They will say "yes" more times than you would imagine to be possible especially if you have found that old-fashioned, product-centred sales techniques don't work for you.

Do the above strictly in the sequence given and your listener will respond by saying: "OK – let's do it".

Summary

Sales techniques have a poor reputation. This is hardly surprising because too many sales techniques are designed to put the buyer on the spot and to increase the pressure until they feel that they have little choice other than to capitulate to the demand that they "buy today". Psychological research suggests that salespeople are too often motivated by their desire to win. They see the prospect as an enemy to be overcome.

Research has shown, however, that where you genuinely have an idea that is in the interest of the listener to accept there is a specific route to agreement that the other person finds both natural and comfortable. Instead of being pushed into making a purchase the buyer is helped to understand exactly what the product, service or idea will do for them. That is ethical influencing and it is more effective than any known combative approach.

No businessperson should ever experience any qualms about developing selling skills. In business we have to sell ideas, products, services, people that we have faith in and, most of all, ourselves. It is essential that you understand the questions and techniques that will make you a superior salesperson.

Every businessperson should recognize that at every step of the process of building conviction it is the *question* that dominates people's thinking.

11

Making change pay

questions of transformation

You cannot manage change. You have to initiate it. Peter Drucker

He is a modest man who has a great deal to be modest about. Winston Churchill (said of Clement Atlee who beat him in the next election)

- Questions that can change a culture.
- The one key question that will get everybody to the barricades when the chips are down.
- Questions that help people to embrace change.
- Questions that show when change is unnecessary.

What you will gain from this chapter

- How to identify when change is needed.
- How to introduce change with the minimum of problems and maximum success.
- How to understand if, when and why people oppose change.

Some important factual questions about change

☑ What are the indicators that change is needed?
  – Are we merely surviving where we ought to be thriving?
  – Are we losing sales in a growing market?

- Are we seriously off target in our attempt to achieve our goals?
- Are we spending too much time solving problems?
- On a scale of 1 to 10 how serious are the problems that we face?

☑ Have complaints from our customers risen?
- By how much have they risen, over what period?

☑ Are we losing good staff?
- Is morale lower than it was a year ago?
- What is our evidence?

☑ Have costs risen?

☑ What would be the cost of bringing in change?
- Have we the money and other resources to implement change effectively?

Behaviour in time of change

"After The World Trade Center nothing will ever be the same again." As the world teeters on the brink of war the doom mongers are out in force prophesying recession or worse. They point to the precipitate response of some airlines and shout, "I told you so". They ignore the fact that anyone like me who regularly flies the Atlantic for less than the cost of a flight to Milan could have told them that the airlines have had problems with their transatlantic routes for years and would have taken action long ago were it not for the fear that a competitor would steal the worthwhile business class part of their business. But when everyone is acting in the same way – no problem. For as long as I can remember automotive manufacturers have questioned the costs and benefits of taking part in the Motor Show. No-one will drop out, however, unless they can be assured that the opposition will not take part. Action is not necessarily an indicator of change. But let's be sensible about this, change is a continuous process and it continues hard and fast.

Peter Drucker added to his fame and attracted my undying affection when, at the end of a three-day conference on "managing change" he rose only to say: "Ladies and Gentlemen you have just wasted three days of precious time. You cannot manage change. You must initiate it".

If you are going to initiate change it might be helpful to understand the motives that drive behaviour in time of change.

Although we blandly say that "people automatically oppose change", this is not entirely true. All through our lives we actively pursue changes. We change jobs, accept promotions, move house, get married or unmarried, have children, leave the parental home and branch out on our own. Change is often an act that indicates personal, business and professional growth.

Sometimes informed opinion is at odds with ignorance where change is concerned. For example, the majority of European business leaders and economists remain in favour of the introduction of the common currency throughout the European Union. Ironically those business leaders who are not in favour tend to be non-Europeans such as Rupert Murdoch who are using populist slogans ("save our pound") to sell newspapers, follow a right wing agenda or both.

Of course, people often do oppose change for either rational or irrational reasons. Psychology suggests three main causes of opposition.

Our everyday behaviour has been moulded by our past successes, great or small

We do what we do because it has worked for us in the past. We value our behaviours because they have made us what we are. Because we value what we have become we are often slow to recognize the need to change. We frequently deny that even major change really impinges on us. So when a take-over occurs we deny the need for change by trying to pretend that the new owners will automatically value the same behaviours as the old. This is true even when the old behaviour may have driven the firm to the brink of bankruptcy, thus forcing the acquisition. This is the denial stage well known to psychologists.

One way to overcome this denial of change is to make change so major that, to put it simply, it gets everyone's attention. At the extreme Bob Townsend, when he took over a company used to seek out the most powerful "pain in the ass" and, regardless of his high position, he would fire him as a clear indicator that the change was real and important. (Cesare Borgia went one further. On one occasion, having taken over the rule of a city, he called the town officials and population to the city square where, without warning, he drew his sword and struck down his own best general and closest companion. He then addressed the crowd. Paraphrasing roughly: "If you dummies think that you can go on just as in the past, forget it. He was my friend, and if I am prepared to do that to him, just think what I have in mind if any of you step out of line.")

The above are fairly extreme examples and not to be followed, but we do need to underline very clearly why a change of behaviour is essential in changing business circumstances, and why change is the only hope of success. ". . . you want job security and I would like job security too. Let me explain something. Did you know that although the average life span of a corporation was around sixty years only ten years ago, business now moves so fast that the average is down to twelve years? We understand how to be one of the survivors, however, and you have an important part to play. The corporations that keep on going are those where people at every level contribute their ideas to make sure that they keep improving the way that they do things. We will always welcome your ideas. We will respect them and use the best of them as quickly as we can."

We fear change and become angry because we fear that we will lose control

Medical research shows that perceived or actual loss of control is the major cause of life-threatening stress.

We can overcome this fear and anger by creating a sense of involvement and control of at least our own small piece of the world. The new science of perception dynamics is aimed at giving people the feeling that they have at least some control over the part of the business that they care about, their own jobs. People do not generally want "empowerment" as it is promoted by "the let my people go" school. What they want is to be listened to when they have an idea about how to do their own job better and, hopefully, more cost effectively. This ties in with the technique outlined above, but if they have been ignored or slapped down in the past, risking the new behaviour may be seen as a high risk. That is why exemplary professional facilitation skills are needed when a company introduces employee ideas workshops. Grim silence or "war stories" are often the alternative outcome if the thing is badly handled.

The cost of change, in terms of extra responsibilities, effort or perceived risk must be paid now

The rewards lie somewhere in the future. We are an "instant gratification society" and we are out of the habit of waiting. Since waiting is now seen as an additional cost we bargain to try and get a better deal.

This is another reason why, when we involve people, it needs very sensitive and skilled facilitation. If we simply appear to encourage the expression of grievances and concerns, we give an impression that we are offering to resolve them. What we need to do instead is to have people tell us: "if we make this work, what do you think would be in it for you?" In this way we emphasize that the "bargain" is that they create their own salvation by doing things in a new and better way and they protect their future by, for example, cutting costs now. What is more, by forcing them to list an impressive range of valued outcomes, we build commitment to the whole enterprise.

- Is there a compelling reason for changing, or are we in danger of changing for change's sake?
  - Are people aware of that reason?
- Are we piling change on change?
  - Are we giving changes enough time to deliver results before we introduce something new on top of untried novelty?
  - Are our people experiencing "change fatigue"?
  - Is the cost of change to the individual greater than the rewards?
- Have people really established what is in it for them if this change is successfully implemented?

- Have we involved enough people in planning the change?
- Have we predicted and put plans in place to deal with anticipated problems?
  - Have those likely to be most affected by the problems been active in their solution?
- Have we refined the change in the light of people's expectations, desires, ambitions and ideas?

The manager who needs to cope with change successfully needs to ask:

- Have I accepted that dealing with changing situations is part of my job?
- Have I got routine work under control so that I can focus on the change?
- Am I sufficiently aware of what is happening in my industry and beyond to know when changes are necessary or beneficial?
  - Do I fully understand the developing and emerging trends?
  - Do I need more information?
  - Do I know where to find what I need?
  - Who can help me?
- Can I stimulate a positive attitude to change by discussing new ideas and issues with my team?
- Do my team raise issues that might indicate the need for change?
- Do I encourage a sufficient degree of future focus without damaging today's results?
- Is my thinking flexible enough?
- Is my leadership style flexible and consistent? (see page 109)
- Can I mobilize my people and resources quickly in a co-ordinated fashion if the unexpected occurs?
- Do I demonstrate that I value creativity over bureaucracy?

Ask those around you when you suspect that change is desirable:

- What's new?
- What do you see as the key issues facing the business?
  - What do you see as our key opportunities?
- What leading edge ideas have you come across lately?
- What would you like to change if you had the power?
  - What are we doing too well to put it at risk?
- What are we doing well that we could do better?
  - How?

- Where could we exert most leverage?
- Where are we falling down on the job?
- If you were a competitor where would you attack us?
- What are the main risks?
- What should we be afraid of?
- What keeps you awake at nights?
- What would keep you awake at nights if you were the worrying kind?

Corporate danger signs

- Out-of-date methods
- Dissatisfied customers
- Late deliveries
- Low volumes
- Low profit margins
- Low productivity
- Dependence on few customers
- Poor industrial relations
- Low morale
- High staff turnover
- Top-heavy management
- Precipitate downsizing
- Industry down turn.

Summary

People respond best to change when they are clear about the reasons why it is necessary right now, understand their contribution and retain a sense of having at least some control. It also helps if they are managed and guided by people who understand the barriers to change and if the management that is leading the change is firm and goals are unambiguous and challenging.

That may seem to be a lot to ask, but in business we ask only for what will make a real difference.

Some readers will have heard of the ancient Roman governor who left a note when he committed suicide that said: "We tried very hard. We incorporated the changes and practised to perfect them – and then they changed it all again."

Always ask the questions that will enable you to give change a chance to work its way through to success and never introduce further change unless the answers that you get convince you utterly that the earlier change is doing harm rather than good.

Lambert's Laws – again

Never consider bringing in a major change until you have the answers to the following questions:

- Will this change make a significant difference to the ability of the business to achieve its goals?
  - Will we achieve our goals more quickly, more cheaply?
- How soon will this pay for itself?
  - Is that soon enough?
  - How can we be sure that it will deliver on time?
  - Is there a less costly way?
  - Would that achieve our goals equally well?
- Will people approach this change with enthusiasm?
  - Will they see what is in it for them?
  - Do they understand the need for change?
  - Do they share the company vision?
  - Can we communicate this change inspirationally?

12
Stop wasting the training budget!

questions of profitable learning

Education, education and education. Tony Blair

The Information Age is already past. Nonaka and Tacheuchi

- Questions to deliver life-long learning – just-in-time.
- Questions to raise the effectiveness of training from near zero to near 100 per cent.
- Questions trainers should ask.
- Questions to ask of trainers.
- Questions to make coaching and mentoring work.

What you will gain from this chapter

- How to make good training pay for itself over and over again.
- How to ensure that all training that you choose to do is good training.
- How to direct training professionals toward making a quantifiable contribution to the success of the organization.
- How to stop wasting money on training.

Some factual questions that some trainers might wish to avoid

☑ How much did training contribute during the last year in pounds or dollars?

☑ What percentage of what is taught is applied in the workplace?

☑ What percentage of training objectives are measured and achieved?

☑ How exactly do you quantify training's contribution?

☑ If delegates were offered additional holiday rather than training, which would they choose?

Building world-class knowledge

World-class organizations are world-class learning communities. Do not be misled by the often meaningless, arguments of the worst sort of trainer and become convinced that training and development are unimportant. We may not need to do more training, but we certainly need to do better training because in an economy that increasingly succeeds on the back of the application of new, but proven, knowledge, life-long learning is not merely an option, it is mandatory if you want to succeed.

With this background it is a tragedy that too much training is in the hands of the glib and the lazy. The attitude implicit in one manager's response to the news that I was taking over training may ring some bells for other line managers who see their people expensively trained to return only to do things exactly as they did them before. The late Don Hambrook is reported to have said: "Great idea. Now that he is a trainer they will stop listening to the bolshie swine. And he'll soon stop trying to change things." Much as I respected Don I hope and believe that he was wrong on both counts. I think they still listen and if being bolshie means that I seek by every method that I can find to do things and have them done better, then I am still "bolshie".

Research

Lucier and Torsilieri

This research programme emphasizes organizational change, rather than the individual transfer of knowledge, but it makes a number of key points. What follows is a summary of the findings and the practical questions that those findings imply. (Findings are in bold.)

It is possible to transform a business through the systematic building and use of the best knowledge throughout the firm.

- Do we encourage the sharing of knowledge or do we inadvertently reward hoarding of information?
  - Do we allow the time and facilities for the sharing of knowledge?

- Are all our people enthusiastic to share what they have learned with their colleagues?
- Have we developed a real learning community?
- Are we prepared to organize the sharing of knowledge and information?
- Are senior management at the highest level ready to share their knowledge?

The organization must learn to learn in a structured way so that people are constantly learning how to learn together.

- Do we follow all learning activities with timely peer coaching to ensure that learning is transferred to the workplace?
- Do our people attend training and development in mutually supportive pairs or teams?
- Do all learning objectives clearly state what people are expected to learn and how they will apply it?
- Do we accept that there may be a short-term fall-off in performance while new knowledge and skills are integrated?

Learning must be related to a specific business objective, not to generalized aspirations.

- Are management, supervision and work teams at every level aware of the business goals and their contribution to achieving them?
- Is training and development a strategic activity specifically designed to meet business objectives rather than a mini "business school" that teaches the well-worn subjects because they always have?
- Can we demonstrate that every training needs analysis activity shows what objectives training will play a major part in attaining?
- Do our supervision position employees effectively before all development activities and debrief and coach them to ensure that they use, share and develop what they have learned?
- Is success always celebrated?

Learning must be undertaken within a "total programme architecture" which includes knowledge and application of effective group and change dynamics.

- Are all employees aware of and committed to the strategic plan?
- Do they understand their personal and group contribution?
- Do they welcome the challenge of striving to become and remain the best of the best?

- Do our managers understand and apply the principles of change dynamics as they apply to this company with its unique culture?
- Have we developed our own process of change?
- What is our evidence that it works?
- Is there a better way?

An example from FedEx (described in detail in Chapter 4).

1. Have work groups affected by change specify what is in it for them if "rough change concept" is effectively implemented. So that they feel as positive as possible about the change from the very beginning and are determined to make it work. Should not employees feel the same way about training? Should they not evaluate training in terms of "what is in this for me?" – and if the answer is "a day or several away from the workplace" is there not something seriously wrong with both the workplace and the training?

2. Specify concerns not as grievances, but as problems to be solved in order to enjoy the benefits of change. Avoid "war stories" and "hidden agendas", but involve people in thinking through what barriers to success will have to be removed.

3. Have teams self-select to find solutions to anticipated major difficulties. Let those with the greatest interest and motivation take responsibility for finding solutions and build the commitment to making solutions effective.

4. Incorporate solutions into change plan.

5. Refine and implement change.

Focus must be on no more than one or two strategic priorities at a time.

- Are we ever guilty of piling change on change to the degree that none is given the time or concentration that it needs to work?
- What systems/attitudes do we have in place to avoid repeating that expensive mistake?
- How specifically will we ensure that everyone focuses on what is important right now in terms of achieving the strategy?
- Have our people learned the value of focusing on developing our strengths rather than mitigating our weaknesses?
- Have we developed a culture of ongoing improvement rather than blame fixing?

Top management must sponsor the initiative because it is a change initiative and if top management do not drive change, who does?

- Are our top management team all committed to being the best of the best in every aspect of the business?
- If not, whom do we have to bring "on board"?
- How specifically will we achieve consensus at senior level without becoming the victims of "groupthink"?

Learning must be measured in terms of the most important factors creating competitive advantage – total cost per unit, asset or employee productivity, sales revenues and profits, new customers attracted.

- Is learning recognized as being a means to an end rather than as something vaguely pleasing for its own sake? (Example: John Egan in his Jaguar days required that all budgets include 10 per cent to facilitate learning so that money was invariably spent effectively.)
- Do we have all necessary measures routinely in place?
- Can our training department put a pound or dollar value on all of their activities?

Summary

My one-time colleague Liese Spiegelberg Tamburrino used to be a vice president of training and education in General Electric. Over a four-year period careful measurement showed that, following training, the average annual improvement in productivity for every employee was 14 per cent. Even in a country in which productivity per worker is increasing at a rate that is twice as fast as most of the rest of the advanced economies, identification of a direct link between training and productivity growth that is two-and-a-half times the national average is significant. It demonstrates the potential that training has to make a difference, but only if it is done properly – if what is learned is transferred to the workplace and used.

Bruce Joyce – University of Columbia, New York

According to methodology used, unsupported training provides a level of transfer to the workplace of between 5 per cent (chalk and talk) and 13 per cent (realistic "practical learning").

Through conference room emphasis on real world problem solving, participants can appear to learn and use up to 80 per cent of the materials taught, in respect of the problem dealt with, but there is little evidence of successful transfer of that knowledge to other problems other than to the very limited degree noted above. While people are adept at using what they are taught in the classroom as long as it appears to make sense in the real world of their experience, there is no evidence that they are generally able to extrapolate to other equally relevant situations without some form of post-training support.

- Can our training people, internal or external, demonstrate convincingly that the methods that they use deliver the optimum level of application of learning in the workplace?
  - What were the training objectives?
  - What must we measure to get the true picture?
    Productivity?
    Time saved?
    Pound/dollar value to the business of problems solved?
    Employee morale?
    Cost savings?
    Sales revenues increased?
    Customer satisfaction?
    Customer retention?
    Profitability?
- If they cannot measure results, is it not time that they were made to?

Xerox

Regardless of methodology, on average 87 per cent of the learning that is transferred to the workplace is lost within twelve weeks if learning is unsupported. (Let me be clear about this, combining Joyce's findings with those of Xerox there is compelling evidence that the "bog standard" every-day training course in which you invest delivers to the workplace, within three months of leaving the conference room, 13 per cent of 13 per cent (1.69 per cent) return on your training investment. Even that low figure is only true if you believe that the whole programme was relevant and worth the overall cost. If some part of the programme was amusing though not particularly useful it is within the bounds of possibility that some of what is remembered and transferred serves very little purpose. I have investigated cases where a heavy reliance on training films that emphasize what not to do more amusingly than they demonstrate the desired behaviour have led to some people, a minority it must be admitted, taking the comedian's antics as a role model for future behaviour.) You might like to ask yourself and then your training people where else that level of return is considered to be acceptable in a business?

- Should we, as an absolute minimum, test how much is learned on all training courses, how much is used at the workplace and how much that which is used contributes to achieving a strategic or tactical goal?

Seward and Gers

In a twelve-year longitudinal study Seward and Gers raised learning transfer to an average of better than 95 per cent and held it there, by:

- Relating training to a specific strategic or tactical goal.

- Ensuring management's informed support by means of a concise, but thorough introduction to what was to be taught and how it was relevant to the attainment of important strategic and tactical needs.

- Ensuring that delegates attended training where possible in self-selected, mutually supportive pairs sharing tactical and strategic goals.

- Integrating peer and supervisor coaching skills and expectations into all programmes.

- Strictly applying behavioural objectives. (Objectives stressed what the delegates "will do" NOT "will be able to do" on completion of the training.)

- Requiring that responsibility for both learning and ensuring application were firmly placed on the shoulders of the trainer, not the learner.

- Warning learners that a short-term fall-off in performance is a normal part of the learning process that is quickly overcome.

- Persuading learners to expect major productivity and quality gains once the learning barrier had been overcome.

- Supplying post-learning information and tools to facilitate ongoing peer coaching.

- Providing a decreasing time schedule during working hours to enable peer and supervisor coaching based on celebrating successful application rather than fault-finding.

- Introducing and supporting mutual contracting to implement and share learning.

- Should we review our training to ensure that it meets the requirements of effective peer and supervisor coaching to ensure transfer of learning to the workplace?

  - Can our internal or external professional trainers develop a method that improves on Seward and Gers results at lower cost?

  - If they can do neither what are we paying them for?

Perception dynamics – Ian Robson

By changing the perception of participants concerning the ownership of learning Robson increased transfer, initially by 30 per cent, and after advice from the author by more than 90 per cent, as measured by quantified financial and non-financial measures.

- Who owns learning in this business?
- How do our people perceive the ownership of what they learn at our expense – or their own?
- Why do people think that they are sent on training courses?
- How do we build a practical learning community based on life-long learning – just-in-time and the enthusiastic and effective use of what is learned?

Improving sales performance – Lambert, Miller et al.

Working with a major insurance company in the UK increased sales revenues by 200 per cent within one year of the training of the sales teams.

The initial study involved three groups – one that received training plus two controls. One control group were given extra cash incentives, the other was given neither training nor potential higher earnings. For three months following training the corporation's external auditors measured the sales performance of the three groups.

The untrained, "unincentivized" group's sales revenues fell by 5 per cent, the other control group increased their sales revenues, short term, by 16 per cent followed by a sharp decline toward the pre-incentive norm.

- The trained group increased sales by 180 per cent.
- After the positive experimental approach, all groups were trained, leading to a year-on-year increase in revenues of 200 per cent.
- Training was limited in duration to one- to two-day programmes, but the number of programmes was subsequently increased to create a developing curriculum supported by "between courses" reinforcement.
- Is it worthwhile for us to treat training initially as a "scientific experiment" and measure the results before rolling out programmes?
- Who, in our organization can produce reliable measures of training effectiveness?
- Who has the capacity to do so without having a vested interest in the outcome? (If you use trainers they are likely to suggest that you have the best of outcomes in the best of all possible worlds. If you look to external "experts" they will have every reason to assure you that nothing is as it should be and that they and they

alone have the answer that you need. Honest brokers are a rarity in a world where too many "experts" have an axe to grind.)

■ How much did we waste on training in the last twelve months? (Another "Killer Question" that I have asked business leaders in Europe and the USA. Invariably the first response is one of shocked silence that is followed by at first a trickle, then a torrent as senior managers catalogue wasted investment and opportunity.)

Mary Broad

The main thrust of Broad's research is into why individuals lose what they have learned and how to reduce the problem. She suggests that there is a normal plateauing of any learning and when participants are not pre-warned that this is a normal part of the learning process they become discouraged and stop using what they have learned.

■ Do we permit anyone in our organization at any level to discourage the application of learning?

■ Do we give new learning sufficient time to bear fruit or do we pile learning on learning just as some organizations pile change on change?

■ Do we ensure that all learners and their management understand the dynamics of applying what is learned and are not pushed off course by a temporary fall in performance?

■ Is learning seen as being a practical tool at every level?

■ Are we ready to implement a practical policy of "Life-long Learning – Just in Time" so that our people learn what they need when the organization needs it, apply it immediately after learning, share it with their colleagues and persevere until new learning is easier to apply than the old way of doing things?

A final review of research

In an extended area of organizational rather than student research Lambert also found that:

■ Organizations frequently insist on speed rather than quality of actions so that individuals are driven to continue to apply old ideas and behaviours that enable quick, though sub-optimal, performance.

■ Individuals at every organizational level, overvalue behaviour that has led to past successes and considerably underestimate the changes in the situation that indicate the need for new behaviours as circumstances change. With the acceleration of the business cycle, changes will become more frequent, increasingly diverse and capable of having a greater effect on the business. The "freezing" by successful groups that leads to the re-use of a tried and tested, but no longer relevant formula will become increasingly dangerous to the business.

■ Colleagues and supervision are threatened by new skills and the newly trained are under peer and management pressure to make less than optimal use of what they have learned.

■ With an accelerating business cycle the need for quick results is becoming essential rather than merely short-term thinking. In this situation the need for training and development is growing, but the need is not for "education for its own sake" or even for "life-long learning". It is for life-long learning delivered, applied, measured and proved – "just-in-time".

Whether you are a training professional, or an executive who believes in or doubts the value of training, ask yourself this killer question often:

■ How much did we waste on training in the last twelve months?

mini case study

Some years ago I was invited by a major corporation to report on why their expensive TQM (yes it was some years ago) programme delivered few if any benefits. I discovered that the sequence of events had been as follows.

First, the company had hired consultants to put in place a Quality Circle programme. To ease the transition the consultants had agreed with senior management that no improvement was to be put into place without first being presented to a committee of executives for detailed analysis and approval. There had been a major and vital problem that had put massive demands on the time of those same executives as they, unsuccessfully as it turned out, sought a solution. As a result, the Quality Circles met and delivered suggestions for improvement. With no time for analysis and approval no improvements reached the implementation stage, but a very considerable backlog of good, bad and indifferent ideas grew. Within the backlog was the solution to the problem that was taking up so much of management's time, but for the harassed executives there was no way of knowing this. As a result the top team concluded that, "Quality Circles don't work".

Since quality is clearly a "good thing" a different approach had to be tried. An engineer was seconded to the training division and was flown away to sit at the feet of Juran and learn all about quality. He returned full of enthusiasm for the considerable amount of enlightening and inspirational stuff that he had learned about the psychology of work and designed a training programme that focused entirely on sharing his new knowledge, first with his new colleagues (many of whom had their own rather different views), and then with the willing, but confused workforce who could not quite see what this all had to do with the price of fish. One thing was clear. Quality Circles were a thing of the past and psychology rules whether relevant or no. But what cannot be measured cannot be managed so few, if any benefits were recorded.

It was next suggested that "since what cannot be measured cannot be managed" a programme of statistical process control should be implemented. A highly qualified team from a relatively local, but very widely respected technical university was given the task of teaching statistical process control to the manufacturing workforce of some several thousand men and women of widely divergent educational attainment and experience. The highly qualified team understood the mathematics, but failed to understand the business. As a result the workers made no use of what was taught, but it was clearly seen to be in place of "all that psychological nonsense" which was now firmly set aside.

On the assumption that quality was still something of a Holy Grail to be sought, the Crosbie organization were invited to produce a "sheep dip" programme to involve all managers. The costs of approximately £1 million (DM3 million) were to be shared between a British and a German division. It did little for the credibility of the team in the eyes of delegates from the automotive world that the leader of those conducting the workshops made it clear that he had last managed a failed motorcycle manufacturer before being recruited into the world of TQM. (That manufacturer that is fondly believed by the automotive industry to have responded to the Japanese challenge by fixing an ashtray to a motorcycle fuel tank.) Those executives that I interviewed who attended the workshops told me that they had learned that "quality is a good thing and that they ought to be planning to do something about it", but they had been left uncertain as to what to do.

What they did was to seek guidance from the Deming Institute, not with the clear information of what had gone before, but giving the impression that they were starting with a clean sheet. The Deming people never stood a chance. Employees at every level had by now developed what I call the "bus queue syndrome" – the belief that this is merely the most recent of a never ending line of arrivals that can be safely ignored if necessary because "there will be another along in a few minutes". The expensive implementation of BS 5750 (ISO 9000) met with a similar display of indifference for the same reason.

Change had been piled on change with the effect that no change, no matter how potentially useful, that could be traced back with the most flimsy reasoning to appear to have a relationship to what had gone before stood a chance of effective implementation. After all, as everybody knew, "there will be another one along in a minute".

The danger is that unless someone is asking the difficult questions training may be piled on training until delegates take the view that "this does not have to be taken seriously. There will be another sheep dip of new knowledge to go through very soon." Once people take that view training will have the same value to them as to the junior supervisor who, when asked why he was attending a training programme answered: "I think I'm being victimized".

Ask yourself

Do we unwittingly suggest to our people that they can ignore this piece of training because there will be another along in a minute that appears to contradict this?

What is knowledge management?

Closely related to training and development is the concept of knowledge management. This is the systematic and systemized gathering, transfer and use of the knowledge that exists within and beyond an organization. It is, in effect, a living library of knowledge resource accessible to all who need it within the organization and accessible to all genuine stakeholders.

The background

In the mid- to late 1990s as Japan slipped from its position of global trade dominance, two academics Nonaka and Tacheuchi sought ways to return to Japanese business a leading edge comparable to that delivered by Total Quality Management in the three decades following World War II. They suggested that the "information age" was already past and that just as information had to go beyond mere data, "knowledge" needed to transcend mere information (see page xiv). They suggested that the "tacit" information within a business (the ideas, creativity, beliefs, expectations, assumptions and hunches of its employees), were as important as the "explicit" information of fact and needed to be captured and used. This initial idea has now developed to where the "tacit" information concerning employees is now widened to include the same levels of knowledge concerning customers, suppliers, distributors and leading businesses in other sectors.

Business purpose of KM

Fully applied knowledge management enables the firm to:

- Adjust the strategy on a timely basis.
- Anticipate and respond to important customer desires as they emerge.
- Involve all stakeholders, including suppliers and distributors in the achievement of the strategy.
- "Leapfrog" competition by implementing and improving on true "global best practice".
- Structure large amounts of information for use by disparate work teams and communities globally.
- Accelerate organizational and individual learning.
- Create a working community committed to "lifelong learning – just-in-time".
- Improve processes, practices and workflow.
- Reduce costs while increasing productivity and quality.
- Do away with perceived "information overload".

The drawbacks

- Knowledge management is, of necessity, systems based and the systems are usually either complex or too limited in scope to be meaningful.
- Knowledge management demands enthusiastic transfer and application by all whose efforts are needed to make it work and the existing culture may require a major re-think before all are enabled or motivated to "buy in" to the system.
- The complexities of the system encourage its use to be limited to "knowledge workers".
- Individuals are often concerned that they are being driven by a system that is out of their control. "Their job" is in danger of merely becoming "the job".

Availability of systems

As with all new business concepts there are a growing number of software firms offering products and consultancy services. Institutes have been set up, some under the full ownership and management of software and hardware suppliers. The difficulty is one of finding an "honest broker" or of having your CIO help the board to investigate a wide range of systems and pick that which most simply and comprehensively meets specified needs.

Establishing a comprehensive and effective knowledge management system usually involves a considerable investment of both time and resources. It is therefore a board responsibility to decide whether the management of knowledge within the business is the best use of resources right now.

Questions for boards to consider

- Do we want and need to systemize the collection, transfer and use of tacit and explicit knowledge?
- What is competition doing?
- Are we keeping abreast of the emerging expectations and desires of our worthwhile customers?
- Are our people and our culture ready for this?
- Do we share at board level a burning desire to dominate our markets that demands that we win the knowledge race?
- Can we accurately assess the need and can we forecast with confidence how quickly we may expect a suitable return on both the financial investment and time required to implement this approach?

- Do we understand the benefits and pitfalls of a systemized approach to KM?
- Are we, as a board, ready to provide the right kind of leadership to make this a success?
- Are we all prepared to let go of the old belief that "power flows to he who knows"?
- If we were to consider implementing a full knowledge management approach would it be because:
  - There is a meaningful business reason for doing it right now?
  - It will pay for itself in a reasonable time?
  - It can be explained in simple and motivational terms to those who must make it work?

How well do we manage knowledge today – a self assessment

Instructions

Against each question give your business a score as follows:

We are totally unsuccessful or unaware of the need (unsatisfactory)	0
We are aware of the need, but perform badly (poor)	1
We are as good as most, but better than none (fair)	2
We could, and do, show competition a thing or two (good)	3
We are the best of the best (excellent)	4

1. Are our people at level committed to sharing knowledge? _____
2. Do we use all the knowledge that exists in the business in a timely and effective way? _____
3. Do operations, departments and divisions co-operate to deliver "communities of best practice"? _____
4. Are we able to actively measure our knowledge performance? _____
5. Are we developing the competencies that we require to fully exploit today's best markets? _____
6. Have we identified the competencies that we will require to fully exploit the best markets of the future? _____
7. Are we able to convincingly imagine, anticipate and invent the future of our business? _____
   - Are we able to create "smart" products and services? _____
8. Have we been able to significantly cut the lead-time from "mind to market"? _____

9. Are we fully abreast of competitive thinking and activity on a timely basis? _____

10. Are we more successful in creating, developing and protecting intellectual property assets than competition? _____

11. Can we demonstrate an ability to build customer loyalty by anticipating, understanding and fulfilling their changing desires? _____

12. Do we have a "continuous learning organization"? _____

13. Are we able to provide our customers, suppliers, distributors and employees with online service and support at minimum cost? _____

14. Have we constructed a corporate knowledge centre? _____

15. Are we adept at exploiting e-knowledge marketplaces and online knowledge exchanges? _____

(Note: Two examples of online "knowledge exchanges" are www.pals.co.uk and www.palsZenith.com where peers and subject experts can come together to exchange ideas to build an international knowledge community committed to sharing and enhancing global best practice.)

16. Could we claim that we have enabled our people at every level to develop and use dynamic, agile, timely and adaptive "sense and respond" capabilities? _____

17. Have we enabled the empowerment of our people within a fully understood framework and with due consideration of their maturity and capabilities? _____

18. Are our processes making full use of knowledge based engineering? _____

19. Are our people constantly producing and sharing new knowledge relevant to the needs of the business? _____

20. Are we better at managing intangible assets such as brands, reputation, image and customer loyalty than competition? _____

21. Do we nurture working teams committed to "working" rather than "warring" competition? _____

22. Are all our people committed to "life-long learning just-in-time"? (Are they devoted to the application, testing and sharing of learning?) _____

23. Are our teams adaptable enough to avoid becoming victims of their own success? (We have the formula and it's always worked, so why consider change?) _____

24. Is our practised leadership style appropriate and the reasoning behind it understood by our people? _____

25. Do our people assume that unpopular decisions are based on valid reasoning? _____

26. Are we adept at "sell and make" rather than "make and sell"? _____

27. Are we finding ways to replace inventories with knowledge? _____

28. Are we skilled at developing and using scenarios in planning and training? _____

29. Have we converted operational know-how into process assets that give us a clear differentiation from competition and a recognized leading edge in our markets? _____

30. Are we first to market when first to market is important? _____

31. Do we use knowledge to reduce risk? _____

32. Are we optimizing our human and intellectual capital? _____

This is not one of those tests that seek to "read your palm" and tell your future, nor is it in the nature of those that say: "if you have marked any question with a zero you need to talk to us about our knowledge management products and consultancy services". It is intended to help the Board to think through this relatively new discipline from a business viewpoint and to make some early judgements. However, if you score less than 128 in total you would be well advised to look at each item that you have given your organization less than 4 and consider what steps you will need to take to stay ahead of the pack. Knowledge management has the capability of delivering superior competitive advantage, but not all systems are of equal quality.

- If you have a knowledge management system in place is it delivering all the potential benefits expressed or implied in the above?

- If you do not have something in place, should you be thinking of it?

- Are the potential benefits compelling in today's business environment?

- Do you need more information from inside or outside the organization in order to make an informed decision?

- Are there gaps in your management and application of knowledge that you should and can address without unnecessary investment?

- If you, after considerable due diligence, decide to invest what benefits, cost-savings and outcomes should you expect?

It is hoped that the assessment may be useful in any discussions with vendors or consultants, reminding members of the top team to ask:

- *How exactly will your product help to give us......................*

- *What does it provide that others do not?*

- *What are the drawbacks in its development or use?*

A simple game plan for success

- Do your homework first.
- Fully assimilate knowledge management into your off-line and online strategic plan.
- Have clear tactical and strategic objectives consistent with the overall business strategy.
- Organize your content for simplicity of retrieval and application.
- Invest heavily in content maintenance.
- Anticipate and initiate change.
- Build the culture in advance.
- Maximize the use of the firm's knowledge resources. Do not leave it to the "techies", knowledge workers, specialists and external advisors.

Conclusion

- Knowledge management has come a long way since the early days, only a couple of years ago. It has, in the best cases, shown itself to be capable of delivering massive present benefits and offers great promise for future commercial and competitive advantage.
- In common with most new ideas it attracts those who seek short-term profits from every fad, fallacy, fake and fairground bunco fraud that emerges.

- It is essential that the board consider KM with the maximum diligence. It is hoped that this unavoidably short, outline provides a basis of careful assessment and decision-making.

Summary

Too much money is wasted on training. The waste results almost entirely from a combination of laziness and ignorance. As a trainer myself I know how exhausting it can be to carry out training effectively. But the fact that something is difficult is no excuse for failure. As the late Ian Mikado pointed out there is no satisfaction to be gained from the fact that Christianity, like socialism has been found to be so difficult that its teachings have not been implemented for the better part of two thousand years.

Trainers are generally too eager to embrace any methodology that enables the delegates to engage in activities that require little or no input from the trainer. They are also given to establishing so-called objectives that state what a trainee will "be able to do" after training rather than take any responsibility for ensuring that what should be done is done.

The situation is compounded by managers who are too lazy and too ignorant to insist that trainers do what they are paid for and supervisors who are unwilling to do what they must to ensure a return on the training budget. The result is money down the drain and, believe me, the wasted money will be the smallest loss if we continue to tolerate "training for training's sake".

13

When others have the answers

questions of choosing and using consultants

If every consultant in the world were laid end to end – it would not surprise me. Robert Townsend

Consultants don't just borrow your watch to tell you the time. They steal it to sell to the next client who also doesn't need to know what time it is either. Howard Shenson

■ Questions that test the consultant's skills and knowledge.

■ Questions to clear away the b***s£$£!

■ The essential questions all professional advisors should ask you.

■ The key questions that you should ask yourself.

What you will gain from this chapter

■ The questions that will enable you to identify and assign the right consultants.

■ The questions and information that could save you a small (or a large) fortune.

■ A clear view of when and how to use external advisors.

■ The questions that consultants will wish you had never asked.

Factual questions about outside advisors

☑ The last time that you used external advisors what was the financial value of the benefits that you enjoyed?

☑ How long did it take to enjoy the benefits?

☑ What percentage of the work done was completed using your own resources?

☑ Can you specify in detail what valuable lessons your people learned from the experience?

☑ Did the consultants leave you with all the tools and knowledge required to continue the work yourselves?

☑ How often did the consultants accurately report progress?

Should I use consultants?

A good and frequently asked question, but one that can only be answered after thinking through a few others that may save you money and grief. Too many managers and executives employ consultants without sufficient thought, with the result that dissatisfaction with the results is often rife, but infrequently expressed. If a manager has spent tens of thousands of pounds or dollars on doing the firm more harm than good they are unlikely to want to talk about the failure. They tend instead to try to persuade themselves and others that things are not as bad as they appear. So the consultant adds the organization's name to his or her client list and moves on to wreak havoc elsewhere.

OK, that is only one side of an often-complex question. Consultants frequently do excellent work and deliver far more than they are strictly paid to do. When that happens it is often down to the client in that they knew in advance what they wanted of a consultant and why the consultant was the right person for the job. Usually this can only be achieved by considering the right questions.

Thought starters

Do we know precisely what we want to achieve?	☐ Yes	☐ No	
Do we lack the people or the expertise to do it ourselves?	☐ Yes	☐ No	
Would it be less than optimal use of our people's time to do it ourselves right now?	☐ Yes	☐ No	
Is what we want to do a real priority right now?	☐ Yes	☐ No	
Would the use of external expertise fast-track the development of our people?	☐ Yes	☐ No	

Are we convinced that there is not a more economical way to develop our people? ☐ Yes ☐ No

Would such development give us a real competitive edge in the real world? ☐ Yes ☐ No

Do we have a clear understanding of how we will use our competitive advantage to damage competition and/or attract worthwhile customers? ☐ Yes ☐ No

Is the cost of using consultants the best use of limited resources right now? ☐ Yes ☐ No

Are we prepared to face up to and use anything that might emerge from an external review? ☐ Yes ☐ No

Are we confident that no key decision-maker will become defensive or protect his "turf"? ☐ Yes ☐ No

Are we confident that we can deliver a "brief" that will ensure that the consultant understands our needs? ☐ Yes ☐ No

Do we know (or know how to find) the right consultants to do the job most effectively and economically? ☐ Yes ☐ No

Do we want to work with these people? ☐ Yes ☐ No

Can we afford the fees? ☐ Yes ☐ No

Have we worked out the cash flow implications of the simple fact that we pay fees now to enjoy benefits later? ☐ Yes ☐ No

Are we prepared and able to live with the time that it will inevitably take consultants to learn about our business? ☐ Yes ☐ No

Only when the answer to each question is an unconditional "yes" can you be certain that this is the right time to use consultants. For any question that you have answered "no" think through what you need to do to change that answer to "yes". No matter what the problem or opportunity, you will get the best out of consultants only when you are fully prepared to use them for optimal effect.

Failing to brief consultants properly can sometimes produce results that are grossly uncomfortable and occasionally fatal. In a wise and witty booklet published by Deloitte Consulting and available free from their website www.dc.com they describe what it is like to let consultants loose in your business and hope for the best. In essence they suggest (with a few additions of my own) that:

- You no longer understand your company's culture because consultants have changed it to the extent that it bears little if any resemblance to "the way we do things around here".

- You are so confused by the rate of apparently unguided change that you sometimes doubt your ability to even remember how you used to do things.

- Your key people don't have time to work any more. They are too busy attending meetings with consultants.

- At most of the meetings the consultants show fancy graphics that no-one understands and that no-one cares to challenge just in case they make sense.

- The rest of the meeting is taken up by the consultants either asking you or telling you what should be done next.

- No-one that you meet in canteen or corridor seems to be older than 23 and they all seem to think that they know more about your business than you do.

- You can't find a space in your once roomy car park because it is now filled with cars that you and your colleagues would love to be able to afford to drive.

- All of your most reliable staff seem to have been laid off to be replaced by consultants.

- Staff cuts and other economies would be saving millions were it not for the fact that the total saving is less than the consultant's monthly bill.

- There is a very real sense of fear that to challenge a cocky 23-year-old about anything would be a dangerous enterprise.

- Someone in the top team is riding shotgun on the consultant bandwagon and is making macho threats to anyone who challenges the usefulness of what is being done.

- The few employees that you have left are wondering why they earn less in a month than the consultant's bill for a day.

- You wonder whether you are too old to become a consultant.

Just in case you think that I and the people at Deloitte are exaggerating, as of course we are – just a little, try reading *Dangerous Company* by O'Shea and Madigan, or my own *High Value Consulting* for some real life cases of consulting turning once prosperous organizations belly-up.

After consideration of all the above ask yourself the following:

- *The last time that we brought consultants in on a project did they fail?*

If your answer is "yes", even a doubtful "yes", it is essential to take a long cool look at why they failed.

- What specifically went wrong?
- Did the consultants lack competence?
- Where you or they uncertain of the necessary outcomes?
- Did they send "boys" to do a "man's job"?
- Did you try to do the job "on the cheap"?
- Did you fail, for whatever reason, to establish and maintain managerial control?
- Were there too many meetings and not enough action?
- Did the consultants withhold bad news?
- Did they try to "report over your head" rather than confront you if the problem lay at your door?
- If you hire consultants again what will you do differently?

If any subordinate has responsibility for deciding whether to employ outside help you may wish to ask him or her the questions rather than to just mull them over yourself, but they need to be seriously considered.

Interviewing consultants

If you are face to face with a prospective consultant that knows the business they will try to interview you. They will ask, and they have excellent reasons for asking:

- Have you used consultants before?
- What did you like about the experience?
- What did you dislike?
- What would be your ideal outcome or solution to this assignment?
- What do you regard as being practically possible?

The consultant's reasons for these questions should be:

- If you have used consultants before you will be more inclined to use consultants again – indeed some people, particularly in government, become "consultant junkies". If you do not use consultants as a rule, they know that they must make clear to you not only the value of using their services, but of using consultants in general.

- Whatever you felt good about they will promise more of when they work for you.

- The proposal or sales pitch will show how those things that gave you problems before will be avoided this time so that you can buy their services with confidence.

- The good consultant will get as close to your ideal outcome as they can without risking over-promising and under-delivering.

- As long as they can reasonably expect to do better than this "practically possible" situation they can expect to have a satisfied client at the end of the assignment.

If you are not very careful the consultant will do nothing other than ask you a series of, sometimes relevant, questions in order to maintain control of the discussion. In their delightful little handbook: *How to Get the Most Out of Your Consultant*, Deloitte Consulting suggest that the following should be thrown in by you to obtain essential information and to throw the consultant off a well-beaten track. The publication of these questions suggests that Deloitte, being a highly professional bunch, have well-rehearsed answers at their fingertips, but the questions are still useful.

- What don't you do well? Any consultant or consultancy that proposes itself as being the ultimate in all the complex areas of a business is kidding either themselves or their clients. We all are stronger in some things than in others and self-awareness has many virtues. However, the thoughtful consultant will pick an area either far removed from your assignment or that is so esoteric that you are never likely to require services in that area.

- Name a client that you wouldn't give as a reference. Why? You need people who are honest and have the ability to learn. That means that they have recognized and learned from a mistake when they have made one.

- How do you plan to leave at the end of the assignment? If the consultant cannot show that they are planning, from the start, to work themselves out of a job and go on to bigger and better things, they probably are not very good at doing much other than imitate a leech. You need to understand just how you will be more autonomous at the end of the assignment than you were at the beginning. If you don't you may find yourself with an expensive friend for life and little to show for it.

- If I don't hire you which of your competitors should I hire and why? This really is a trick question. The ill-prepared will avoid the question. The stupid will blurt out an unnecessary recommendation for a competitor. The smart may just take the opportunity to convince you that they, and they alone, are the people to hire.

Once you have the consultant's attention you might wish to ask:

- What have you learned about our important customers?
- Who would you rate as our most threatening competitor(s)?
- Have you ever tried to talk to our call-centre? What did you conclude?
- What do you think of our website?
- What do you think of the places where we sell our products?
- Who would you consider to be the experts on our industry?

You may or may not receive real pearls of wisdom in response to these questions, but you will at least know that they either have, or have not, taken the trouble to do a little homework.

mini case study

the "lost" Australian

When George Feiger was heading McKinsey in the United Kingdom he quickly assessed that British people, having been the recipients of appalling soap operas from Australia tended to assume that Australians were not the brightest lamps in the street. When visiting a potential client, George took advantage of this undeserved low opinion by getting "lost" on his way to the meeting. As he asked his way he chatted to a random sample of employees and he would add their comments about the firm to his understanding of the industry, the firm's reputation among suppliers and customers and the strengths and weaknesses of competition. He had done his homework and then put a little cream onto the top of the trifle. As a result he reached the meeting almost certainly better informed about real attitudes in the organization than were the directors he was to address.

If you want to hire consultants that can fast-track the learning process and show a real interest in your business the "lost" Australian might be the role model for those that you hire. So ask questions such as the above that will assure you that the consultants that you are hiring have taken the trouble to learn a little about your business. If they take the trouble to learn before billing you, they are likely to be quick learners when you are paying them to learn – and you nearly always have to pay them to learn about the specifics of your business.

The learning curve costs money – and it is your money

When I was running a consultancy in the USA the delight that the client experienced at the end of an assignment was often less influential on their decision to hire us again when something bigger and better turned up than the simple fact that they did not have to pay us to learn about their business a second time. They would add to their brief something along the lines of "what has changed since last time" which helped to remind me, if I needed reminding that their situation was neither what it had been, nor was it just like some other client's situation. In some crucial ways their needs were absolutely unique to them.

You need more than detachment

If you consider the use of consultants you need to be assured that they will tell it just like it is. You need a detached, objective view of your business. You also need, however, to have an honest and trusted advisor, so that when things are not as they should be he or she brings the problem and its possible solution to you even where the objective view is that you are personally responsible for causing some or all of the problem. You need a "team-mate" who will do whatever it takes to make you and your team successful and you need an honest critic who makes you face up to difficult decisions.

It is worth asking the prospective consultant the questions:

- On an assignment where does your ultimate loyalty lie?
- If you found that I was the cause of the problem what exactly would you do?
- How would you contact my superiors if you thought that was necessary?

Even if you receive the answers:

- To the company and since you represent the company to you personally.
- I would come directly to you, without discussing the matter elsewhere and work with you until we found a solution.
- Only through you and with you.

Be careful, we consultants ought to be fast on our feet and come up with satisfactory answers. If you don't receive answers similar to these, however, be very careful indeed. The balance that is essential to your working relationship may be difficult to establish and impossible to maintain.

| *mini case study* |

Figgie Corporation – consultants can be bad for your health

The Figgie Corporation had been the darling of Wall Street. It had grown from modest beginnings to become a billion dollar operation with a wide range of products and services. It had grown to be a complex conglomerate with products and services ranging from aircraft parts to paper cups. It was moderately profitable, but the expectations of investors had not been fully recognized and Wall Street was increasingly unwilling to support acquisitions as unquestioningly as they had in the past. On revenues of $1.3 billion they were enjoying profits of around $65 million a year on average. Not bad, but not good enough.

The boss of the corporation was an autocrat who had been a consultant before he took on a real job. He decided that hiring consultants would cure what ailed him. He hired first one, then most, of the large consultancy firms. His car parks were flooded with consultants' fancy cars, his top management were called upon to attend a series of fruitless, frustrating consultant driven meetings that seriously affected their ability to get any work done. The cost of this consultant mania was $75 million in fees, several times that in lost executive productivity and the corporation went to the wall. (For detailed analyses of what went wrong at Figgie and a salutary lesson for consultants and executives alike you may want to take a look, as suggested above, at *Dangerous Company* by O'Shea and Madigan and my own *High Value Consulting*.)

Ask yourself if you have the time and ability to manage consultants in your business, because if you haven't, assigning a big name, or even all the big names, may not be enough to stave off disaster.

Had the Figgie management had the freedom and the nous to ask the right questions, the corporation might well have prospered. As it was the questions were not asked and the results have been well documented.

Danger signs

- Your consultants agree with everything that you say.
- Your consultants disagree with everything that you say.
- Your car park, designed for ten years of rapid business growth is suddenly full of consultants' BMWs.
- The consultants who seem to fill every available cubic inch of space in your premises constantly demand meetings to decide: "where do we go from here?"
- At every meeting with your consultants there are faces that you have never seen before.
- The newcomers clearly know nothing about your business, but they all want to speak at length and all have ideas to express.
- The lead consultant has not been seen for weeks or longer.
- Your consultants make all the presentations and speak mainly to each other.
- You are receiving and checking so many consultant invoices that you don't have the time to check on the status of the project.
- New consultants come and go with such frequency that you never learn their names.
- Work plans proliferate with such abandon that there is no time to do the work.

- Consultants raise ideas based on the movie that they saw last night.

You may think that I am attempting to inject a little humour. Sadly I am not. The above is a brief factual summary of some of the things that apparently happened at Figgie and which, to a greater or lesser degree, I have seen happening elsewhere.

Key reasons for using consultants

- An objective assessment of the operation.
- Fresh ideas culled from current research or international best practice.
- Skills, knowledge and experience that you and your people lack.
- An extra pair of expensive but willing hands.
- Highly specialized abilities that it is not economic to have constantly on tap.
- A "fall-guy" to take the flack for unpopular or difficult decisions. (This is a perfectly reasonable way of using consultants as long as you are up front about what is expected of them.)

You need to develop specific questions that will enable you to assure yourself of the ability of your prospective consultant to meet your needs. For example:

- If I asked you to investigate a problem and you found that my behaviour was making it worse what would you do? (See above – this question is so important that I repeat it intentionally.)
- What should we be aware of that will affect our industry in terms of changing knowledge and practice?
- What is your experience of . . . ?
- Would you regard yourself as operational or strategic in your approach?
- How do you feel about your personal popularity in businesses where you work?

These may at least start a worthwhile exchange of views. Try to avoid questions that baldly say: "this is what we are looking for", because most consultants will latch onto the opportunity to assure you that they can, and will do practically anything. Keep them guessing just a little and you will keep them honest.

Think about making a very short, but telling speech

If, after asking and carefully considering the replies to all of the above you decide to hire me or someone like me, you may want to clearly establish the ground rules. A few words along the following lines should make the position absolutely clear.

- Our relationship will be one of absolute candour. I will hold nothing back from you that you need to know and I expect you to hold nothing back from me.

- If you believe that I am at fault I expect you to tell me. Not my boss, not my team, not even your colleagues – I expect you to tell *me*.

- I guarantee that you will not be kicked off any assignment that I give you for expressing your views frankly and honestly to me.

- I will fire you immediately, however, without compensation, if I ever discover that you are talking to others without discussing my behaviour with me.

- If we have a problem we will work together to find a solution.

- If and only if, my behaviour is clearly damaging to the company and I, fully aware of its implications, refuse to alter it are you free to discuss the matter with my superior.

- I expect the simple courtesy of being present at any such meeting.

These questions are more important than they might seem at a glance. The relationship of mutual trust that exists between a good consultant and a good client is essential to a worthwhile outcome. You don't have to like your consultant, but you must respect each other. After all else has been covered ask yourself:

- Can I work with this person?

Believe me, any consultant worth his or her fees is asking himself or herself the same question about you. If you can't work together you cannot hope to succeed together.

When assigning the consultant

Ask yourself

- Am I clear exactly why I am hiring this very expensive person? (If he or she is not relatively expensive are they likely to have the skills, knowledge or experience that you need? Sam Goldwyn said that a verbal contract is not worth the paper it is written on. A cheap consultant is rarely worth hiring. We are in an information-driven business in which only the cheapskate can afford to be cheap.)

- Is he or she equally clear?
- Are they well qualified to solve my problem or show me how to exploit the opportunity?
- If they fall under the proverbial bus, how will I continue the project?
- If something unexpected emerges are they fully supported by appropriately qualified colleagues?
- Are they clear on what I am prepared to spend and creative enough to find solutions within my budget?
- Will they challenge my assumptions and ideas to find the optimal solution at lowest cost?
- Are they assertive rather than aggressive or arrogant?
- Will their presence be acceptable to my team and my bosses?
- Will they help me to communicate progress to others in a way that promotes my interests not theirs?
- Will I be more autonomous when they finish the job than I am now?
- Will they get the hell out of here when their job is done?
- Will they give me adequate support, only if asked, if I need further advice or explanation when they have finished the job?

Clients have rights

All my consultants, I call them "mine" because I train them, manage them and support them in the field, work to a code of ethics and absorb a client "Bill of Rights" until it permeates all that they do. A copy of the Bill of Rights may give you a flavour of the way that consultants ought to treat their clients.

Client Bill of Rights

- You have the right to manage your personal and business life in accordance with your personal values and judgement.
- You are answerable to no-one but yourself and your employers for your progress.
- You can demand information that will enable you to make informed judgements concerning what, if any, path of advice you choose to follow.

- You are free to decline help without having to justify your decision to anyone outside your organization.
- You have a right to seek help from as many sources as you choose without experiencing pressure of demands for exclusivity.
- You are entitled to feel afraid from time to time without fearing the attitudes of others and without fearing fear itself.
- You have an absolute right to avoid those things or people that make you frightened.
- You can expect help from allies in overcoming your fears.
- You alone have the right to decide if, where and when you should confront your fear.
- You must not be touched, physically or emotionally without your consent.
- You alone decide whether to speak or remain silent.
- You can accept or decline feedback, suggestions or interpretations at all times.
- You can ask for help in a specific area of your life without having to accept help with everything.
- You are free to challenge any crossing of your boundaries and are empowered to seek and receive help to stop any trespass.
- You can demand explanation of any communication that you do not readily understand.
- You are free to express disagreement or concern to anyone at any time.
- You have the right to acknowledge your feelings.
- You cannot be pressured to explain your feelings if you do not wish it.
- You are free to resolve your doubts without deferring to the views or wishes of others.
- You have the right to regard any therapist, mentor, consultant or counsellor as your personal coach, not as your boss.
- You have the right to receive expert, confidential and sympathetic help in healing from your therapist.
- You have the right to the assurance that your therapist, consultant or coach will never have a relationship with you that is unprofessional, whether social, business or sexual.
- You are secure against any disclosure about you except with your consent or in answer to a court order.
- You have a right to your therapist's or consultant's undivided loyalty when in their care.

- You may expect full, informative answers to any questions concerning your therapist's or consultant's accreditation, mediation or qualifications.

- Your personal safety must always be a primary responsibility for your therapist.

- Your financial, emotional and physical well-being must be the primary concern for your consultant, mentor or advisor.

- Other than in circumstances of habitual criminal acts by you or the creation of situations that might endanger your therapist your support and treatment is not conditional on your continued "good behaviour".

- You may expect to be taught therapeutic or business skills and to be given appropriate help to enable you to practise them for best effect.

- You have the right to reasonable physical comfort during all sessions.

- You can expect that communications in time of urgent need, to your therapist or consultant outside formal appointments, will receive a timely response.

- You have a right to expect that your therapist, consultant or coach will leave you more autonomous and self-reliant at the end of any intervention.

- Where your chosen therapist, consultant or mentor is less than fully qualified to deliver your needs it is their responsibility to help you to find a qualified person or team with whom you feel comfortable.

Don't let the references to therapists disorient you. My consultants are hard-bitten businesspeople. We are, however accredited to a number of institutes including one that works in the field of psychology, both business and therapeutic. Doing so reminds us all that we are working with human beings and need to have their best interests at heart in everything that we do if only because by understanding people we are able to do our best for the business. Frequently mentoring work leads qualified consultants into pathways that are, or are very close to, therapy. That is another reason why it is essential that no consultant should ever accept an assignment for which they are not fully qualified. Some things cannot and must not be learned at the client's expense.

For the sake of completeness I include a copy of our Code of Ethics, which every consultant signs and by which each of us works under the eagle eyes of our independent third-party assessors.

Accredited consultant code of ethics

The client interest will be placed ahead of that of the consultant at all times.

Confidentiality of client information will be absolute including a requirement that the consultant will not publish in any form the fact that he/she is working, or has worked, for the client unless they have the express permission of the client, in writing, to do so.

The consultant will take no financial advantage of insider information in relation to the client business.

No member of the Institute at any level will accept an assignment for which they are less than fully qualified. Any doubts concerning qualifications will be referred back to the Institute to ensure proper client and consultant support.

At the end of any consultancy assignment the member will ensure that the client is enabled to continue the work or use the outcomes without further external intervention.

The client will be formally informed of the progress of the assignment at least monthly and immediately should the need arise.

The consultant will not serve two or more directly competing clients at the same time without the knowledge and permission of each.

The consultant will respect the autonomy of their principal and will give sensitive information to the client immediately, frankly and completely.

The consultant will inform the potential client of any circumstances that may influence the consultant's judgement or independence.

Where possible, the client will be made fully aware of the cost of the intervention in advance.

The consultant will not solicit or accept commissions for recommendations for equipment or software not previously tested and approved by the Institute.

The consultant will not introduce colleagues or other professionals into the assignment without the specific permission of the client and of the Institute.

The consultant will not recommend anything to a client which:
Is not of real, measurable benefit to the client organization;
Cannot be implemented by the client or their employees;
Cannot be explained to the client in simple language that will enable the
client to make an informed judgement.

Summary

In a complex and fast-moving business environment it is essential to draw on all sources of information, assistance and advice that are available to you. It is also essential that you satisfy yourself that this is the appropriate source of advice and support; that it is economical and that it develops your autonomy rather than diminishes it.

As business becomes increasingly complex nobody can hope to know it all and that goes for consultants as much as it does for executives, managers and knowledge workers. So "buyer beware" becomes the client's watchword. As Figgie shows, the purloining of your watch may prove to be the least of your problems.

If you need the help of consultants Lambert's Laws still apply.
The use of outside help must make a significant difference to achieving worthwhile goals.
The intervention must pay for itself in a reasonable time.
It must engage the co-operation and promote the growth of your people who will make it work.
The consultants must leave as soon as the job is done – and they must leave you with the tools to continue as far as you wish or need to go.

Glossary (and soapbox)

Too often words are used as a barrier to enable specialists to pursue their speciality without "undue" interference from line management. With this in mind this glossary goes a little wider than the text and offers some additional food for thought for thoughtful businesspeople. It also gives me the opportunity to reiterate those things that I believe are important for managers, executives and directors to consider.

A

Above the line Marketers love talking of above-the-line and below-the-line activities to confuse the unwary. Above the line is mass marketing – such as advertising, below the line is addressed to individuals.

Accrual accounting The method usually used to record sales and expenses. Sales and expense are recorded when earned or incurred rather than when received or paid.

An example of the simple things that can be wrapped up in a fancy phrase to befuddle the innocent. "Oh we use accrual accounting methodologies – I wouldn't expect a non-professional to understand." A lifetime of dealing with specialists of all kinds, but particularly finance people has taught me to use the simple question, "Why don't you try me?" A Nobel prize winner, Leo Szilard, put it better when he said: "Why don't you assume total ignorance and unlimited intelligence?"

Activity-based costing The key to effective costing of business activities is to separate those that add to customer delight and to regard such costs as an investment. The old approach of allocating costs to products tends to produce a product-centric rather than customer-centred approach and is being replaced in forward looking companies where everything is related to delighting the customer at minimum cost.

Adjacent sector/segment A market segment or sector that could be serviced with existing products or services at relatively small cost and that is often used to extend the life cycle of a product or service. As a prelude to redesigning any product or re-vamping any service it is useful to ask: "Could we sell this elsewhere just as it is?" and "Is the cost of selling it elsewhere a worthwhile investment?" and perhaps "Would selling this elsewhere delay or damage our ability to dominate the really important markets?"

Affinity marketing Having your product or service recommended to their customers by an honest broker that has a similar customer base, but completely non-competitive products or services. A low cost/no cost form of marketing that has emerged due to the rich opportunities provided through the rich flow of information online.

Assets Anything of value owned by the business and recorded on the balance sheet. In modern theory the market value of the company should be a high multiple of the assets because knowledge and competencies add value. Cash assets have recently become a temptation for asset strippers as dot coms with little prospect of turning a profit often have considerable cash reserves supplied by once over-optimistic, now panicking, investors. The accrual and protection of assets was at one time the focus of interest of finance professionals. In the modern firm physical assets are of less value than intellectual assets and the market value of any company should be a high multiple of its asset value both as a defence against take-over and as an indicator of its knowledge base.

Asset stripper The massive, often short-lived cash assets of some dot coms are becoming a happy hunting ground for a new breed of asset stripper who wisely seeks cash rather than stuff. Sadly, too many dot coms were woefully inadequate when it came to relevant and valuable intellectual capital. Could this be because they failed to ask the "killer question"? (See **Assets** above.)

Audit After Enron it is being questioned whether an audit is any longer an "examination of the company's financial statements by an independent third party". Unless audit becomes independent again it is difficult to see the point in the process. In spite of denials, audit was far too often used in the past as a means of getting the company's consultants through the door. Recent scandals have accelerated the distancing of consultancy from audit and if no further good comes out of it, that alone is a major step in the right direction.

Auschwitz syndrome Feelings of guilt experienced by the survivors of downsizing that lead them to covertly damage the firm that they see as making them complicit in their colleagues' job loss. Any firm considering downsizing should be asking "how will we avoid the Auschwitz syndrome here?" For details of one successful, relatively low cost approach please see page 60.

Average total cost Variable costs plus fixed costs divided by the number of units produced. Some accountants and others prefer this as a basis for deciding on prices. You should never forget that pricing, once profitability can be ensured, becomes a strategic issue.

B

Balance sheet A snapshot of company health showing what is owned, what is owed and what is left for the owners and the basis of all essential financial ratios. But the transient nature of the information should lead managers to always question when the balance sheet was put together and the business circumstances prevailing at that time.

Balanced product offering The assurance that a product:

- Works as it should;
- Is available when required;
- Has the unique and recognizable qualities of the brand.

Barriers to entry The quality of your service to customers should be a barrier to entry for your potential competitors that causes them to over-spend, lose money and withdraw. That is market dominance. If you identify an exciting market opportunity you should be asking "What barriers to entry could/should we erect?" and "How do we erect them at the lowest possible cost?"

Below-the-line marketing PR, point of sale, demonstrations and similar activities aimed at buyers one at a time. A question that has haunted me all my life in marketing is: "what does it matter to the normal business person whether something is described as above or below any line?"

Body In e-mail terms, the part of the message containing the most textual content, sandwiched between the Header and the Signature. Make no mistake about it, the use of e-mail in the United Kingdom is currently doubling each year, while in the USA e-mail marketing has seen massive growth, and not only as a result of the "anthrax in the mail" scare. It is a cheap way to reach customers who "opt-in" requesting information. The trouble at present is the wide variance in what list owners claim is "opt-in". Always ask a list owner, at the very least, "what did they opt-in for and when did they indicate their desire to be provided with information/opportunities?"

Bookmark Virtual bookmarks work pretty much the same as the real ones. They record a URL or web page to enable you to refer back to at a later date. An essential adjunct to asking the right questions is to have up-to-the-minute information. Business research sometimes reiterates the obvious, but sometimes findings fly in the face of what we like to think of as common sense. The internet is an unsurpassed, often free, storehouse of knowledge. You need to be able to use that storehouse with the least effort.

Boston Consulting Group Matrix The categorization of product, services and even customers (in private) as cash cows, stars, question marks or dogs. Cash cows should be looked after with loving care. Stars and question marks should be market tested and should attract investment. Dogs should be helped to die.

Brand Is the accumulation of highly visible qualities of a product or service that are promoted to differentiate the offering and assure consumers of consistent and high quality. In a marketing strategy branding is intended to be used to ensure the company of customers who are also of high and consistent quality. Branding is important, but too often those without the will or the capability to do otherwise produce fancy but impractical websites to "build the brand". An advertising executive recently told me that I was a brand. My question is: "Should I be flattered or was he merely being biblical and suggesting that I was overdue for burning?"

Brand awareness The often self-indulgent measurement of the percentage of consumers who recognize a brand. This is usually reported by advertising agencies who omit the essential information of whether the consumers who recognize the brand are prepared to buy it. In a hypothetical brand awareness study if every consumer said, in effect, "Yes we recognize that brand, but we wouldn't buy the product because it's rubbish," the marketing department would be congratulating themselves from here to Carey Street.

Business process re-engineering Is an approach that, at its best enables a company to improve processes and remove duplications of effort. At its worst it has become an excuse to reduce headcounts, damage morale and loyalty, damage the long-term viability of the business and make huge bonuses for hatchet wielders who have the good sense to abandon each sinking ship that they leave behind every eighteen months or so. Like so many fads it has had its successes, but these have been outnumbered by failures. Always seek out the successes before using a tool and ask the questions that give you clear answers to "why did it work here in spite of failing elsewhere?"

Budget A tactical plan expressed in financial terms. A budget enables you to achieve objectives. If the mandate to cut a budget is considered a key question is "since the objectives were worthwhile, how much more would it cost to achieve them now and is that still a good deal?"

Business to business (B2B) Providing goods or services to other businesses rather than to the consumer. Sometimes we are given the impression that business to business marketing begins and ends with the internet. It does not. Currently only 20 per cent of British business procures online. But, and it is a potentially important but, it is estimated that 80 per cent will be procuring online by 2006.

C

Capital The money invested in an enterprise so that more money can be made. Working capital should make money and enhance cash flow. Fixed capital may attract asset strippers if the application working capital is questionable.

Captive demand Creating a market advantage such that the customer has no choice but to come to you. If Amazon had exclusive rights to a Tom Lambert book all my many fans would have no choice but to go to them. (Sadly no-one offers me millions to write exclusively for them. Perhaps I should be asking: "why not?" You, on the other hand, should be asking how you might establish captive demand when it comes to your products or services. Captive demand by definition is market domination.)

Cash cow A mature product that offers high revenues with little investment usually in a low growth market. Cash cows should have unstinting protection when they still have potential, but when they grow too old they should be recognized as "dogs" and dumped.

Cash flow The inflows and outflows of cash. It enables the day-to-day management of funds. It is essential that funds are never idle they are there to make more money. Negative cash flow is potentially more dangerous to a business than lack of profit, so always be prepared to ask "when will cash flow be positive?" This is a slightly different way of looking at the first of Lambert's Laws that any investment should pay for itself in a reasonable time.

Change agent A process consultant who "acts as a catalyst" to bring about change in a company. What worries me about such worthies is that like the catalyst to which they compare themselves they may induce change in others without experiencing any change themselves. (Another way of saying that some of us never learn.)

Change management The process (usually expensive and protracted) of changing the culture of a business. Research in the USA and the UK suggests that between 1970 and 1995, 75 per cent of such attempts failed to achieve their objectives. Before incurring expense, managers should ask "what precisely are any shortcomings in the present culture costing?" and "is there a cheaper, more reliable way?"

Client A "posh" word for a customer intended to denote that the user is in a "profession" rather than a trade. The purpose of any business, trade or profession is to create and keep a customer.

Competencies What the firm is good at doing. A key part of strategic planning for market dominance should be devoted to assessing:

What competencies will enable us to best exploit current markets? Which do we have and which must we build? What competencies will we need to exploit the most exciting markets of the future? And what competencies do we need to build to create the rules by which others have to play if they wish to compete?

Competitive advantage Usually taken by marketers to be a cost advantage, a price advantage or both. On the internet savings can produce major cost advantages that can be applied to ensure that customers are so delighted that they see no need to even look elsewhere for what they buy from you. In the real world competitive advantage is a matter of doing things better at lower cost and is a function of productivity combined with customer and staff loyalty.

Conglomerate Usually an international corporation with diverse business interests. Now loosely used to replace the word "multi-national".

Consortium A strategic alliance, sometimes short-term, to offer a better range of competencies to the marketplace than any one member is able to offer alone.

Core workers (knowledge workers) Those who have the capacity to make a major contribution to the success of the firm. Core workers have too often been limited in some company-think as the technical experts. This is fine as long as it does not lead to a low estimate of the worth of others. Arie de Geus has shown that firms that prosper for hundreds of years treat all their people as "knowledge workers" and develop a culture enriched by life-long learning.

Corporate Alzheimer's The loss to a company of essential, but unrecorded knowledge when downsizing has occurred and those with the most experience have left taking their understanding of customers, markets and systems with them.

Critical success factors The key areas of focus in a business. A firm that loses focus is heading for trouble as it applies its resources ineffectively.

Culture "How we do things around here." An unwritten set of rules and values that dictate corporate behaviour. Like a company's image it is expensive and difficult to change.

Current assets Those assets of a company that are, or can be, readily turned into cash (cash at bank, share/stock holdings in other companies, current stocks and debtors).

Customer proposition Why a particular segment or sector should buy your product or service in preference to any other. The customer proposition should always be clearly stated online or off. In simple terms it is the offer that should persuade customers to come to you first and stay with you. It should answer the question "from the customer's point of view what makes us different and better?"

Customer retention Research by Reichheld of Bains and Company has shown that customer retention is the key to employee retention, investor satisfaction and profitability. The essential is to attract and retain the right customers and that suggests that you need to ask questions that will lead to the effective targeting of customers, because some customers are more trouble than they are worth.

D

Database Details of your customers and the computer software that facilitates the keeping and updating of the records. Properly speaking the software is a databank. With the growth of interest in Customer Relations Management the value of an efficient database cannot be overstated.

Debenture Investment in the form of a long-term loan guaranteed by specific assets.

Delayering An ugly word usually taken to be the removal of unnecessary levels of bureaucratic management. In e-commerce it can also mean the removal of unnecessary intermediaries. Almost every advance in e-commerce is opposed by intermediaries who believe that they will lose out where customers can get a better deal at lower cost. Instead of bemoaning the potential reduction of margin, some would be wiser to ask "how can we do more business at lower cost and deliver a real win-win service to the customer?"

Development capital Investment that is intended to fund growth rather than start-up of a business.

Direct costs The actual cost of materials and direct labour used in making a product.

Domain name Unique address identifying each site on the internet, usually of two or more segments separated by full stops. In e-commerce terms there has been a fashion for thinking up even sillier domain names than names of pop groups. This is a serious mistake. Search engines increasingly look for domain names that match a product or service that the user has entered to search against. Is there really any sense in having a domain name (or expensive television advertising) that gives the prospective customer absolutely no idea of what you offer?

Downtime Time when an employee or machine is not working efficiently. In most companies much longer and more frequent than is admitted. The Auschwitz syndrome often causes employees to look busy while in effect "firing the company" by wasting time. One disadvantage of the internet is that it can provide an alibi for "goofing off".

E

Electronic mail or e-mail Method of communication whereby an electronic message is sent to a remote, or not so remote (people sitting at adjacent desks have been known to send each other e-mails), location and received by another user at a specific e-mail address. Internally in many companies the novelty and convenience of e-mail has led to its use for numerous non-business communications to the degree that workers, encouraged by the press and to the delight of consultants are complaining of "e-mail overload".

Opt-in e-mail where your customers invite you to keep them up-to-date with news about products or services on a regular basis is a key feature of e-commerce. But as the billion dollar industry of e-mail marketing continues to grow at a massive rate, be sure that you ask the right questions to assure yourself that "opt-in" really is opt-in and not a meaningless response to novelty.

Equity The capital invested in a company by its owners. Investment bankers and venture capitalists buy equity in the business when they invest the millions that we business owners always think that we need. If you look briefly at a balance sheet and deduct what a company owes from what it owns the resulting figure is the owner's equity. This creates an imbalance in something that must balance and so the mystery of why "goodwill" appears as a liability is solved.

F

FAQ (Frequently Asked Question) Lists of frequently asked questions (and their answers) covering all manner of topics can be found across the world wide web, allowing the user to search for a query to which somebody has already found the answer. In marketing off-line as well as online, we often use (or invent) FAQs as an apparently transparent, unbiased way of passing information to the customer.

First-to-market advantage The theory that the first supplier in any market can build and sustain competitive advantage, but only if they are able to deliver high customer satisfaction rather than pursuing high short-term profits. But let us add a note of reality about short-term profits and particularly about early positive cash flow. Investors are becoming increasingly impatient to get a return on their investment. Management is under increasing pressure to achieve rapid results. Short-term thinking may be more and more frequently an essential prerequisite to surviving long enough to enjoy the long term.

Fixed assets Those assets of a business that are held, not for conversion into cash, but as a semi-permanent resource for enabling the business to continue. (Buildings, land, plant and machinery.) A temptation to asset strippers if the company is failing to make effective use of them especially as property prices continue to rise.

Fixed costs Costs that have to be borne regardless of levels of production. (Rents, local taxes, administration costs.)

Four "Ps" of marketing Price, Place, Product and Promotion. To which some add a vital fifth, People. The people in a business deliver customer delight which is why Reichheld's research that shows that the relationship between loyal staff, loyal customers and loyal investors leads to massively increased profit potential is so important.

Fragmented market A market in which there are many competitors of whom none has a dominant share.

G

Gearing The relationship between investment capital provided by the owners of the business and long-term loans.

Globalization Where customer tastes, expectations and desires are sufficiently similar world wide to be satisfied by a global product or service.

Having a global strategy in terms of costs, resources, people and production facilities to minimize costs and, in theory at least, maximize customer satisfaction.

H

Hawthorne effect The tendency for results to improve for no better reason than that they are being researched. A sort of placebo effect for business scientists. Where change has been introduced into an organization the managers responsible for that change frequently over-estimate the benefits while those not directly involved tend to underestimate them. Only asking the right questions of all the right people will lead to a proper evaluation of what has been achieved and what remains to be done.

Headhunter A consultant who finds usually senior people for a business for a considerable fee that is usually a multiple of the first-year salary package.

Holding company A company that owns at least 50 per cent of a subsidiary company or which controls the composition of the subsidiary's board of directors or, more usually, both.

Hub and spoke system A distribution system where a central facility supplies a number of smaller warehouses that in turn supply customers or distributors.

Hyperlink In world wide web pages, hyperlinks are highlighted text or images which, when selected (usually by clicking the mouse button), follow a link to another page. Hyperlinks can also be used to automatically download other files as well as sounds and video clips. Hyperlinks often speed online research.

I

Indirect cost (overhead) Costs of running the business which are apportioned, more or less fairly, to all or most commercial activities.

Inertia selling The practice of sending unsolicited goods through the mail in the expectation that the recipient will pay for them rather than take the trouble to send them back. It seems to work for charities and book clubs.

Inventory Stocks that are usually a mixture of current and useful, surplus and doubtful and obsolete and useless which is why finance managers have a healthy disrespect for any stock figure in the books unless it has been physically counted and the rubbish has been written off.

J

Jargon All specialized subjects have their own jargon; a somewhat cryptic language describing technical details. Jargon serves three purposes: it provides a shared language that brings people together; it delivers communication short-cuts to those in the know; and it identifies and excludes "outsiders". Some jargon is explained in this glossary to help reduce the third effect and help you to encourage those who would blind you with jargon to begin to speak plain English.

More generally, jargon tends to be used by members of an in-group as a means of indicating who is in and who is not. Jargon has the advantage (to those who understand it) that it is often a succinct and economical way to express complex ideas. It is an interesting fact that there is no such thing as a simple language. All languages have to be sophisticated enough to express any thought that the speaker may have.

K

Knowledge industry A business in which the key competitive advantage lies in having knowledge denied to others.

A business that exploits the internet's unique ability to publish and sell information online at virtually zero cost.

L

Liability What the company owes.

Life-long learning In a rapidly changing world, life-long learning is no longer an option – it is a prerequisite for survival. Learning that is not used, however, is rapidly lost, so forward looking companies develop a learning strategy that delivers "Life-long learning – Just-in-time". It is essential for managers when, for example given the opportunity to attend or send an employee on say, a training programme to ask how soon can we usefully apply what is learned. Research by Xerox suggests that 87 per cent of what is not applied within twelve weeks of learning is lost.

Liquidity The ability of the company to meet its immediate debts.

Long-term loan Any loan that does not have to be repaid in the next twelve months.

Loss leader Goods sold at a loss or at a reduced profit to attract customers. Retailers should be careful not to annoy existing customers by offering bargains only to new prospects and deny loyal customers who rightly feel that they deserve recognition for keeping the firm in business for years. Never underestimate the value of loyal customers. Find ways of turning loyal customers into proactive advocates of the business.

M

Market leader What every firm should aspire to be whether globally, locally, in a carefully chosen segment or a niche. Market leaders must remember, however, that they are there to be "shot at" and they should be consistently looking to improve their customer service at a lower cost to make it difficult for others to compete. The value of the "customer for life" is that they provide employees with the knowledge, motivation and opportunity to do more for the customer at lower cost.

Market research Analysis of buying intentions. This is often of less practical use, though far more expensive than, market testing. (Putting an offer to the customer, quickly and cheaply, and seeing if he "bites your hand off".)

Marketing strategy "The biggest single waste of corporate time and money", according to one writer, but the most important business activity, far too important to leave to marketers alone, if you are to believe me. But be careful not to become so strategically minded that you forget the tactical actions that will not only bring success today, but will also provide a sound platform for tomorrow's strategy. With my clients I always suggest that we fill the order books with worthwhile business *then* turn our attention to a distant strategic horizon rather than leaving today to chance while we dream about tomorrow.

Mission What a firm is in business for – what customer desires it exists to satisfy – what makes it different and superior – how it treats its stakeholders – what challenges it to be the best of the best – the values that drive and guide the decisions of all employees.

N

NPV – net present-day value The value of future cash flow at today's prices. Equally important is to consider the question of how soon those cash flows will be enjoyed.

NRV – net realizable value The market value of assets less the cost of selling them.

O

Overtrading How to go broke while making a profit. Trading that places unsustainable demands on the finances of a business. To sell more you have to make more. If to make more requires more working capital than you have, you are overtrading. Meanwhile cash flow is negative while uncollected profits appear to soar.

P

Packet Information moves around the internet in "packets"; chunks of data each with their own destination address. Think of packets as sealed envelopes containing data, with addresses written on them. They all go through the system and usually end up at the correct destination. The more envelopes the system must handle, the slower the process becomes.

Payback period The time that you wait to collect the benefits of investment of money or resources. If an investment will not pay for itself in a reasonable time it should not be made.

PEST+ analysis A useful technique for assessing the business environment that includes specification of the political, economic, social, technological and legal factors that might impinge on the business in any market.

Positioning Finding a market position for a product that emphasizes what makes it different from and better than the offerings of competition.

Price/Earnings ratio The relationship between a company's profits and its share value.

Pricing strategy Price is an important strategic issue that few seem to optimize. The customer should drive the price and simple demand curves beloved of economists are not always borne out in practice. Some people prefer to pay a price premium if they perceive it as being indicative of quality and desirability. When I was a youngster in Harpenden there were those motorists who parked on double yellow lines not because of any shortage of parking spaces, but as a snobbish indication that they could afford to pay traffic fines. There are many workable pricing strategies that can add to revenues and/or profits. A comprehensive description appears in my *Key Management Solutions*.

Profit An essential prerequisite of being in and staying in business.

Public domain Refers to software that anybody can use or modify without authorization as well as to research and opinion that anyone is able to use. For example, all the research quoted in this book is either my own or in the public domain. By writing up my own research in this book I effectively give any reader the right to use it as they see fit.

Q

Question marks The fruits of research and development that require major investment and that have yet to prove themselves in the marketplace. Potentially the stars and cash cows of the future, but possibly a major drain on resources if they have not been developed with the customer in mind. Simply asking the questions: "who will buy?" and "why will they buy?" can turn brain children into money machines.

R

Relationship marketing Knowing customers well enough to be able to satisfy their desires more quickly and economically than competition can hope to.

Relative market share Your share of your chosen market divided by the share enjoyed by your largest competitor. When your share is a considerable multiple of that of the best of the others you are on your way to market dominance.

Repeat purchases The cost of winning the first order is relatively high. Companies should be focusing on encouraging repeat purchases that are both more frequent and bigger as the key to low cost growth. They should also look to increasing the size of initial orders, possibly through risk reversal. In other words the supplier rather than the customer assumes the risk of the initial purchase in return for a larger, more profitable order.

Research and development (R and D) Too often a group of devoted people for whom even the best is not quite good enough. As a result of their pursuit of perfection many products reach the marketplace "too late and too expensive". Conversely, of course, they may be the guarantors of the future of the company. The right questions asked at the right time can encourage the "boffins" to become business brains.

Resource Those assets of a company that are used strategically and tactically to delight customers at a profit. People are not a resource of a company, but their commitment, loyalty, knowledge, skills and behaviours often are.

S

Sales force People whose views should always be listened to, but never acted on without verification. All right I am being a little unfair, but only a little. Reducing all prices at a stroke will not usually bring in more or better business. The sales force should be encouraged to identify the most profitable opportunities, to keep abreast of the most important emergent needs and desires of customers and to communicate this information along with all the supportive evidence. They should then be provided with all the tools that they need to win the most profitable business.

Sector A carefully defined part of the market with needs and desires that you have, or can readily acquire, the competencies and strengths to fulfill.

Segment A specified part of the total market with needs or desires that are satisfied by your existing product or service.

Share capital Used to be the money that was invested in a company by its *risk-taking* shareholders. A growing burden of legal claims initiated by disappointed stockholders increasingly suggest that risk is a long way from their expectations.

Star A relatively new product in a high growth market that is showing considerable sales growth, but requires serious investment to achieve its full potential.

Strategic alliance An agreement between two companies to co-operate, sharing knowledge and sometimes resources to achieve a pre-determined set of business objectives that are to their mutual advantage.

Strategic management The effective application of resources to achieve long-term objectives. This implies the equally effective use of resources today in order to survive to enjoy the long term. Arie de Geus has shown that companies that are successful over long periods tend to be frugal in the short term. It is essential for any company in an ever-faster moving business environment to ensure that they do well enough today not merely to survive, but also to build a fund to finance future changes of direction as the markets change.

Surfing What some at least of your employees waste your money doing if current research is accurate. You might wish to take a lesson from a World War II catchphrase and ask: "Is your access really necessary?"

T

Teleworker The current in-word for what used to be called a "home-worker" or "telecommuter". The internet with its capability for almost instant communication at minimal cost enhances the opportunities to make teleworking work. The need to reduce costs and enable a work/home balance may provide greater impetus as employers seek ways to avoid building the monument to bankruptcy known as corporate HQ.

Tertiary brand A product made by an obscure manufacturer that is designed to sell entirely on the basis of price to capture sales from well-known brands and the retailer's "own label".

Third generation idiot A twenty-five-year-old business postgraduate whose studies have been under the direction of a thirty-year-old postgraduate lecturer reporting to a thirty-five-year-old postgraduate professor, not one of whom has ever held down a real job in the real world. It is easy to spot a TGI in the workplace. They wave their hands a good deal when they talk (which is most of the time), and compare every situation to an ancient case study: "Wow, this is just like Polaroid France –1971'!"

Time to market The time taken to get a new product into the market-place. Hamel and Prahalad recommend that a new product should be available to buyers as quickly as possible even if it means that necessary refinements and design improvements lead to a large number of models in quick succession (cf. Toshiba and their early range of laptop computers). It is equally arguable, however, that the product or service ought to reach all customers, including early adopters in a condition that delivers satisfaction. Failure to do so often leads to the second to market winning greater market share in a shorter total time.

Time taken to deliver goods or services to the online customer including any time required to answer requests for information.

Turnover Annual sales revenues. By dividing turnover by the investment capital and multiplying the result by the net profit percentage you can get a good rule of thumb assessment of how well capital is being applied.

The rate at which any resource of the company turns over whether labour or capital. The combination of e-commerce and a total commitment to retaining the worthwhile customer should play a major role in reducing the turnover of labour while accelerating the turnover of capital as measured in Return on Capital Employed and Return on Working Capital and

Return on Investment. If it fails to improve turnover ratios it is reasonable for top management to ask "What are we online for?" or even "What are we in business for?"

U

Undercapitalization The opposite of the profligate investment in daft dot coms that was the norm before the "crash" of 2000. When seeking capital investment to cover, for example, the first year of trading, a company is well advised to assess how long it takes to obtain the capital injection and add that period of time to the date at which cash flow is forecast to become positive and profits start to accrue. This gives a buffer period during which further funding can be sought if necessary. Remember that there is no mileage in an over-optimistic forecast and as David Myddleton has said: "A forecast is what would have happened if what did happen didn't happen."

USP (unique selling proposition) The benefits of your offering that your competitors either cannot match or do not promote that will persuade the customer to come to you first and stay with you. If you fail to develop a compelling USP you may have little choice other than to sell purely on price. Those who sell on price alone are normally destined to be a follower in the marketplace rather than a leader as they try to match or beat any price reduction offered by any competitor anywhere. This approach is only viable in the long term where there exists a recognized "low cost niche" as, for example, in the airline business.

V

Value chain The addition of identifiable customer value at every stage of development, production and distribution. Michael Porter identified five critical success areas: research and design; development; production; marketing and distribution. Each should contribute quantifiable added value.

Variable costs Costs that vary directly with the levels of output. High productivity reduces labour costs and therefore variable costs as well as enabling fixed costs to be more readily absorbed, but too many organizations seek productivity on too narrow a front. The real art of management is to increase and reward productivity throughout the business. That includes productivity in the boardroom. Years ago Bob Townsend charged directors for their time, the consumption of paper, food and alcohol (?) that resulted from board meetings. He claimed (*Up the Organisation*) that board meetings became infinitely more productive as a result. The Synectics organization promoted the idea that all areas of board discussion should be subject to a predetermined time guillotine. Better than 90 per cent of attenuated discussions were never raised at a future meeting. Draw your own conclusions.

W

Working capital Short-term funds to be turned over rapidly as they enable the firm to carry out its day-to-day trading. Business growth frequently places increasing demands on working capital that can, in extreme cases, have such an effect on cash flows that the company fails.

Index

above the line marketing 229
Abrahams, Mike 64
Accenture 13, 124
accrual accounting 229
achievement motivation 94
activity based costing 229–30
adjacent sectors/segments 230
advertising 152–5
   and recruitment 38–9, 40–1, 42
affiliation 94
affinity marketing 230
airlines 188
American Marketing Association 150–2
Andersen Consulting 13
appraisal 52–3
asset strippers 230
assets 230
   current assets 234
   fixed assets 236–7
   return on total assets 136
attitudes 70, 185
audits 230
Auschwitz syndrome 59–60, 230–1
average collection period 135–6
average total cost 231

balance sheets 135–6, 231
balanced product offering 231
barriers to market entry 231
behaviours 71, 185
Belbin, Meredith 67
below the line marketing 231

benchmarking xv
best practice xv
best use of the best people 26–7
Bill of Rights
   for clients 224–6
   for employees 37
body language 181
bookmarks 231–2
Borgia, Cesare 189
Boston Consulting Group Matrix 232
BRAD 153
branding 232, 233
Broad, Mary 203
budgets 136–8, 232
burn out 35
bus queue syndrome 205
business cycle 130–1
business process reengineering (BPR)
   103, 232
business to business marketing 232–3

capital 235
   return on capital employed 136
   share capital 242
   turnover of capital 135, 243–4
   undercapitalization 244
   working capital 132–3, 233, 245
captive demand 233
cash flow 132–3, 233
change xvii, 100, 185, 188–93,197–8, 233
   bus queue syndrome 205
   cost of change 190–1

More power to your
[business-mind]

Even at the end there's more we can learn. More that *we* can learn from your experience of this book, and more ways to add to *your* learning experience.

For who to read, what to know and where to go in the world of business, visit us at **business-minds.com**.

Here you can find out more about the people and ideas that can make you and your business more innovative and productive. Each month our e-newsletter, *Business-minds Express*, delivers an infusion of thought leadership, guru interviews, new business practice and reviews of key business resources directly to you. Subscribe for free at

● **www.business-minds.com/goto/newsletters**

Here you can also connect with ways of putting these ideas to work. Spreading knowledge is a great way to improve performance and enhance business relationships. If you found this book useful, then so might your colleagues or customers. If you would like to explore corporate purchases or custom editions personalised with your brand or message, then just get in touch at

● **www.business-minds.com/corporatesales**

We're also keen to learn from your experience of our business books – so tell us what you think of this book and what's on *your* business mind with an online reader report at business-minds.com. Together with our authors, we'd like to hear more from you and explore new ways to help make these ideas work at

● **www.business-minds.com/goto/feedback**

[www.business-minds.com
www.financialminds.com]